My Amazing Mom

Chicken Soup for the Soul: My Amazing Mom
101 Stories of Love and Appreciation
Amy Newmark

Published by Chicken Soup for the Soul, LLC www.chickensoup.com

The publisher gratefully acknowledges the many publishers and individuals who granted Chicken Soup for the Soul permission to reprint the cited material.

Front cover photo courtesy of iStockphoto.com/Zerbor (©Zerbor)
Back cover photo courtesy of iStockphoto.com/laflors (©laflor)
Interior illustration courtesy of iStockphoto.com/Krimzoya (©Krimzoya)
Photo of Amy Newmark courtesy of Susan Morrow at SwickPix

Cover and Interior by Daniel Zaccari

Distributed to the booktrade by Simon & Schuster. SAN: 200-2442

Publisher's Cataloging-In-Publication Data
(Prepared by The Donohue Group, Inc.)

Names: Newmark, Amy, compiler.
Title: Chicken Soup for the Soul : my amazing mom : 101 stories of love and appreciation / [compiled by] Amy Newmark.
Other Titles: My amazing mom : 101 stories of love and appreciation
Description: [Cos Cob, Connecticut] : Chicken Soup for the Soul, LLC [2018]
Identifiers: ISBN 9781611599763 (print) | ISBN 9781611592764 (ebook)
Subjects: LCSH: Mothers--Literary collections. | Mothers--Anecdotes. | Mother and child--Literary collections. | Mother and child--Anecdotes. | LCGFT: Anecdotes.
Classification: LCC HQ759 .C454 2018 (print) | LCC HQ759 (ebook) | DDC 306.874/3--dc23

Library of Congress Control Number 2017964356

PRINTED IN THE UNITED STATES OF AMERICA
on acid∞free paper

25 24 23 22 21 20 19 18 01 02 03 04 05 06 07 08 09 10 11

My Amazing Mom

101 Stories of Love and Appreciation

Amy Newmark

Chicken Soup for the Soul, LLC
Cos Cob, CT

Changing your life one story at a time®

www.chickensoup.com

Table of Contents

❸

~What a Character!~

❹

~Recipes for Life~

5

~My Role Model~

6

~The Sacrifices She Made~

7

~Special Memories~

8

~Thanks, Mom~

9

~A Lasting Legacy~

Introduction

Did you ever notice that MOM spelled upside down is WOW? That's because our moms are just AMAZING.
~Author Unknown

I worked on this collection of stories while living through the final "firsts" after losing my mother a year ago: the first Christmas without her, the one-year anniversary of her death a few days ago, and today, the one-year anniversary of her funeral. I worked through a lot of my grief as I edited this book, meeting all the amazing moms in these pages and feeling the same happiness, sadness, and pride as their grown children — the talented, selfless writers who shared these personal, moving stories with us.

It was a difficult, but enlightening experience, and when I posted about it on Twitter I got a thoughtful response from one of our long-time Chicken Soup for the Soul writers — James Warda. He shared a wonderful piece of wisdom from his sister. After their father died, she told James, "I feel his absence but feel his presence more." Isn't that brilliant? And so true.

A mother's influence never stops. Whether she's in the trenches raising young children, or she's counseling her grown children, or she has passed on, the kids will always feel her support, try to make her proud, and follow her advice, even if they pretended not to be listening when they heard it. And that applies to grandmothers, and stepmothers, and mothers-in-law, and all the other mothers in our lives, all of whom are represented in these pages.

What a wide variety of tales you are about to read! In Chapter 1,

"Just What I Needed," you'll see how Timothy Freeman's mother-in-law gracefully stepped in to the role when his mother died, telling him, "You've still got a mom when you need one." He says he started crying when she told him that, and I did too!

Chapter 2 is about "Lasting Lessons" and it's for all the moms whose sons and daughters are still rolling their eyes when their mothers try to share some wisdom and guidance with them. Laurie Carnright Edwards confesses that her mom embarrassed her terribly when they went car shopping together, insisting that there was a better deal to be had and forcing Laurie to stride out of that dealership even after two price reductions. But Mom always knows best. That car salesman called Laurie later and met her mother's terms.

Everyone's mom or grandmother or mother-in-law or stepmother is a bit crazy, in a wonderful way, and we have one wacky lady after another in Chapter 3, which is called "What a Character!" Jill Keller tells us about the wild day she had when her mother insisted over and over again that Jill was pregnant — because she had dreamt it. Jill knew she wasn't pregnant but her mother saw confirming "signs" all day long. You can guess who ended up being right!

We all have our favorite mom or grandma foods, and we have a whole chapter about that, too, but these "Recipes for Life" go deeper, because there's usually a backstory to these kitchen memories. Beth Krone-Downes tells us how she finally came to understand why her great-grandmother's recipes were so variable as to ingredients and so imprecise as to measurements. She had been a refugee who escaped to the United States from Germany and went through many tough times. Beth realized that her great-grandmother never knew where she'd be cooking next, or what would be available to her, so her recipes were fluid and flexible, adaptive to her circumstances. Great-Grandma Johanna never told Beth how hard her life had been — it was the recipes that revealed the truth.

Talk about struggling — we have numerous stories about mothers and grandmothers who bravely went through tough times and came out the other side, and we shared many of those stories in Chapter 5, "My Role Model." Savannah D. Cassel is one grateful daughter who recounts how her single mother struggled financially to raise her. But as soon as their situation improved, her mother turned around and filled up her car with groceries for another family going through a tough time.

Many of our stories are about children whose mothers never made it obvious to them how difficult their lives were. Chapter 6 is called "The Sacrifices She Made" and it's filled with stories of children having epiphanies about their selfless mothers. Elaine Herrin Onley, for example, always had the right clothing for school and social events. It wasn't until she came home from a party one night and spotted the ragged nightgown that was usually hidden under her mother's robe that she realized how much her mother had been sacrificing to keep her children looking good.

We all become our mothers, right? And once we're old enough, we welcome that. In Chapter 7, we share all kinds of "Special Memories" of good times with Mom, including a cute story by Dorann Weber about how hard she resisted learning her mother's hobbies—knitting and crocheting—to the point where she refused to even wear the sweaters that her mother knit for her. But then that moment that all mothers wait for occurs: Dorann became a mother herself. And everything changed. She donned one of the sweaters her mother knit for her and she started knitting herself. That's the sweet revenge we all talk about, right? "Just wait till you have a child of your own...."

I learned to just soldier on, dispensing that unwanted advice while the kids were growing up, and smiling occasionally when they'd quote my own advice back to me as if it was something they had just thought of themselves. So every teenager should read Jocelyn Drawhorn's story in Chapter 8, "Thanks, Mom." Jocelyn tells us about a very wise teacher, Mrs. D, who was always available to help her during the school day, especially during those awkward times when her so-called friends were being mean to her. Mrs. D told her not to let her friends' problems become her own, saying, "Never let the insecurities of others determine who you are." Jocelyn says she has carried that advice with her throughout her adult life, thanks to Mrs. D, who, she reveals, is her mother.

We close out the book with Chapter 9, "A Lasting Legacy." This was the hardest chapter for me to edit as it kept reminding me of all the good things that my mother did and the lessons and characteristics that are her legacy to me. One way to keep a mother's legacy alive is to support her favorite cause at her funeral. In my family, we did that by requesting donations to the local animal shelter in lieu of flowers, and that's why I included a story by Xochitl E. Dixon in this collection. Xochitl and her family asked the guests attending their mother's memorial service to bring coats and gloves and hats to honor her, a teaching assistant who had always made sure to equip a few of her students each winter with the outerwear their families couldn't afford. At their standing-room-only service, they collected hundreds of coats, hats, and gloves for their mother's students.

I guess that is symbolic of all our mothers — they are the providers of the coats and hats and gloves that we need as we navigate life, and I'm not really talking about clothing. I'm talking about the emotional outerwear they provide when we leave our homes and interact with the world — the comfort and support and morals and strategies for life. Our mothers are our cheerleaders, our chief advisers, and our role models for how to be the very best human beings that we can be. This book is a great big thank-you to all the moms out there. You are truly appreciated by your families.

~Amy Newmark
January 7, 2018

Chapter 1

My Amazing Mom

Just What I Needed

A mother is the truest friend we have, when trials heavy and sudden fall upon us; when adversity takes the place of prosperity; when friends desert us; when trouble thickens around us, still will she cling to us, and endeavor by her kind precepts and counsels to dissipate the clouds of darkness, and cause peace to return to our hearts.
~Washington Irving

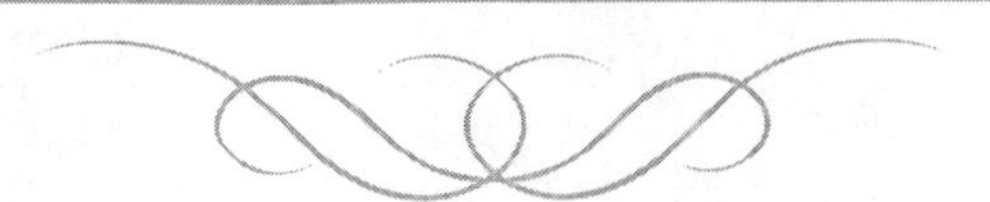

Peggy Sr.

Thank you… for gracing my life with your lovely presence, for adding sweet measure of your soul to my existence.
~Richard Matheson

We walked to the end of the hall, neither of us saying a word. We'd just been down to her room, and my mother-in-law knew it was going to be the last time she could hold my mama's hand, ask her how she was doing, brush her hair back off her forehead and give her a kiss on the cheek. It was the last time she'd make her laugh by giving her a wink and a grin and asking her "Does he belong to you?" while pointing at me on the other side of the bed. By this time, all Mama could do was nod her head and chuckle when the woman I call Peggy Sr. said, "Well, he's a pretty good fella… I think we ought to keep him around." It was the last moment they shared together.

Her daughter and I had already been married twelve years, but it was there in that hospital, at the end of that hall, that I realized how much this woman loved me and how much I loved her. She didn't say a word before she got on that elevator; she just held my face in her hands and gave me a smile that said everything I needed to hear: "This is bad… this is sad, but you're going to make it 'cause I'm right here." I put my head on her shoulder, feeling like the gravity of this whole episode was knocking me to my knees. But she was there to catch me.

My hands were shaking because moments before, I'd signed a

DNR just like I always promised I would when the time came. But in that embrace, there was a rub on my back and a kiss on my cheek… and my hands quit shaking. She took her arms from around me and put her hands on my face, staring hard into my eyes. Again, without words, I knew what she was asking.

"I'll be okay," I said out loud. "I'll be okay."

Later that afternoon, Mama was moved into hospice care. She was gone the next morning.

A couple of weeks later, we were standing in my in-laws' driveway, saying goodbyes after a good meal and a relaxing evening together. I got in my truck and rolled down my window, waiting for my wife to finish a chat with her dad. Seeing an opportunity to speak to me privately, Peggy Sr. came over, leaned in my window and said, "I need to tell you something. I would never, ever pretend to take the place of your mother. But I want to make sure you know how much we both love you. I know you miss her, but you're not alone. You've still got a mom when you need one." I assured her I needed one almost every day, and then I cried like a baby all the way home.

Mothers-in-law have long been punch lines and clichés. But the only thing you'll hear me saying about mine is that I thank God for her every day. I call her Peggy Sr. and my bride Peggy Jr. because they're birds of a feather. Peggy Sr. spoils me rotten, makes me laugh, and has the most extensive "Crimson Tide" wardrobe of anybody living east of Tuscaloosa. She'll holler "Roll Tide" anywhere from the grocery store to church. She makes the best deviled eggs on the planet and has a hat collection that would shame any woman parading around Churchill Downs. She loves gospel music and sings it perfectly, too. But the thing she does best is what she did there in that hallway at the hospital — look right into the soul with a mother's tender eyes and calm whatever storm she finds brewing.

~Timothy Freeman

A Birthday Letter

You give but little when you give of your possessions. It is when you give of yourself that you truly give.
~Kahlil Gibran

I was a young, stay-at-home mother and there never seemed to be enough money to go around. Thus, on my mother's birthday, I found myself lacking a present. My father had died when I was in my teens, and my twin brothers lived far away, so if I didn't acknowledge my mother's birthday, likely no one would.

My mother worked during the day, and I had a family to cook dinner for and then a young son to put to bed, so a visit seemed impractical. I thought about a quick phone call to wish her a happy birthday but that didn't feel like enough. Then I realized I could bake her some cookies. I would take them to her house and leave them with a little note for her to find when she got home.

Sitting down to write a few words of good wishes got me to thinking. My mother and I had not always been close. I resented things that happened in my childhood, and I held them against her. Pouring out words of love and respect seemed insincere, but there were plenty of things that I did appreciate, so I decided to list all of them. Pretty soon, I had several pages of genuine heartfelt thoughts, so I wrote a letter to my mother expressing my appreciation for the things she and my father had taught us as children.

They had taught us to live within our means, and not to go into debt other than a mortgage. They taught us that the color of someone's skin was irrelevant. My mother taught us that helping others in need was its own reward. She taught me to value the elderly by encouraging me to make May Day baskets and valentines for them. My father taught us to be good neighbors by taking care of our home and helping others if they needed a hand. My parents taught us how to work. They taught me that putting a huge dent in the car was an opportunity to learn how to use body putty and paint. My mom taught us how to see the shapes in the clouds and how, if we were patient, we could see shooting stars on a summer's night. She taught me to appreciate the way the air smelled after a rain.

The list went on and on.

By the time I had finished the two-page birthday letter to my mother, I realized that I had been given everything I really needed as a child. My mother had not been perfect, but overall she was a good mom. My letter had expressed my love and appreciation after all.

I put the cookies on the table in her kitchen, arranged the handwritten letter beside it, and went home. That evening, she called and thanked me. She said it was a wonderful birthday present, and she loved me wholeheartedly. I was busy with dishes and getting my son ready for bed, so I didn't spend a lot of time on the phone with her and I didn't understand just how much that letter meant to her.

Two years later, she suffered a fatal heart attack. While cleaning out her house, I came across a photocopy of the birthday letter I had written to her. It was in the drawer of the bedside table in the guest room. I was confused as to why she would make a copy and stash it in the guest room.

But then I got my answer. Room after room, drawer after drawer revealed more photocopies of the same letter. There was one in the kitchen drawer and one taped to the inside of the kitchen cabinet. I found one in a drawer in both bathrooms and another in the sofa table in the living room.

The last room I cleaned was her bedroom. By this time, it had become a treasure hunt. I already held nine copies of the letter in my hand when I sat down on her bed. I was bawling by this time and I opened the drawer beside her bed, looking for a tissue. There I found an old handkerchief and as I pulled it out a wrinkled piece of paper fluttered to the floor.

It was the original birthday letter. It had been smoothed over and over again. I realized that my homemade birthday gift was the best present I could have ever given my mother. It seems that the best things we gave to each other weren't really things at all.

~Marcia Wells

At First Sight

Anger makes you smaller, while forgiveness
forces you to grow beyond what you were.
~Cherie Carter-Scott

It was hate at first sight. My fiancé Jake and I stood in his mother's dim kitchen. The scent of old coffee filled the air as my future mother-in-law looked me over.

She turned to her son and announced, "It's her or me."

I stepped back in surprise and looked at Jake.

He squared his shoulders, and a muscle twitched in his jaw. His face reflected the same stubborn look his mother wore.

Jake grabbed my arm and steered me toward the door. As we walked out, he called over his shoulder, "It's her."

Months of mother/son separation ensued. Even though they lived in adjoining towns, Jake and his mom refused to visit or even phone each other.

I'd heard the term "stubborn as a Missouri mule." Well, the mules could take a lesson from those two.

"Mom, why don't you and Jake make up?" Jake's sister asked.

"No. He chose that woman over me."

Jake's sister tried again. "Why don't you like her?"

Mom thought for a while. "I don't know," she admitted. "She just rubs me the wrong way."

After Jake and I married, visiting my in-laws during the holidays felt like torture. Jake's mom veered between ignoring me to icy politeness, but she showed genuine love for Patty, our four-year-old daughter from my first marriage.

My sister-in-law's twin girls were the same age as Patty. Mom showered them all with gifts, cookies, and love.

Still, no matter what I did, my mother-in-law liked me as much as a hernia.

If I bought her a present, it was the wrong color.

If I brought food, it was cooked incorrectly.

In the Great Cucumber Debacle of 1989, she disassembled my vegetable platter to slice the veggies thinner.

My bitterness and anger grew, leaving Jake stuck between two warring camps.

In the movies, a life-changing event transpires, and two adversaries lay aside their differences.

For me, it wasn't an action flick or spy-drama occurrence.

My life changed completely when I turned it over to the Lord. I told my husband, "From now on, I'm thanking God for all the blessings in my life. Even your mother."

Jake raised one eyebrow. "You're thankful for my mother?"

I hesitated for a moment, slowed by newfound honesty. "Well, I'm grateful she gave me a wonderful husband. That's a start."

I focused on gratitude each time I thought of my mother-in-law. Her influence had produced my husband's compassion, kindness, and thoughtfulness. Plus, I felt grateful that she accepted Patty as a beloved granddaughter.

Although it wasn't a dramatic movie-scene turnaround, a softening had begun in Mom's heart and mine. As the years passed, our once-prickly relationship grew into love.

Visits didn't seem like torture anymore. Mom and I would snuggle side by side on her plush living-room sofa. I'd wrap myself in a blanket and breathe in the scent of baking cookies. She, always warm, would rub my terminally cold hands with hers.

"Don't you ever get cold?" I asked.

She shook her head and smiled. "I've always been too warm. I used to stand barefoot in the snow to cool off."

One day as we sat together on her sofa, she took my hand and sandwiched it between both of hers. I waited for her usual, "Your hand is so cold."

Instead, she said, "I'm so glad you married my son. He couldn't have found a better wife."

I wrapped my arms around her, my heart overflowing with gratitude at her sweet words.

Life took a drastic turn when Mom went into the hospital for a cardiac ablation to correct her abnormal heart rhythm.

Instead of a routine procedure, she wound up with a nicked liver and a punctured heart. The surgical team worked frantically to save her. She lived, but she had gone without oxygen for far too long.

Despite therapy, she was plagued by physical issues and memory problems. She'd ask the same questions repeatedly. She, who'd always been so hot, couldn't get warm.

As time went on, her health declined.

She'd still touch my hand and say, "Oh, your hands are so cold." She'd cup my chilly hands in her icy ones and try to warm them, saying, "There, that's better, isn't it?"

"Absolutely, Mom. So much better."

In odd moments, she'd turn to me and say, "I'm so glad you married my son."

The night before she passed away, Mom and I spent some time alone in her dim hospital room.

She tossed and turned, restless and in pain. The beeping monitors and antiseptic smells added to her discomfort.

I held her hand and prayed quietly over her, then whispered, "I love you. Thanks for raising such a great husband for me."

She stopped thrashing and looked at me in a brief moment of clarity.

I leaned close as she squeezed my hand and murmured the last words she spoke to me.

"I'm glad you married my son."

"Me, too, Mom," I whispered. "Me, too."

The moment ended, and she began her agitated rocking again.

The next morning, Mom was gone. I was grateful she wasn't suffering anymore. Grateful for the years we'd spent as friends. Grateful for the husband she'd given me. Grateful for her impact on my life.

Yes, it was hate at first sight, but I'm so grateful it was love at last sight.

~Jeanie Jacobson

Step by Step

Stepparents are not around to replace a biological parent, rather to augment a child's life experience.
~Azriel Johnson

I suppose it wasn't easy for either of us in the beginning. Welcoming an out-of-control fifteen-year-old boy into one's home would be difficult for any stepmom. Walking into a new family in a different house in a strange city could tip any teenager over the edge. It did for me, but Judy placed her apprehension aside and embraced me. She saw the good in me, even if it lay buried under years of pain and distrust.

It certainly helped that three great kids came with her. The two boys and I hit it off right away. They were athletes even at a young age, and we played indoors and out every day. The older daughter pecked at me whenever she could, but I gave as good as I got. We all grew close over time.

Judy was a busy working mom, but she always made time to inquire about her kids' worlds. I don't think it was idle conversation either; Judy always showed genuine interest.

She and my dad met at the tail end of two troubled marriages. They loved each other enough to throw everything into a bag, shake well, and plow ahead with life. They began as two adults with three kids. Then I came along, and after that one of my brothers. They bought a bigger house, got everyone situated, and ran with it.

I remember one day talking with Judy's sister on the phone. We got onto the subject of my mom and dad's split, and I mentioned how sad I felt for my mom. "But isn't it wonderful that your dad is happy now?" she said. I'd never thought about it like that before. From then on, I saw Judy in a new way—as a companion for my dad, a guy who'd had his own share of troubles. I began to love her as a person and as my stepmother.

I trudged through high school and community college, and flailed around here and there, not really accomplishing anything. I'm sure Judy and Dad had a few conversations about me, but I think Judy always saw the spark. Judy always looked for the good in everyone.

I stumbled through my "idiot years," as I like to call them. Everyone threw up their hands, and rightly so, but I'd like to think Judy held onto a silent hope that maybe I'd finally straighten myself out. I can see it in her eyes these days, and in that beautiful smile: true happiness and honest motherly pride. I'm a university professor and an author of children's fantasy novels.

She knows how much I love my cats. She e-mails me pictures and videos of cute felines, and buys me kitty-cat Christmas presents. One year, she bought me a 365-day magnetized kitten calendar for the refrigerator—a simple gift, but one with great meaning for me.

Judy sends birthday cards to everyone in the family; she never forgets. She gets as much pleasure out of it as the recipients. She also loves to entertain. Having the clan over for Christmas is a joy for her. The family has grown substantially—eight kids, most with their own kids. Throw in grandchildren and great-grandchildren, and you could have the neighbor's kids at the party and no one would ever know. And no one plays Santa better than Judy.

She takes care of my dad now; he's ninety-five years old and surprisingly alert, but physically slowing down. I'm sure it's doubly tough on her; she has to watch a man she loves deteriorate before her eyes, and she's taken on the lion's share of the domestic workload. I wish I could pay her back for all the little things she's done by sending a maid over twice a month.

For now, it will have to be simple gestures. We held a family birthday party recently. I sat and talked with her grandson, a young man who lost his father a couple of years ago. He has challenges ahead of him, but with the right nudge he might find his path.

Judy sent me an e-mail thanking me for spending time with him, but I recognized that I was just like that grandson way back when. Everyone needs someone to talk to about life's challenges. I think Judy sees the same spark in him that she saw in me many years ago. I'm sure she'll never give up on him either.

We talk periodically. Whether by e-mail or by phone, I can always envision her smile in the background. On different days, that smile might be directed at her husband, her children, friends, co-workers, or the hostess at a restaurant. She gives it away freely. Judy wants everyone she meets to be happy.

Sometimes, I felt self-imposed pressure to refer to Judy as my mother, especially since my own mom passed some years ago. However, I now realize the folly in that idea. Judy is my stepmom, and she's fulfilled her role with dignity, patience, and deep devotion. I love her for being exactly that, and I feel privileged that she became a part of my life more than forty years ago.

~Kevin Gerard

Every Age and Stage

I would maintain that thanks are the highest form of thought, and that gratitude is happiness doubled by wonder.
~G.K. Chesterton

Being born into a military family set the stage for me to have many mothers in my life. It would be a challenge to identify the one who had the greatest impact, because they were all perfect for me at the time they stepped forward to mother me.

My mother died when I was seven. One of my cherished memories is hearing her merrily singing popular Broadway tunes as they came on the car radio. Few things have brought me greater joy than belting out the lyrics to musicals with my own children.

My first stepmother happened to have been my older brother's fifth-grade teacher the year my mother passed. While her stay in our lives was a mere six months, I vividly remember her hand clasping mine as we stood in line to see *The Sound of Music*. That memory impressed upon my young heart that simple acts of concern, care, and compassion can go a long way toward bringing hope and reassurance to a grieving soul.

My second stepmother entered our lives in a fashion that would have been comical if it hadn't bordered on desperate. On the verge of deployment to Vietnam from his assigned base in the Caribbean, the obvious need for someone to watch his three children may have nudged my father into a hasty marriage to a recently divorced mother of four.

A backyard wedding was followed by a honeymoon cruise through the nearby islands. The seven children, from six to sixteen years old, began exploring our new life together. One of the most fascinating aspects of this arrangement was how nonchalant the involved adults appeared to be over the obvious language barrier. Our four new stepsiblings were native Spanish speakers, and the three of us, fairly new to the island and mostly isolated on the military base, spoke only English. Over the next few months, we somehow managed to come up with our own version of Spanglish and communicated fairly effectively over the next five years.

Our new stepmother impressed upon us the value of determination and hard work. She added to the family income through both her small tailoring shop (an impressively self-taught skill) and the beautician service she ran in our screened-in carport-turned-salon. In addition to the responsibilities of raising the seven children of a blended family and running those two businesses, she also kept an immaculate home. She managed all of this largely on her own while my father volunteered for three back-to-back deployments as he pursued his military career and the extra pay that helped to keep our motley crew afloat.

A final tour to Europe and my father's retirement seemed to strain the union, and another marriage dissolved into divorce. Through this new set of circumstances, the love of another kind of mother came into my life — a foster mother.

Friends of mine were about to be stationed in the Pacific Northwest. While helping them clean, organize, and prepare for the arrival of the moving company (skills that often become second nature to military brats), my friend's mother looked at me tearfully and said, "I'm going to miss you so much! Why don't you come with us?"

Phone calls were made and meetings ensued, which included legal guardianship and money to cover travel and living expenses. And thus I came to experience the love of this new kind of mother. She may have had no biological or marital obligation to care for the child she was "fostering," but she embraced mothering another soul simply because she had it in her heart to do so. What a special kind of blessing it is to be so loved!

Several years and another foster mother later, my college education was interrupted by my own marriage. Here I found the love of yet another kind of mother—a mother-in-law. My mother-in-law had seven children of her own. Her only son was my new husband, and she had six daughters ranging in age from twelve to twenty. In the midst of her own bustling life, she had the heart to welcome another daughter into her circle. Through her example, I learned we can always make room in our hearts to love someone new—even when our cup is full!

Almost four years of infertility revealed to me that a mother's instinct can be powerful enough to propel a woman to overcome tremendous obstacles. When my firstborn child arrived after a challenging pregnancy, the kaleidoscope of love from all the mothers in my life seemed to arrange themselves into a beautiful pattern, illuminated by the dawn of my own motherhood. Early motherhood insecurities gave way to joy as our family grew over the years, through birth and adoption, to seven children of our own. Now I have experienced the joys and sorrows of being a natural mother, an adoptive mother, a mother-in-law, and more recently, a grandmother.

A friend of mine shared with me once that her mother had commented about me, "She is a natural-born mother. It comes to her like falling off a log."

She obviously had no idea how the very thought of being a mother had caused me to break out into a cold sweat as a young woman. But the host of beautiful mothers who helped me navigate through a variety of situations and circumstances encouraged me along the way—as only mothers can.

I marvel at all the mothers who have touched my life. Those mentioned here, plus grandmothers, pastors' wives, and nurturing friends, have all provided what I needed during the different stages of my life. I've been blessed beyond measure by each of them.

~Donna Lorrig

The Driving Lesson

A well-balanced person is one who finds both sides of an issue laughable.
~Herbert Procknow

At sixteen, I possessed something every teenager dreams of… a learner's permit. But unlike most kids my age, I was terrified by the thought of navigating almost two tons of crushing steel.

"Do you want to drive home?" Mom asked when she picked me up from my after-school house-cleaning job.

I hesitated. "Really? Are you sure?"

Mom nodded with confidence. "You'll do fine."

"Okay." I hopped into the driver's seat of our Ford Galaxie 500.

"You've got plenty of room to back up," she said while I maneuvered in Mrs. Carlson's driveway.

The car bumped over potholes down the long dirt drive. When we reached the county road, I stopped. "Now, look both ways," Mom instructed. "Turn your wheel to the left. Give it some gas, but take it slow. We're not in any hurry."

I pulled onto the narrow two-lane road. We rolled along fine until a pickup truck barreled up behind us. Mom stiffened her back and leaned forward. I glanced in the rearview mirror. I guess it didn't occur to the man driving the blue rust bucket to slow down as he crowded our bumper. When I failed to speed up, he blasted his horn. My fingers clenched the wheel.

Mom pointed. "You'd better turn into the next driveway and let this guy pass."

Before I reached the place where I needed to turn, the guy laid on his horn again. In a panic, Mom exclaimed. "Turn, turn here. I said turn!"

I could see I wasn't close enough to make the turn, but I did as instructed. I jerked the steering wheel with a hard crank to the right and our car plunged into the ditch alongside the road. My foot slammed down on the gas pedal, and the engine bellowed like an angry bull. Our old Galaxie flew airborne up the other side of the ditch and plowed through a fence.

Mom yelled, "Hit the brake!" We bounced in the seat as the car landed with a thud in the middle of a pasture.

My hands dropped from the steering wheel. For a moment, we sat silently. I took several deep breaths, afraid to look at my mom.

Finally, she asked, "Are you okay?"

"Yeah." I turned to face her. I expected a harsh scolding, but when our eyes met, we burst into hysterical laughter. We threw open the doors and climbed from the car. Still laughing, we leaned against the fenders to steady ourselves.

Two brown horses stopped munching grass in the adjoining field. They trotted over to the wire fence to observe the strange happenings. If horses have eyebrows, theirs were certainly raised. They tilted their heads and stared, mouths agape. Their funny expressions triggered more giggles.

"Excuse me," a man's voice interrupted. "Excuse me. Are you ladies okay?"

We spotted the blue pickup parked in the driveway and an older man hiking toward us, totally confused at what was so funny.

Mom quickly pulled herself to a more dignified pose. Still shaken, she staggered through tall clumps of grass toward the irritated truck driver. "Yes, we're fine. I was just giving my daughter a driving lesson."

"I'm so sorry," he said. "I would never have honked my horn if I'd known a teenager was behind the wheel."

He checked the car over and didn't see any damage. However,

the tires had sunk into the soft ground, leaving us stranded.

"Well, I'm in a hurry. As long as you ladies are okay, I'll be on my way."

"Thank you for stopping to check on us," Mom said.

We watched him hop into his truck and drive off. "You'd think he might have offered us a ride," I said.

The property owner didn't answer the door when we knocked. Mom scribbled a note with our name and phone number and wrote we'd be back to claim the car and have the fence repaired. Then we walked to her friend Jeannie's house, which wasn't far.

After a cup of tea and a good chuckle, Jeanie drove us home.

When Dad arrived home from work that evening, the first words out of his mouth were, "Where's the car?"

Mom and I exchanged a knowing smile, sealing a new bond between us. She told Dad what happened and admitted being partly at fault for overreacting to the situation. For the first time in my life, I saw her as a person, not just my mother.

And, thanks to Mom, that was not my last driving lesson.

~Kathleen Kohler

Love Engraved

A gift consists not in what is done or given,
but in the intention of the giver or doer.
~*Seneca,* Moral Essays: Volume III

When my brother Paul and I were in middle school, we ordered a "personally engraved Mother's Day plaque" for our mom a few months before the big day. Being teenagers, we forgot all about it until one Saturday morning when we found ourselves face to face with a tough-looking teenager at our front door holding a small plastic-wrapped object stamped "C.O.D."

"You ordered a plaque cash on delivery," he said.

We were broke, so I did the only thing I could — stopped Mom in her slippers and asked if we could borrow twenty dollars.

"What for?" she asked suspiciously.

"We can't tell you."

Sensing our desperation, she turned and went into the bedroom while the three of us — Paul, I, and the plaque dude — waited awkwardly.

We heard her muffled conversation with my dad.

"What do they need it for?"

"I don't know."

"Who's at the door?"

"I DON'T KNOW."

Our parents came out cautiously. Mom handed me a tightly folded twenty-dollar bill. I gave it to Plaque Man, who released the shrink-wrapped tribute like a little hostage and left without another word.

"Happy Mother's Day!" I said to Mom, handing over the mystery object.

Mom opened the plastic wrapping and stared at the plaque, which was much tinier in real life than it had appeared in the catalog. She fingered the thin plate on which her own name was cheaply etched.

My father blurted out, "THIS cost TWENTY dollars?"

Over the next few years, I saw that plaque displayed prominently in the living room, then on a bedroom shelf leaning on some books, and later, beneath the books.

My mother's name rubbed off in a matter of weeks, and the plate developed sickly green spots, like moldy bread. The plaque ultimately migrated to the garage, and finally vanished.

Looking back, the plaque was pathetic as tributes go, but then the same might be said of Mother's Day itself. How can an entire year's worth of appreciation be captured in one day, one card, or one gift?

My mother can't cook well, rarely offers advice, and is uncomfortable with excessive human sentiment. Her maternal instinct is limited to a small range, with worry on one end and denial on the other. But she showed me one thing: what it means to be unconditionally supported, no matter what I do.

The memory of that awful, cheap plaque struck me suddenly last week as I accepted a handmade Father's Day card from my daughter. I thanked her as if it were the most valuable gift she could give me — and indeed it was.

Impulsively, I called my mom. I told her that, in my mind, no one can hold a candle to her — and not just because it would light her liberally applied perfume on fire.

She had no recollection of the plaque incident and when I reminded her, she responded in a way that brought the moment instantly back to me: "I can't believe I gave you twenty dollars!"

She never asked for that twenty back, maybe recognizing that the memory — and the intention attached to it — is now worth much more. That's a true motherhood instinct if there ever was one.

~Joel Schwartzberg

Dear Mothers

Mothers hold their children's hands for a short while, but their hearts forever.
~Author Unknown

Dear Mother,

You were utterly unknown to me. I imagined your face, your hair, your touch, but you were merely wisps of smoke, and I played a child's guessing game.

You gave me life when you didn't have to; you carried me, nurtured me, nourished me inside. Then you let me go.

***

Dearest Mother,

You longed for me. I was a dream in your heart that couldn't come true. Yet you found a way. You believed that if you wanted something truly enough, purely enough, it would come to you. You traveled far for me at a moment's notice.

You brought me into your life and gave me a home. We shared the same birthday, and you said I was the greatest gift you ever received. You cared for me, nurtured me, and helped me to grow. You were there for my first step, my first day of school, and my first period. When I was sick, you sang to me — off key.

You taught me to ride a bike. You taught me to celebrate my successes. And when I had failures, you commiserated with me, encouraging me to try again. When my heart was broken, you held me and cried with me. But you never promised me it wouldn't break again.

We were a real family, as real as any other. You told me where I came from while still making me feel loved. And when Daddy died, you made sure that I still felt safe and adored. When I needed him, as a willful adolescent, you did all you could to take his place. I gave you more kinds of grief than I could count, but you loved me anyway.

When I became engaged, you rejoiced for me. You welcomed my fiancé into our family without hesitation and began planning a beautiful wedding. My heart broke in a million irreparable pieces when you died before you could walk down the aisle with me. I realized that we're never too old to need our mothers.

***

Dear, Dear Mother,

You embraced me when I married your only son. You took me in as your own daughter, even though you had two others. You have always been there for me. When I became a mother, you shared your wisdom as my own mother would have but couldn't. You gave me a family when mine was gone and made me feel a part of something bigger than myself. And you got to be something my mother never did: a grandmother.

***

Now I'm a mother. I endeavor to live up to the examples set by all the mothers in my life, I hope that the young women I am raising will become mothers like the ones who came before them.

~Audrey RL Wyatt

Stuck

A mother is a daughter's first best friend.
~Author Unknown

My mom says that when I was a toddler, she carried me everywhere on her hip. "You would sit right here and wrap your legs around me like a little koala," she says. "I had to cook while holding you, vacuum… sometimes I even used the bathroom like that because you wouldn't let me put you down."

I used to cringe whenever she reminded me of this, especially in front of my friends from high school, but it's very true. I've always been close with my mom, and I love spending time with her. We're a lot alike, with frizzy auburn hair, freckled skin, and the same goofy sense of humor. Growing up, it was just the two of us, and I always looked up to her. To me, she was not only the coolest mom in the world, but also the most amazing friend.

She taught me all about classic rock, from Pink Floyd to Queen, and let me eat ice cream straight from the carton. She had an endless supply of jokes and knew all about the best rides at Disneyland. She was fun and silly, and worked hard to keep me happy.

As a preschooler, I remember fighting to stay up past my bedtime because I didn't want to miss any time with her. I would beg her to read me story after story before lights out. Some nights, after I was supposed to be asleep, I would sneak out of bed. I would hide on the stairs and watch the evening news with Mom as she sat on the couch, oblivious to my presence behind her.

One night, when I was about six years old, I tiptoed out of my room and sat on the stairs. I remember thinking, as I sat, that the TV screen looked blurry from my hiding space. It had always looked a little fuzzy from my spot on the stairs, but that night I could barely make out the news anchor. I squinted and then opened my eyes wide, but nothing seemed to work. I leaned forward, trying to get as close as I could by pushing my head against the stair railing. Still, though, the screen didn't look right. I leaned forward a little more and… *pop*. My head went through the railing to the other side of the staircase.

No big deal, I thought. *I'll just pull it out.*

I leaned backward and felt pain on the sides of my head as I pulled against the metal bars. I was stuck!

After another minute of trying, I gave up.

"Um, Mom?" I called out. I knew I would be in trouble for being out of bed, but I had no other choice but to give away my hiding spot.

She looked around, confused.

"I'm up here."

Mom stood and turned around. My vision was still blurry, so I couldn't see her face very well, but I'm sure she was disappointed.

"Jilly, what are you doing out of bed?" she said in a stern tone.

"I don't know," I said, now embarrassed.

Mom climbed the stairs. "Why are you sitting like that?"

In my mind, I like to imagine I said something cool and sarcastic like, "What, like this? I'm super comfortable," but instead, I began sobbing as I admitted, "I can't get out."

"Really?" she said.

"Really."

She bent down on the steps to be at my level. "Are you okay?" she said. "Does it hurt?" and finally, "How did you get in there?"

"I couldn't see the TV, so I leaned forward," I said through tears.

She was silent for a moment, looking from me to the living room below. "You couldn't see the TV from here? Maybe we should get you to the eye doctor."

Great. My head was stuck, I was embarrassed, and now I needed glasses.

I pulled my head back, trying again to free myself, but it still wasn't budging.

"So you really can't get out?"

I shook my head back and forth, at least as much as I could considering my limited range of motion.

"Are you sure?"

"Yes."

Mom finally stood up. "I guess we'll have to call the fire department."

I didn't know if this was just a threat, but I was unnerved by the prospect of firemen coming into our home. I imagined reporters catching wind of my embarrassing problem and seeing myself on the evening news the next day, big, burly men in uniforms using a saw to cut apart the stair railing. I was horrified. Panicked, I yanked my head back as hard as I could once more, ignoring the pain. Finally, my head slipped through the metal bars, and I fell back onto the step.

After a moment of shock, I broke into laughter. Mom started laughing, too.

The sides of my head were sore and my ears ached from being folded forward, but I was free!

Mom scooped me up and checked my head for any injuries, both of us giggling as she pushed my hair out of the way to check for bruising.

"I think you're good as new. I hope you learned something today," she said, still smiling. "Come on, let's get you to sleep."

She walked me upstairs and tucked me in bed again.

That night, I certainly did learn my lesson: not to stick my head through the stair railing (and that I needed glasses). But I didn't stop sneaking out of bed to watch the news with Mom. I always wanted to spend time with her, and to this day I'm so happy I was able to appreciate her, even back then.

Now in my twenties, I look back and I'm in awe of how well she handled the challenge of being a single mom. She gave me fun memories full of laughter and plenty of ice cream, and even managed to scrape together enough money to take me to theme parks and concerts.

Now I live in a condo on my own, but I'm still very close with her. We talk on the phone most days, or at the very least I'll send her a text to say "hi." But at least one evening a week, I drive to my mom's house and have dinner with her. Then, we sit on the couch and watch the news together.

~Jilly Pretzel

My Mother, My Teacher

The mediocre teacher tells. The good teacher explains. The superior teacher demonstrates. The great teacher inspires.
~William Ward

It is often said that the best teachers are those who are able to form a genuine relationship with their students. This was never a problem for my second-grade teacher, as she viewed all of her students as family. Of course, in my case, it was actually true, because my second-grade teacher was my mother.

I know that in many schools this would not be allowed, but I attended a Lutheran school in a small town. At the time, I was not so sure it was a good thing to have my own mother as my teacher, but I was only in second grade — what did I know?

I won't lie and say the year was easy. At times, there were difficulties starting the school day with a clean slate as teacher and student when there had been an issue at home as mother and son. The same can be said for after school when my mother just happened to know every little thing that happened during the school day. At times, it could be confusing to determine whether I was talking to my teacher or my mother.

My mother decided to move me up to the third-grade reading class. I used to joke that it was simply because she wanted me out of her classroom for part of the day, but I knew better. She had too much respect for education to do such a thing. The faith she had in me to challenge my reading stuck with me as I began to share my mother's love of books. Looking back at my life, it is easy for me to see that the year with my mother as my teacher was the point when books became a central component of my life — first reading, and later, writing.

Even as she was in the hospital dying of cancer, my mom was teaching me. I will always cherish the conversations we had in those last few weeks. In spite of everything, my mother, the teacher, still made me check in to see how her students were doing as the school year wrapped up. She also continued to press me about my future writing projects to make sure that I never gave up on my dreams, as well as checking that the plots all made sense. Even as it became clear that the end was close, she was working to make sure that everything from the funeral plans to the bills was in order. The example she set in those last days, as she never wavered in putting others first, taught me more about living a life of faith than any other lesson I have ever learned.

I'll always remember and cherish that about her: She was a pure teacher. She didn't do it because it was expected of her, but because she was called to teach. She didn't do it because it was easy, but because it was hard, and she was gifted. She didn't do it because of the money, but because it was vital. Few things made my mom smile more than a former student's success in life. She was always able to look back to remember her former students and share stories with them about their time in her class. Every Christmas, our tree and house would become a walk down memory lane for my mom. The smile wouldn't leave her face until all of the decorations from students had been placed properly around the house. That was her pure love of teaching.

I know that some people might balk at the idea of having their mother as a teacher as I did at first, but looking back I can tell you I am grateful for that opportunity. In fact, she was my best teacher. She taught me in the classroom, but I also had the privilege of her teaching me every single day of my life. While telling time and counting change are important lessons, they pale in comparison to the lessons Mom taught me about faith, love, and family. Those lessons were at the core of who she was and are cornerstones of my beliefs because of her. She was my favorite and best teacher, and she never stopped teaching me those lessons, right up to the very end.

~David L. Bishop

Angel, Grandma, Friend

A grandmother is a little bit parent, a little bit teacher, and a little bit best friend.
~Author Unknown

It all started at a birthday dinner for one of the moms from daycare. We had balloons and ribbons and confetti all over the table—and no kids.

Okay, technically, there was one kid: my second child was only eight months old, so I brought her with me that evening. The restaurant was busy, as usual, so my baby was tucked out of the way on the floor in her car seat. I was happy to be out for a nice dinner with friends, and I didn't mind that I would only be able to half-participate.

I chatted happily until I was interrupted by little chirps from the floor. When I plucked my baby girl out of her seat, I could see that she was not sleepy, nor was she hungry. "I think she just wants to see what's going on," I said to the mom nearest me.

After settling my baby, I tuned back to the conversation, which had moved on from where I left off. As I scanned the faces across from me, looking for a place to jump back in, I noticed a woman across the restaurant weaving her way through the tables. She was heading straight for me.

"I would never have known there was a baby in here if I hadn't seen you walk in carrying her. She's being so good," the woman said with a wide smile. "Oh, she is such an angel. Can I hold her?"

I froze. It would be rude to say "No," wouldn't it? My child's safety comes first, of course, but I'd been taught all my life not to be rude. This woman seemed brash, but harmless.

"Sure," I said. Even as I write this, that moment of uncertainty still makes me catch my breath.

As she gently cuddled the baby in her arms, she told me about missing her grandchildren in Montreal. My own mom had passed away before meeting her first grandchild. I relaxed a bit, realizing that holding this baby was a gift that I could give to this other grandmother.

"I can watch her for a bit while you enjoy celebrating with your friends," she offered.

Now I had found my line in the sand. No. This was not an option. "That's a wonderful offer," I managed, "but I'll have to feed her in a few minutes, anyway. Thanks, though."

Not put off in the least, the woman took a few more moments to enjoy snuggles, then returned my baby to me. "If you ever need a surrogate *grand-maman*, please give me a call," she said, handing me her number. "*Au revoir*."

We have a supportive family on both sides, but we live on Vancouver Island, and our aunts, uncles, and grandparents are scattered across Canada — spread from the east coast to the prairies to the west coast. I know that it takes a village to raise a child. I chose to reach out, rather than retreat. Prior to this, I had seriously considered checking out the local resources for surrogate grandmas, but had never actually done anything about it. Now I had one drop into my lap! Could it be that easy?

I agonized over that phone number like a teen agonizing over a crush. A few weeks later, I called her. "Hi, Dee. Remember me and my baby girl from the restaurant in Coombs?"

Much to my surprise, it was that easy. In no time, we had arranged a play date in the park: Dee, my two children, and me. And then another date for coffee and a muffin at a café. And then one at the beach, and another… and another…

And then I agonized over how easy it was — how easily this random person fit into our family's life. *If it seems too good to be true, it probably is,* I thought on many occasions. But I resisted the thought and continued on this journey, despite my misgivings.

And that's how Dee became our surrogate grandma. She's a young, spirited *grand-maman* who has adopted my children as her own grandchildren. When I'm stuck with too many places to be in too few hours, she gently reminds me, "Isn't that what a grandma would do?" When she needs a break from her own life stresses, she borrows the kids for water-gun fights and obstacle-course races and picnic suppers on the beach. And each time I pick up the kids, *she* thanks *me*—for trusting her with my children, for giving her that special pleasure reserved just for grandparents.

And Dee doesn't just take the children off my hands; she sometimes takes my hand, too. "I think we deserve a nice dinner out," Dee said to me six months later. "What say we go celebrate Mother's Day together?" So we did. We enjoyed a glass of wine, an unhurried meal and easy conversation.

A year later, Dee insisted that my partner and I needed some time away from the kids. "Go. Make a reservation. Just let me know the dates and make it happen." So I did. I left the children with Dee so Mom and Dad could enjoy a weekend getaway in Tofino.

It's been nearly two years since that fateful meeting at the restaurant. If I had brushed off this perfect stranger, I would never have Dee. She often reminds me, bluntly but firmly, what a wonderful family I have and how lucky I am.

There is no question I made the right decision in the restaurant: to trust that there are good people in the world, and maybe even angel-friend-grandmas among us. I'm learning from Dee, so I can be someone's surrogate grandma one day, too.

~Nicole Muchowski

Alone in the Airport

Being there at the moment is everything.
~Author Unknown

It was my first job interview. I was wearing the new business attire my mom had bought me for Christmas and holding the leather padfolio I had borrowed from my dad. I felt so official. I sat at the airport, head held high, the twenty-two-year-old college student who was going to have a job after graduating. A church had called me for a last-minute interview; I was one of two candidates being flown out to Florida for the spot. I was determined to win them over.

Checking my watch, though, I was starting to get anxious. My flight was running late, and I needed to make a connection in Atlanta.

"We are so sorry, ladies and gentlemen. There is really bad weather in the Atlanta area, so your flight is being delayed."

I had a little leeway in my timing, but with each subsequent announcement, my confidence diminished. Finally, I knew it. I would miss my connection. I couldn't help but wonder if this church would still consider me, the twenty-two-year-old college student, when I couldn't make it on time for an interview.

I called Mr. Clark, the man who asked me for the interview, and gave him my choices—fly out to Atlanta that night and get to Fort Myers, Florida, by morning, still being able to make most of the interview slots they had planned, or schedule a new weekend to fly down.

"We will get you a hotel in Atlanta. Fly down there, and we'll see you in the morning when you get here."

They still wanted to meet me! My phone buzzed with a confirmation number for a hotel room in Atlanta, and I sat calmly in the boarding zone until my flight was cleared to go. Sure, this wasn't exactly the plan, but it was going to work out. I would still stride in confidently, wearing new business attire, holding a padfolio, looking fresh and ready for this interview—the twenty-two-year-old college student who was going to have a job out of college.

The plane touched down in Atlanta at 11:00 p.m. I was ready to get to the hotel and crash. As I exited the plane, I was struck by the immense number of people crowding the airport. I knew Atlanta was a huge city, but this place was packed. I made my way to the taxi and shuttle services, and gave the hotel a call.

"Hello, I have a room reservation for tonight, and I am just wondering how I get to your hotel. Do you have a shuttle service from the airport?"

"You don't have a room," an apathetic voice responded.

"What do you mean, I don't have a room? I have a confirmation number." I couldn't help but notice how small my voice began to sound.

"A ton of flights have been re-routed tonight. So I'm sorry, all of our rooms are taken. You don't have a room." The apathetic voice didn't sound sorry.

I hung up. Frustrated, but determined. What would a confident twenty-two-year-old out of college do? Surely, she wouldn't cry. I called Mr. Clark to let him know about my situation, and I found a wall of hotel listings.

I heard everyone making phone calls around me, and they were all saying the same thing. "There is nothing." The airport seemed bigger, there were people everywhere, and I had a horrible realization that I was on my own. I knew no one in Atlanta. I was going to have to sleep on the floor in an airport before my first job interview. This twenty-two-year-old college student began to want her mom.

Was this a closed door? Would I even get a chance to interview for this position?

My cell phone rang.

It was Grandma.

Why was my grandma calling me at 11:30 p.m.? Anxious to keep my line free but also a little worried about what this call would entail, I answered.

"Hello?"

"Are you in the Atlanta airport?" my grandma asked.

"Yes." I had no idea how she knew that. She lived in Orlando, and I hadn't told her anything about my flight situation.

"Well, I was flying back from Oklahoma on business, and my flight got re-routed. I am in the Atlanta airport, too."

I told her where I was and waited for her to find me. I couldn't believe my grandma was in the airport. But when she found me, I was thrown into further shock.

"Ronni, my flight to Orlando was boarding, and as I got up to get on the plane, I had this sudden feeling that I needed to get off this flight. God told me that you were here in this airport, and I needed to get a hotel room and find you."

My grandma gave up her seat, booked a flight for the next morning, got a hotel room, and had found me in the mess of the Atlanta airport. The door was still open — I was going to make it to my interview.

That night, I got three hours of sleep because my grandma's new flight was at 5:00 a.m. After that incredibly stressful night, I expected to be exhausted and not in great interview shape. Thankfully, God gave me another miracle, as I had the energy and endurance of someone well rested throughout the interview process. And two weeks later, I got another phone call that changed my life — the church offered me the position. This twenty-two-year-old college student did graduate with a job!

~Ronni Meier

My First Away Christmas

The greatest thing you'll ever learn is just to love and be loved in return.
~Eden Ahbez

In the winter of 2015, I spent my first Christmas away from home. When I say away from home, I mean everything that goes along with home too. I was away from my mom and dad, my sister and nephews, my pets, my Christmas tree — everything.

I was worried about spending such an important holiday away from the people I love so dearly. I was afraid I'd be a nervous wreck. I was scared I wouldn't be able to appreciate the holidays as much. And to top it all off, my family (for the first time ever) was going to spend the holidays somewhere warm. They were visiting Florida to spend Christmas on the beach. And I was choosing not to go.

All for the new love of my life: Devin.

I am from Ontario, and Devin is from Nova Scotia. Our two hometowns are roughly 2,000 kilometers apart from each other (1242 miles for you American readers). Although Devin and I were both going to school in Ontario, we knew that the distance between our families was something that was going to be a challenge for the rest of our relationship. But we knew we *had* to spend this Christmas together.

Devin and I had both had a rough semester at school. And we were both really good at supporting and comforting each other — we just couldn't imagine being away from each other during our first Christmas together as a couple. My family said they understood, but from their not-so-subtle hints, I knew they were trying to get me to reconsider going to cold Nova Scotia instead of warm Florida right up until our flight left Pearson Airport. But I was resolute: Devin and I were meant to spend this Christmas together and, though it would be a bit of a sacrifice on my part, I wanted to see it through.

We landed in Nova Scotia to hugs, kisses, and squeals of joy from Devin's mom and dad. I was so happy that they were pleased to see me. From the first moment I stepped off the plane, I felt immediately welcomed into Devin's family. They plied us with appetizers and finger-foods when we got to Devin's childhood house, and his mom treated us to her famous "silver bells"—a holiday drink made up of milk, Kahlua, and some other tasty spirits. The house was decorated to the nines. Even the bathroom had Christmas decorations! My family was usually not so enthusiastic in their decorating.

But even though Devin's family was supportive, loving, and excited—more than I could ever hope for in prospective in-laws—I kept finding myself drawn to the bedroom or to the television. I felt myself get upset with Devin more quickly than was normal. I got a little quiet and sullen. I felt depressed. My family kept sending me beautiful pictures of their Christmas vacation in Florida. And I kept sending them pictures of Nova Scotia snow banks (which are beautiful in their own way, I suppose).

Devin's family did things a little differently than mine. In my family, we have one big dinner with our extended family and that's it. The rest of the holidays are time for our immediate family. My mom and I would play board games, my dad and I would go to the movies, and my sister's family and I would play in the snow. My sister's husband has an amazing tradition of creating a "snow track" around their back yard, where he uses his tractor to pull as many people as can fit on a sled around the track. We usually go until we all fall off.

In Devin's family, there are several family dinners. There are maybe two or three big dinners with extended family and several smaller dinners or get-togethers in smaller groups. Now, I know I might be sounding completely ungrateful—but it got pretty stressful! I am used to holidays where we try to relax and recharge, but instead I felt like a piece of cargo getting shipped from one Christmas event to the next. And trying to remember all of the names and faces—impossible!

Christmas morning arrived and I was surrounded by Devin's family: his mom, dad, sister, brother-in-law, and his little nephew. We watched his nephew open all of his amazing presents, and he loved every one of them. Then came our presents: and I was completely and utterly overwhelmed. Devin's family piled gifts on me: clothes, jewelry, fancy soaps, chocolates—it was amazing. All I could do was say, "thank you so much" over and over, but I felt like it didn't fully express the gratitude I felt to them for including me so whole-heartedly in their Christmas. And I tried to tell them over and over that they didn't need to get me all those gifts. I already felt so loved and accepted by them; that was gift enough. They reminded me that although I was "away," I had a new home with them.

But there is one gift from Devin's family that will remain in my heart's memory for a long, long time. During one of the big family get-togethers, Devin's grandma approached me with a gift.

Now, Devin's grandma, Dodie, is the sweetest, loveliest lady I think I've ever met. I loved her from the first time I met her; I felt that we instantly connected—just like she was my own grandma. She is full of stories and knowledge; she's caring and compassionate and her family is her greatest source of pride and joy.

She approached me at the party with a gift and I instantly felt guilty: I didn't have a gift for her. But she insisted I accept and open the gift she brought me.

The party was loud, children were playing, grownups were drinking wine and beer and "silver bells" and catching up on the latest family news. New babies were being cooed over, folks were sitting on chairs and couches nibbling on food. The room was buzzing with noise, and even though it was chaotic, it was clearly filled with love.

And in a quiet, unacknowledged corner of the room, I opened the gift from Devin's grandma. Inside a lovely box was a piece of delicately twisted, knotted colored glass. It looked like a small piece of art. With the glass, there was a card that read:

> *This knot represents a never-ending connection. This gift unifies the giver and recipient; it links our fate and binds us together.*

She looked into my eyes, beaming and smiling.

"As soon as I saw this I thought of you," she said. "We love you so much. Welcome to our family."

~Emily Bednarz

Chapter 2

My Amazing Mom

Lasting Lessons

Our mothers give us so many gifts. They give us
the precious gift of life, of course, but they also
leave treasured lessons that can guide us
along our journeys even when
they are no longer with us.
~Maria Shriver

Better Late Than Never

My mother… she is beautiful, softened at the edges and tempered with a spine of steel. I want to grow old and be like her.
~Jodi Picoult

As a child, more often than not, I woke to the familiar burnt-aluminum smell of another kettle whistling itself to death on our electric range. It was the starting-gun odor of my mother's daily race from behind.

Mom was chronically late, always doing "one more thing." She'd pick up a ringing phone, or have to place dishes in the sink, or lose her car keys. And heaven help my sister or me if she sent us to wait for her in the car. Then, there'd be no one to remind her there wasn't time to dust the coffee table.

I remember standing outside the elementary school every Tuesday, assuring my Brownie troop leader that Mom hadn't forgotten me. Mrs. Williams would snort a response that let me know she had more important places to be.

I was late for school, doctors' appointments, band practice, sleepovers… you name it. Each incident made me more uncomfortable and less forgiving. How hard was it to get out the door on time? Thank goodness, Mom's boss was tolerant. She charmed him with her quirky sense of humor and strong work ethic once she arrived, but the shadow of disciplinary action always loomed over her employment. In her defense, I'm sure her role as a single, working parent didn't help, but I wasn't ready to entertain that as a valid excuse.

My wedding was the icing on the three-tiered cake. After a thirty-five-minute delay, the guests were fidgety. My side of the crowd collectively rolled their eyes when my mother rushed in and raced to her seat. I walked down the aisle, tense-lipped, a few minutes later.

In my late twenties, Mom became seriously ill. She had battled sarcoidosis since shortly after I was born. The disease builds scar tissue on major organs in the body. In her case, it had begun attacking her lungs. For years, she'd disguised its symptoms and powered through its debilitating exhaustion without complaint. None of us had known how hard it was on her.

My husband and I made the decision to move her into our home, and I began to comprehend tardiness. I juggled a new marriage, an ailing parent, and a job. I struggled to be on time for *anything*.

When my son was born two years later, it was even worse. Mom's chronic "one more thing" became *my* life. Every time I needed to be somewhere, Mom required my attention, or my son needed a diaper change, or the new puppy threw up the diaper I just changed because I left it on the floor. Then my husband would call from work to ask if I could please make him a doctor's appointment. Meanwhile, my own appointment scheduled for thirty minutes earlier was long lost.

I finally understood Mom's years of failed punctuality. The phone that rang on her way out the door was a friend who needed advice, or my sister forgetting her gym clothes. And Mom's never-ending search for lost car keys? Well, that was a daily occurrence for me now. I even understood the dust on the coffee table. Once noticed, it had to be dealt with because later she'd be too tired. Mom had been responsible for it all as a single parent while suffering a chronic disease. And she'd done it valiantly with smiles and jokes that vexed me to no end as a child.

I apologized to her once in the midst of scavenging my son's diaper bag for my darn keys. Near tears, I looked up to find her holding them out to me.

"Oh, Mom, I'm so sorry. I used to get so mad at you when I was a kid."

She squeezed my shoulders. "Honey, we're all judgmental jerks when we're young. I knew you'd outgrow it."

What could I do but laugh?

When Mom passed, our family arrived early for her memorial service. We were greeted by a funeral director with a slight sheen of sweat on his lip, although it was a chilly October day.

"I'm afraid I have some distressing news," he said. "There is a problem with your mother's ashes. They will not be available until tomorrow."

Mom had managed to be late for her own funeral! My sister and I burst into laughter. We laughed until we cried, and then we giggled some more. Mom was more with us in that moment than if her earthly remains had arrived. As mourners entered the church, the news spread that an empty urn sat next to my mother's picture. People suppressed grins and whispered, "Of course." Mom had made sure we smiled in the midst of our grief.

After the service, I found myself alone in the sanctuary. It hit me how much I had taken for granted that Mom would always be there… eventually. I desperately wanted a few more minutes to make sure she knew how much I admired, appreciated, and loved her. But I was too late. Somehow, though, I knew she understood.

And now, when my son is hurrying me out the door, or I've forgotten his lunch money, I remind myself it's okay to fall short sometimes. My mother taught me that perfection has nothing to do with being an amazing mom.

~Leigh Smith

One Day We'll Laugh About This

In school, you're taught a lesson and then given a test.
In life, you're given a test that teaches you a lesson.
~Tom Bodett

After attending Catholic school through seventh grade, I was introduced to a whole new world when we moved and I started attending a public school. There I discovered that men could be teachers and some folks unabashedly ate meat on Fridays! These revelations and others provided a bit of culture shock, but one discovery made this thirteen-year-old girl's heart gleeful. Having a wardrobe comprised of more than plaid skirts, white blouses, and navy blue knee socks was cool. Very cool.

This lack of a dress code tested my mom's seemingly uncomplicated child-rearing philosophy. She believed that unless one of her six children's requests would result in physically or morally threatening consequences, she would grant permission. I know this makes her sound pretty hip, but she was Irish Catholic, so the "morally threatening" component covered a lot of territory, including dressing immodestly.

After deeming my fashion choices no threat to my immortal soul, Mom gave the green light, and I relished all the colorful, fashionable choices I had. That is, until I purchased a teensy red halter top and a pair of very tight pants.

I knew this ensemble would take my mother to her knees (literally), so upon modeling it for her, I wasn't surprised when she stated calmly, "We'll talk about it later." I knew she would make a prayerful decision about allowing me to wear it, and she would get back to me when she'd received her answer.

Within a couple of days, Mom informed me that I could wear the outfit, but only around the house or to a friend's house. It was not to be worn in mixed company and most definitely not out in public. As long as my girlfriends could see how "with it" I was, I was satisfied.

The opportunity to strut my stuff came that Saturday when Caroline, the most popular girl in eighth grade, invited me and five other girls to hang out at her house. The squeals of approval upon my arrival did not disappoint, and we settled in to gossip and giggle. All was right with the world until one of the girls suggested we walk into town. I knew that "walking into town" meant walking past the homes of several cute boys and then hanging out in the park by the busiest intersection in town. I also knew that explaining I couldn't walk into town would be social suicide, so I chimed in, "Great idea!"

All too soon, my companions and I arrived in town, and they took their places on the park bench, leaving me standing there in that skimpy halter with my navel peeking out for the world to see. As if on cue, Mrs. Behner, our next-door neighbor, emerged from a store and waved at me before getting into her car. I had no doubt she would immediately report me to my mother.

I told Caroline I wasn't feeling well and we silently trudged back to her house. When her mother dropped me off at home, who did I see through the kitchen window but my mother and Mrs. Behner! I hoisted up my pants, hoping to cover the offending navel, offered a prayer to my guardian angel, and walked in.

"Did you have a good time?" my mom asked. I checked the women's faces for any sign of conspiratorial alliance. Nothing.

"It was okay," I said, and my mother and Mrs. Behner returned to their cribbage game, leaving me confounded but relieved. I silently thanked my guardian angel and prayed my luck would hold.

Caroline held no grudge for the ruined visit to town, and the following week at school, she accepted an invitation for an overnight on Friday. Mom agreeing to an overnight on Friday should have been a red flag, but I chalked it up to her being pleased that I was settling into my new school and making friends.

"In here!" Mom called from the kitchen as Caroline and I bounded into the house after school that Friday. "I'm making you girls root-beer floats."

My mom was indeed making root-beer floats. She was making root-beer floats dressed in a denim miniskirt, an off-the-shoulder peasant blouse, a psychedelic headband, and round, tinted granny glasses. I was aghast. Moms were supposed to look like moms!

"What are you doing?" I stammered. "What are you wearing? Where did you get that?" Caroline slurped her root-beer float, riveted by my outburst and the peculiar spectacle of my mother.

"Do you like it?" she asked. "Just a little something I picked up a couple of days after you visited Caroline."

"I don't know what to say, Caroline. I'm so embarrassed." I hoped my eyes conveyed the serious need to keep this incident between the two of us. "My mom doesn't dress like that, I swear! I don't know why she's dressed like that!" But, of course, I knew exactly why she was dressed like that. Message received loud and clear.

Caroline shrugged and said, "She seems nice. Sometimes moms are weird."

Decades later, dementia robbed my mom of her independence, most of her memories, but never her faith or easy laughter. Searching for photographs and trinkets from years gone by in hopes of making a connection, I found those tinted granny glasses at the bottom of the grandkids' dress-up box. I slipped them on, peered over my nose and asked, "Remember these, Mom? How do I look?"

She smiled softly, and I took her hands in my own. "I remember, Mom," I said, caressing her paper-thin skin gently with my thumbs. "I remember it all, and I am grateful."

~Maureen Hart

Catch a Grateful Habit

It is not happiness that makes us grateful.
It's gratefulness that makes us happy.
~David Steindl-Rast

My mother has a hobby of being positive, and it is quite contagious. One day, I took Mom to the doctor's office. As the nurse took Mom's blood pressure, she asked, "How are you?"

Mom answered the usual: "Fine, thank you."

The nurse gave the general answer, "That's good," while routinely pumping the blood-pressure bulb.

Later, when we got in the car to go home, Mom said, "Bet that nurse didn't even hear my answer."

"What do you mean?" I asked.

"The nurse probably asks all the patients how they feel," Mom said. "The usual answer is, 'Fine, thank you.' The next time someone asks how I am, I'm going to answer differently."

I asked her, "What are you going to do?"

"I'll think of something," she said.

The next time Mom had her blood pressure taken and the nurse asked the usual "How are you?" question, Mom gave a new answer: "I'm grateful!"

The nurse flashed a big smile and said, "Oh, I like that!"

Mom told me later about a time when she walked into the library office where she volunteers. The receptionist smiled and said, "Hi, how are you?"

Mom answered impishly, "Not well."

"That's good," the receptionist said cheerfully… then paused to think a moment. "Oh, I'm sorry. What's wrong?"

Mom laughed and explained she was testing various responses to "How are you?" and wondering if the person asking really hears the answer. She said, "From now on, I'm answering, 'I'm grateful.'"

The receptionist beamed and said, "Oh, me, too. That's wonderful."

So, now I am into this grateful "hobby" of my mother's. Often a person asks me, "What are you grateful for?" It's easy to come up with a positive answer.

Depending on the day or circumstances, I'll say, "I'm grateful for the sunshine (or rain) today." Or, "I'm grateful to be here talking with you!"

In *A Whole New Mind*, author Daniel H. Pink suggests that once a year on our birthdays, we write something that we are grateful for that particular year. Each year, we should add a new grateful item to the list.

Pink also suggests starting a Grateful List on a young child's birthday. The child should be old enough to understand the project. Years later, the child can look back to see the history of his or her gratefulness.

A guest on a noted doctor's TV show remarked that people who log in their Grateful List every day are twenty-five percent happier than those who don't.

Since I've taken up Mom's hobby, the reaction to my "I'm grateful!" answer is often a double take or a pause, and then a delightful response. There is always a smile! Here are some of the responses I've received:

Really? I like that.
That's a great response!
Love it!
How refreshing!
Awesome response!
Oh, I'm stealing that!

When the secretary at my local gym smiles and asks how I am, she knows my answer. If I ask her, she'll echo back.

Yep, this hobby is contagious for sure!

~Sylvia Brich Thompson

Do As I Do

I actually think that the most efficacious way of making a difference is to lead by example, and doing random acts of kindness is setting a very good example of how to behave in the world.
~Misha Collins

About a year ago, I was walking out of the grocery store and noticed an elderly woman putting groceries in her car. Instinctively, I walked up to her and offered to put away her shopping cart. She was pleasantly surprised and more than happy to receive my help.

After I put away her shopping cart, I got in my car, looked over at my daughter and came to a touching realization.

My mother *never* explicitly said to me, "Whenever you see an elderly person putting away his or her groceries, offer assistance by putting away the shopping cart." Instead, I learned the art of compassion and empathy through my mother's actions.

As I gazed into my daughter's eyes, I silently prayed, "Please let me be the kind of mother who teaches my daughter the most valuable life lessons through my actions, not just my words." If I instill half as many values within my girls as my mom instilled within her children, I know they will turn out just fine.

~Denise LaRosa

A Not-So-Faraway Reality

My mother's gifts of courage to me were both large and small. The latter are woven so subtly into the fabric of my psyche that I can hardly distinguish where she stops and I begin.
~Maya Angelou, Mom & Me & Mom

In the summer of 2003, my world was ripped apart. *Harry Potter and the Order of the Phoenix* had finally been released, and I had waited all day for my mom to get off work and pick me up to go to the bookstore. When she finally arrived, she honked from the driveway, not even bothering to come inside to change out of her scrubs.

The entire drive, she listened contently to my chatter as I summarized Harry's adventures thus far for the millionth time. It was a story far removed from her reality, but she was happy I loved to read.

We parked outside the bookstore and I hurried my mom inside. Just as we were entering, a man was exiting with a shopping bag swaying at his side. The alarm went off and we paid no mind because we were entering the store. But then we heard a man yelling at us, and we froze instantly.

"STOP!" cried a man, his pale face splotched with red as he stomped toward us. "Wait! Don't move!" he commanded.

Behind us, the man with the shopping bag was rifling through it looking for his receipt. But the man who was yelling didn't even notice him. His beady little eyes were too focused on my black mother and me.

"Open up your purse!" puffed the man, stabbing his finger toward the worn leather bag slung over my mother's shoulder. A pin on his chest glinted in the fluorescent light. It read: Assistant Manager. The man with the shopping bag shrugged and left.

My mother recoiled. "What? Why?"

It was as if a light bulb flickered on in his mind, illuminating the narrow pathway leading to reason. The assistant manager looked at the entrance, saw the white man exiting, and then looked back at my mother. The color drained from his face. It was then he realized he had made an assumption — a sick, hurtful assumption.

"Uh, let me see your phone," he said, a poor attempt to undo the damage he had done. "S-sometimes they, uh, t-trigger the alarm." But I already saw the proverbial steam shooting out of my mother's ears.

This man had summed up my mother in a matter of seconds based on something as superficial as the color of her skin. My mother, the registered nurse, who had worked tirelessly on her feet all day attending to the needs of others and rushed home to take her daughter to the bookstore. My mother, who worked and went to school, while raising a daughter by herself, was nothing to this man but a common thief. All her sacrifices and accomplishments were nullified because this man saw only the color of her skin. And even though I knew he was wrong — so incredibly, disgustingly wrong — I pleaded with my mother.

"Please," I whimpered, but to no avail.

"How dare you!" she yelled back, her voice a thunderous roar of pure outrage. I slinked a few steps away to the table covered with the deep blue covers of the latest edition of *Harry Potter,* and my heart felt heavy. Before all of this, I only cared about what was happening in the wizarding world. After all, Voldemort was back! But reality and its frothing hatred had reared its head and seared its way through the fantasy.

At that moment, I wished I had my own wand made of gnarled wood and dragon heartstring. I wished I could cry out *Stupefy!* to send the assistant manager flat on the cool linoleum floor in an immobilized plank, wide-eyed and mouth ajar. I wished I could cast *Silencio!* to render my mother's words of truth into nothingness as if they didn't need to be said. But I was helpless and confused, caught in the crossfire.

People stopped and stared on their way to the checkout line. Some shook their heads with disapproval. Did they care that my mother had been profiled the instant she entered the store?

Finally, a woman arrived on the scene. Her pin said Manager. She calmly asked what happened. My mother took a deep breath and explained in exasperation the injustice that had occurred. The woman looked at her employee, whose eyes had shifted downward, and then looked at my mother. She said, "I'm sorry."

The man didn't apologize.

We left the store without the book we had planned to buy. Back in the car, my mother looked at me with eyes reddened with suppressed tears and said, "I'm sorry."

We drove fifteen minutes to another bookstore. This time I didn't prattle on about Harry Potter's world. We entered the store, and I plucked the book from the display in the entryway. But as we walked to the checkout line, I realized something had changed.

I had coveted this book for what felt like a lifetime, but the excitement I should have felt as soon as its velvety cover touched my hands had been diminished. In pursuit of this book, I had experienced racism for the first time in my twelve years. Before, racism was something safely tucked away within the shiny pages of textbooks. Those black-and-white pictures were of a faraway time, so far removed from my reality. But now, I had seen it firsthand, and I had also seen my courageous, indignant, hardworking mother be the victim of it, but also its conqueror. She became my hero, capable of stopping a bad man in his tracks. As Harry Potter would say as he cast a spell to ward off evil: *Imperio!*

~Cassie Jones

By My Side

A mother is she who can take the place of all others but whose place no one else can take.
~Cardinal Mermillod

After she was diagnosed with terminal cancer, my mother chose to go home to die. Family and friends helped my brother and me give her round-the-clock attention so she could remain there until the end. That time gave each of us the opportunity to talk candidly with her, and we used it gratefully.

About two weeks before Mom passed away, I sat quietly by her bedside watching her sleep. I thought of all the things she had done for me over my lifetime, and I began to cry. She woke and saw the tears streaming down my face. Her immediate reaction was to comfort me. For just that fleeting moment, I felt like a small child again. She took my hand and said, "Oh, honey, don't cry for me. I've had a wonderful, full life, and I have no regrets."

I sobbed, "Mom, I'm not crying for you; I'm crying for me. I don't know how to go on without you. You're my mother, my friend, and my partner, and I'm scared to live without you." I felt selfish and embarrassed.

She squeezed my hand with the little strength she had and reassured me in a soft voice, "You're the strongest woman I know. It is I who have been leaning on you these past years. You'll be just fine."

Several years earlier, my husband had died suddenly and unexpectedly, leaving me alone to raise our two young children. At the same time, my father was suffering from terminal cancer. I remember my mom saying that never in a million years did she think I would be a widow before her. She became one a year later, and she relied on me heavily for a while, until she learned to live alone as I had.

The two of us fell into a new relationship. We were already mother and daughter and best friends; we now became partners in the raising of my children. She was always available to drive or pick up one of them from sports or dance class. She attended school concerts, dance recitals, and hockey games. When someone was sick, they stayed home with her. There was nothing I couldn't count on her to do for us, and helping us gave her life new meaning.

We spent a lot of holiday time together as well. Sometimes, it was just long weekends at the cottage. My kids always took a carload of friends along for the fun. My mom and I cooked them huge meals and kept a lid on their shenanigans. This routine carried on well into their teenage years. Occasionally, we travelled out of the country. Mom was always there to back me up, and my kids came to think of her as their other parent.

My mother was also my voice of reason. I remember one instance when my son was in tenth grade. He had done something he knew I would not approve of, so instead of coming home, he went to his grandmother for backup. She brought him home and came in the door first. I will never forget the words she whispered quietly, "I know you are not going to be happy, but just remember, it's only hair. Pick your battles carefully." She opened the door, and there stood my son sporting a huge mohawk. I was horrified at first, but I realized she was right. There were more important issues in life than a hairstyle.

Several weeks later, we were having coffee together, and I asked her why she had been so relaxed about her grandson's haircut. I said, "I remember when I wanted to get my ears pierced in high school, and you almost had a fit. You said they were your ears until I was sixteen, and you didn't want holes in them. It seems like a very similar situation to the hair."

"You're absolutely right," she said, "and do you remember what happened?"

I thought for a moment and said, "Yes, I told you I hated you, and you were mean. We stopped speaking for weeks, and a friend at school pierced my ears for me anyway."

"That's right," she said quietly. "Your words and silence hurt me more than you could ever know, and I realized you were only trying to be in style. Every generation has their thing. I had to admit to myself that I had overreacted."

I smiled knowingly. "I guess we do learn from our own mistakes. Thanks for not letting me make one."

At Mom's funeral, her four grandchildren spoke about her. They each had their own little secrets about things she had let them do when they were younger. We laughed at these tales that could now be told. I could see her in my mind, laughing loudest of all, knowing there was nothing anyone could do about it now.

Mom was cremated just as she had wished, and the beautiful urn decorated in flowers and butterflies that held her ashes was lowered into the ground above my dad's casket. I remember her stating adamantly before she died that we should not come to the cemetery to talk to her. She declared bluntly, "I will not be there, but I will be with each of you every day, wherever you are." She was right. I still feel her by my side.

~Penny Fedorczenko

She Ironed Underwear

My second favorite household chore is ironing. My first being hitting my head on the top bunk bed until I faint.
~Erma Bombeck

I inherited some of my mom's good qualities, but organization was not one of them. I have eleven standard locations for my keys. Mom, on the other hand, dusted everything every Saturday morning like clockwork. She loved housekeeping, and her routines ensured every corner was immaculate.

If it went through the washing machine, Mom ironed it. Her grandmother took in ironing for a living and taught her how to iron. I slept on ironed sheets, our tablecloths were ironed, I blew my nose on ironed hankies, and, yes, I even wore ironed underwear. My father was a plumber, and he went to work every day in freshly cleaned and ironed clothing.

One day, in the summer before I left home for college, I walked through the kitchen. Mom was ironing. She summoned me to come to her. I had an inkling I was about to learn something I had no desire to know. I said, "No thank you," and kept walking. Mom rarely raised her voice, but I experienced one of those rare occasions that day. "Young man, you stop right there." I stopped, but I came no closer to her or her ironing board. Her dark brown eyes stared holes in my soul, and she emphatically thumped the ironing board with her forefinger.

That was the day I received my first lesson in how to properly iron pants and shirts. For the rest of the summer, I ironed not just my pants and shirts, but my brother's and my father-the-plumber's pants and shirts. Mom's older son wasn't about to be launched into the world looking like a ragamuffin.

In my four years of college, I tried my best to keep my skill with an iron a secret. For the first two years, I managed pretty well by doing my ironing while the rest of the guys in the dorm were partying. Eventually, word got out that I was better at ironing than the girls in the other three dorms. I didn't like doing my own ironing, and now I was warding off guys who wanted to hire me.

My wife thanked Mom repeatedly for teaching me to iron. My mom was indeed special, and in this small way, she made me a good husband, in spite of my natural disorganization and my sloppy tendencies.

My mother died twenty years ago, and the entire family felt the enormity of our loss. It was, however, several years later that I realized just how far Mom's reach extended. I took over responsibility for doing my father's ironing. One day as I ironed his retired-plumber's pants, my nephew's girlfriend walked through Mom's kitchen. She came over and watched me iron. After four or five minutes, she asked me to teach her to iron pants and shirts.

Uncle Ed was suddenly passing on the skill his mother taught him. This took place in the same kitchen, in the same location, where I learned this skill I had tried to avoid learning.

Incidentally, I never learned how to iron underwear. Mom spared me that burden. Maybe even she knew that some traditions aren't worth passing on.

~Ed VanDeMark

Mom Knows Best

Everything is negotiable. Whether or not the negotiation is easy is another thing.
~Carrie Fisher

As a first-time car buyer, I had brought my parents along for moral support. It was a cream-colored AMC Renault Alliance and *Motor Trend* magazine's Car of the Year. My mom had been researching how to bargain with a car salesman, and she was determined to help me get the best deal possible.

I was satisfied when Mom convinced the salesman to go inside to see his manager the first time, and he came back to say he could knock a few hundred dollars off the sticker price. But not Mom! She had read that they could always come down from their first offer. I was sweating at this point. But, sure enough, a second trip inside to visit his manager, and the salesman was prepared to offer us an even better deal. *Good work, Mom!* I thought. *Now let's do this thing!*

But my mom was sure she could get the salesman to give us an even better deal. He vowed that he could not. Mom stood there and argued with him. Meanwhile, I was trying to shrink into the pavement. *Please, Mom,* I thought, *you're starting to embarrass me.*

And then she did it; she crossed the line. Mom started to walk away, saying we would take our business elsewhere. And that was when I thought I was going to die of embarrassment. In my view, this person had given us a good-sized chunk of his time, and he had interceded with his manager twice on our behalf.

But my dad was walking away with her, and I wasn't going to stand there to negotiate the deal all alone. I followed my parents and shrunk into the back seat of their car as we drove off the lot.

"Mom! What on earth are you doing? Now I'll never get that car! He let us walk away, so that's it!"

"Trust me." She said. "He has our contact information. He'll call us and offer us a better price. Believe me, he wants to sell us that car."

Yeah, right, I thought. The twenty-minute ride home had me beside myself. Not only had my mother embarrassed me by making a scene and walking off the lot, but she had caused me to lose the car of my dreams. I was fuming.

We walked into the house, and I sat sulkily watching the phone. We weren't in the door five minutes when the phone rang. It was the car salesman. "Miss Carnright—you've got yourself a deal!" I got my dream car at a very good price—and I learned a hard lesson. Even when you're the ripe old age of twenty-five, sometimes your mom still knows best!

~Laurie Carnright Edwards

Learning to Laugh at Yourself

To make mistakes is human; to stumble is commonplace; to be able to laugh at yourself is maturity.
~William Arthur Ward

In the spring of 1991, the phone in my studio apartment rang. Upon answering, all I heard was my mother's laughter. Laughter being contagious, I began to chuckle a bit and asked her what had happened. She continued to laugh so hard that nothing she said was audible.

"I'll call you back" were the last words I heard before she hung up.

Knowing that it must not be serious if she was laughing, I went about my business, wondering what she had done this time. The phone rang again and this time she was able to say a few words between the laughter.

"I put my head in the ceiling fan." More laughter.

"What?" I was starting to laugh myself. "Why would you do that?"

"I saw a cobweb up on the shelf in the kitchen…" Laughter. "So I stood on the chair to wipe it away… then *whomp, whomp.*"

I exploded into laughter, and soon tears began rolling down my cheeks.

I could hear more laughter coming from my father. It was just like my mother to do such a thing. We were all laughing at this point, and I tried to ask if she was okay, but gave up. If she was laughing this hard, then she was fine. Just an average day for my mother.

Over the years, she has done some pretty hilarious things, and she always comes out laughing at herself. Ever eager to share her stories, she is often the topic of conversation at family gatherings. Being able to laugh at yourself is one of the lessons that my mother has taught me.

I have learned to take note of her antics. For example:

1. Don't put flour on strawberries. It tastes bad and is difficult to wash off. Use sugar instead.
2. When heating up hot water, do not blame the microwave after the timer goes off and you remove your cold mug. The kitchen cabinet was not made to heat water.
3. When you are unable to find the milk in the refrigerator, try looking in the cupboards.
4. When taking out the trash, don't leave it downstairs. The garbage man does not have a key to your house, and it might start to smell after a while.

Her hijinks aren't limited to the house — parking lots are another source of amusement. One time, she and my father went to the movies at the local mall, and freezing rain was coming down as they left the theater. Not wanting to get her hair wet, my mother started jogging to the car. With the slippery pavement, it wasn't long before she fell onto her stomach and slid quite a distance, past a group of teenagers heading into the mall. She was laughing, but clearly remembers hearing one of the teens ask his friends, "Did you see that old lady?" It only made her laugh harder.

She can often be seen walking the rows of automobiles, looking for her car because she forgot she drove my dad's. Once, she even unloaded her groceries into the wrong car, not knowing it until she got into the driver's seat and realized, "I don't have bucket seats." Quickly, she retrieved her cart to unpack her purchases and went in search of her car again.

Another favorite tale from the parking lot: While walking to my uncle's car in Florida, she was talking with my aunt and not paying much attention. She got into the back seat of the car and closed the door. In the front seat, a little old man she had never met turned around and asked, "What are you doing?"

Shocked, she said simply, "Oh, wrong car." As she opened the door to leave, she offered the man some advice: "You should really lock your doors."

My uncle and aunt were standing by the correct car, laughing. My mother scurried over and got in, laughing the entire time.

Cars and Florida are a bad combination for my mother. After finishing a game of golf, my parents, uncle, and aunt stopped at a restaurant for dinner. My mother was changing out of her golf shoes in the back seat as my father parked, got out of the car with my uncle and aunt, and locked the door behind him. With the child-resistant locks on, and unable to reach the locks on the driver's side door, my mother was locked inside, the Florida sun beating down on her. The others had entered the restaurant and were seated before they realized she was not with them. Looking out the window next to their table, they spotted her banging on the rear window, waving frantically and laughing. They all burst out laughing, too, causing other customers to notice my mother locked in the car. My father made his way outside and unlocked the doors. When they returned to the restaurant, all the customers and staff were still laughing.

My mother offers much humor to this family and to others. Laughter is the best medicine, and with her background in nursing, it is no wonder that she uses laughter to make people better.

~D.K. Laidler

My Grandmother's Candy Dish

Some people can't believe in themselves until someone else believes in them first.
~From the movie Good Will Hunting

My grandmother had a small, two-bedroom apartment on the second floor of a building in Youngstown, Ohio. Her face lit up when we arrived, tired from hours of driving. I remember her soft, lilac-scented lap, smooth dusting powder, tightly curled white hair and low-heeled beige shoes.

My parents would stay the night and then leave me for a longer visit. Grandma Myers and I would spend several days, just the two of us. We usually visited Fellows Riverside Gardens at Mill Creek Park. My grandmother loved walking through the extensive flower gardens. From her, I learned the names of roses, lilacs, impatiens, petunias and daisies.

Each visit, I would perch on one of her two couches and look through old, loose photographs, older generations of our family intermingling with newer ones in the disorganized drawer of her breakfront. She would sit beside me, naming people, so that I learned my family's faces without ever meeting most of them. After several years, I knew who they all were. I loved looking through those photographs, most of them black and white, seeing my mother as she grew up. My mother had passed away when I was four, and we were each other's only remaining connection to her.

On Grandma's coffee table was a leaf-shaped candy dish, full of colorful, hard candies. Some were in clear wrappers, and some had wrappers that resembled strawberries. I would eye her candy dish, but she never invited me to have one. One day, when we were talking about going to visit her sister, she noticed me eying her candy dish.

"I always keep candy here," she said, smelling sweetly of Lily of the Valley talcum powder and wearing a belted dress. "I told your mother that the candy was for guests, and she never touched a single piece. I was very proud of her for resisting the candy." My grandmother fixed her hazel eyes on me behind their cat-shaped, rhinestone glasses. She looked at me a while in silence to see if I understood what she was saying.

I thought over her words. She was not inviting me to eat the candy. Rather, she was suggesting I should not eat any of it at all. I thought this was a bit cruel, and I was sad at first. But I realized that my not eating the candy was very important to her, and so I did not eat one piece. We dropped the subject, and I never asked her for any.

When my grandmother's niece came for a visit, she offered her and her daughter Becky a piece of candy. Becky was near my age, and she happily unwrapped one and popped it in her mouth. I was jealous at first. But then I was proud. I realized that I was not a guest in Grandma's house. I was family; I belonged.

After a while, I hardly noticed the candy dish, and I did not feel tempted by it. Her eyes gleamed with approval in the evenings, when she would look at it and notice it was still full.

Looking back over the long years, I realize she taught me willpower. I would not have believed I could be in the room with candy and not eat a single bit. My stepmother used to hide Snickers bars, not trusting any of us, but I knew from the clink of the good flatware that she had hidden them in the dining-room buffet. My grandmother left candy out in plain sight, and there it stayed. She believed in me, and I didn't want to disappoint her. I still look at that hard candy in stores, knowing it's not for me. I can live without it.

I take my kids to botanical gardens, and I teach them the names of flowers: salvia, hydrangeas, lupine, and foxglove. These are the scents of my grandmother, and it makes me feel close to her.

~Brenda Davis Harsham

The 33 Things My Mother Taught Me

All women become like their mothers. That is their tragedy. No man does. That's his.
~Oscar Wilde, The Importance of Being Earnest

My mother passed away from pancreatic cancer two years ago. Naturally, the grieving process has been hard, but I'm now to a point where I can think of all the wonderful things my mother tried her best to instill in me during the glorious thirty-three years she was in my life.

I often catch myself doing something that my mother taught me — be it an unorthodox organizational technique or a quick and sensible hairstyle — and I chuckle to myself remembering how wondrously idealistic some of her advice was. But that was my momma — a sweet, spirited woman who was never opposed to looking silly or going against the norm in order to solve a problem. She even went so far as to wear a fanny pack, because her number one rule was to be prepared.

My mother kept useful things close at hand for those "just in case" moments, whether they turned out to be a cut, a bruise, a toothache, or a zombie apocalypse. Everything was neatly organized into individual plastic sandwich bags (along with a few extra bags just in case, of course). And although I've forgone rocking a fanny pack, I've been known to carry my purse essentials in separate Ziplocs. Thank you for that tip, Momma.

Here are thirty-two more awesome tips, tidbits, and life lessons that my mother shared with me throughout the years, one for each year I knew her as it turns out. Some of these things, she simply told me. Others are things she had to "shake" into me (figuratively, and sometimes literally). All of these things she showed me through her beautiful spirit and shining example.

1. Always clean the house before leaving on a trip. It can be a huge letdown to stay at a luxurious hotel for a week, and then come home and be reminded of your own housekeeping inadequacies.
2. Staying at home with your children (as I do) is a true gift that many parents don't have the opportunity to receive. Don't take it for granted.
3. Keep a flashlight on your key ring.
4. Keep a roll of paper towels in your car.
5. There's nothing more important than spending time with family.
6. If you can't tell anyone about a particular activity, it's probably not worth doing.
7. Reading is fun.
8. Always keep an apple corer and a melon baller in your kitchen utensil arsenal. You never know when you'll need to make a fruit salad.
9. Have an option to weigh? Write down the pros and cons. It may seem cheesy, but it works.
10. Who in the heck cares if you wear white after Labor Day? Wear what you want.
11. Be sweet.
12. You're never too old to learn a new trade.
13. Traditions are a wonderful thing. Be they huge family dinners or regular holiday rituals, traditions allow you the opportunity to create memories that children will carry for a lifetime.
14. Never be afraid to try something new. Doing the same thing all the time is boring.
15. Learn to bake.

16. Save curse words for when you're really, really, REALLY angry. That way, they have more impact. I never heard my mother curse until I became a teen. When she did it, I was scared to say anything to her for the rest of the day. Her point had been taken.
17. Always make time to stop and smell the proverbial roses.
18. Keep wet wipes in your purse. They come in super handy.
19. Ask for help when you need it. It's OKAY to need help sometimes. (I'm still working on this one.)
20. Your husband is the leader of the household… or at least make him think that he is.
21. If you have multiple children who like to tamper with their gifts under the Christmas tree, write a code name on the gift tags. I was Frosty, my sister was Rudolph, and my brother was Dasher. The trick is remembering who's who on Christmas morning.
22. Seafood is awesome.
23. Clean up as you go. There's nothing worse than cooking a full Southern meal, sitting down to eat it, getting the sleepies, and realizing that you have a sink full of pots and a grubby counter that aren't going to clean themselves.
24. Learn how to change a tire.
25. Positive thinking and prayer can lead to miraculous things.
26. Good music can be the soundtrack of your life.
27. There's nothing wrong with faking it till you make it.
28. Wearing someone's nice hand-me-downs or decorating with thrift-store items can actually enhance your frame of mind and put you in a headspace to go for the things you may not have now.
29. Be different.
30. Always continue to educate yourself.
31. Don't be afraid to stand up for what's right. The day my mother yelled, "THIEF! THIEF!" after she witnessed two men stealing from the front table of Macy's was the day I learned

this. *(Mom, they could've KILLED you!)*

32. If you lie, you'll probably cheat; if you cheat, you'll probably steal. Don't lie.

~Kesha Phillips

Clarity in the Fog

If nothing is going well, call your grandmother.
~Italian Proverb

His blue eyes gleamed with excitement. "Will you marry me?"

"Yes!" I exclaimed. As we hugged, I stared at our initials carved into the tree. Immediately, a sick feeling came over me. What was I doing? I was only nineteen. I looked down at my hand where the ring sparkled as the sun shone through the trees. Was I too young for this?

It had been a whirlwind romance. I only met him a few months before he proposed. We attended the same university, met at a Bible study, and spent nearly every day together from the moment we first met. It seemed picture perfect. At first. Then the controlling behavior began. The constant calls to "check in" when we were apart, the jealousy, the obsessive need to know all of my passwords… It all happened so subtly that I didn't even realize these were all red flags. The next thing I knew, we were making plans to move to Oregon after the wedding, and I was being stripped of my car and my family. I was in too deep.

"Are you sure you're ready for this?" My mother's eyebrows rose with concern.

"Of course! I'm fine!" I wanted to prove that I was old enough to make this life-changing decision on my own. She knew he wasn't a good fit for me, as did the rest of my family. They would drop subtle hints that they were worried, but they didn't want to push me away in case I did end up married to him. They saw the controlling tendencies and how I had changed, but I was so swept up in the moment that I couldn't see the warning signs. I proceeded with the wedding plans out of embarrassment and stubborn pride.

My dreams haunted me. Friends appeared to me in my dreams saying: "You shouldn't marry him. You hardly know him." In one dream, I stood at the chapel the day before the wedding, but the decorations were being torn down. At first, I ignored the dreams, but deep down I was doubting my decision. Even so, I buried the doubt far enough that it would take more than a dream to shatter my determined resolve.

Three months before the big day, I took my fiancé to visit my grandmother in the nursing home. In her state of dementia, she couldn't recognize me and barely put a few words together, let alone a sentence. No matter whether she knew me or not, I loved visiting my granny. I wanted to show her the ring on my finger that used to belong to her mother — the ring that she had passed down to me. As we settled into the comfortable couch, sitting on either side of her, I began telling her about the wedding plans.

"You're getting married?" she asked. I was shocked at the clarity with which she put the words together. It was the most she had spoken in months. She looked at me as if she knew me but couldn't say my name and didn't know how we were related. I told her how we wanted an exotic wedding in Mexico, then chose a beach wedding in Oregon, before finally settling on a chapel at home in Montana.

"You're getting married?" She stared down at the save-the-date and the invitations that were to go out the following week. I told her about the wedding colors and the beautiful red roses I had just ordered.

"You're getting married?" By the third time she asked, that uneasiness in my gut grew even stronger. Was she trying to tell me something?

Granny sat staring at our picture, stroking it with her wrinkled, delicate hands. Suddenly, she looked up, stared at me straight in the eyes, and said, "You're too young to get married."

Shivers went down my spine.

She was so cognizant in that moment. Was this a message from heaven? On top of my deeply hidden doubt and the dreams warning me not to go through with it, this was the last straw. I knew exactly what I should do.

The following week, I went to visit my fiancé in Oregon over Spring Break. As I drove to Bridal Veil Falls, where I was to mail the invitations, I stopped in front of the post office. I stared at the pile of invitations in the back seat, but I couldn't bring myself to carry them in. I turned around and drove home.

I never saw him again, and I never looked back. When I returned, my grandma was on her deathbed. As I sat by her side, listening to her raspy breathing, I was able to tell her that I was home, I was safe, and that she was right all along — I was too young to be married.

Thanks to that miraculous moment with my grandma, I have never regretted my decision to call off the wedding. Would I have canceled the wedding without my grandmother's comment? Probably not.

Six years later, I wear that same ring on my finger, only I'm married to the man I waited for, the man of my dreams. And we have a beautiful baby girl who may someday wear the same ring.

~Brooke Bent

Chapter 3

My Amazing Mom

What a Character!

To describe my mother would be to write about a hurricane in its perfect power. Or the climbing, falling colors of a rainbow.
~Maya Angelou

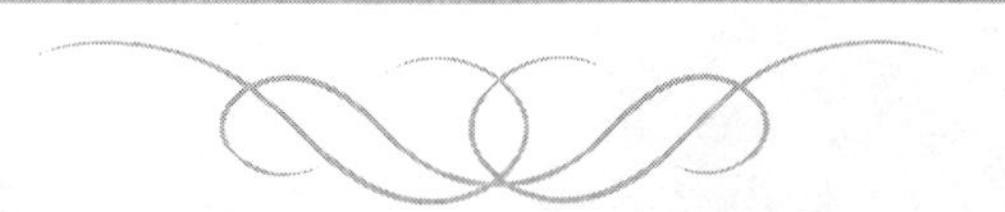

A Dreamy Pregnancy

Mommy knows a lot, but Grandma knows everything.
~Author Unknown

My mother and I have a tradition each spring. We wake up at 4:30 a.m. and spend our early Saturdays searching through people's unwanted possessions at the community yard sales. This is something I remember doing since early childhood and it has become a dear tradition to me.

One year, my mom came to pick me up and had the strangest smile on her face. As soon as I sat down in the car, she exclaimed, "You're pregnant!" Since I had zero symptoms of any pregnancy and was actually feeling my monthly cramps, I laughed at her. "No," she insisted, "you are! I had that dream again, and the dream is never wrong. I can feel it; you're pregnant!"

She went on to tease me unmercifully at every yard sale that held tiny baby clothes, beautiful baskets, like-new swings and adorable strollers. She would jab me with her finger and say, "Look, that's a great deal, and you need that! You have to buy it!" I told myself she was crazy. I had learned long ago how to shrug off my mother's silly antics, even the more persistent ones.

The sun had not even risen yet, and I had already been poked and teased a dozen times. All I could do was grunt and grumble and try to stay awake. I even woke up my husband, texting him about how crazy my mom was!

I was too tired to get out of the car at one sale, so I stayed in the seat and closed my eyes. I was startled awake by frantic knocking on the window. It was my mother, eagerly wanting to tell me something.

"You have to get this! It's a sign!" she exclaimed. I followed her pointed finger to an item that was apparently a sign of some sort. It was a Snow White and the Seven Dwarfs figurine.

"Huh?" I looked at her. "What kind of sign is that?"

"You always said the theme for your next girl would be Snow White. I had the dream that you're pregnant, and now there's your sign. You have to get it!"

I reluctantly went over to the table. "That's from Disney World," the yard-sale lady told me. "I bought it years ago to display."

My mom smiled and nodded, as if my obsession and adoration for Disney World was an additional sign. I asked how much it was, expecting it to be quite expensive. It was a vintage item, and I would later see it on eBay for seventy-five dollars. "I'll take five dollars," the lady said. Of course, I couldn't resist.

"You're pregnant, you're pregnant, you're pregnant," my mom chanted as we walked back to the car.

Nearing the end of our circuit, we stopped at a church that was hosting a household sale. There, I found my dream double stroller for only five dollars. My mom knew it was my dream stroller and got even more excited. "That's your stroller! You have to buy it," she insisted. "It's meant to be! I told you that you were pregnant," as if the stroller sitting there near the inside doorway was a pregnancy test that just turned positive. "It's a sign from God," she continued, shaking my arm and pushing me toward it. "It's even in church!"

I looked at the stroller, almost hoping that something was wrong with it. It was big, it would be hard to get back to the car, and I felt silly. I wasn't pregnant. In fact, I was cramping badly enough to be wishing that I had stayed in the car. But the stroller looked almost new. No flaws, no rips, no stains. I turned to a church worker and made sure it was still for sale. It was late in the day, and I was surprised that no one had already picked up this $600 stroller in such great condition. "I'll take it," I said as I pulled out a five-dollar bill, and my mom grinned.

We loaded up the car and stopped to meet my husband, who was taking me to the doctor. Our toddler daughter had collided with me days before and given me a black eye that ended up getting infected and swollen. I said goodbye to my mother, and then had to explain to my husband why there was a double stroller in our trunk, and why I was cradling a fragile Snow White figurine. Then I forgot about my crazy morning as we checked in to urgent care.

Forgot, that is, until the nurse taking my information asked me if I could be pregnant. "It's very unlikely," I told her and decided against saying that it was a possibility just because my mom had a dream that I was.

The doctor determined that I needed antibiotic eye drops to help my eye get better, but before he was able to prescribe them, they asked me to take a pregnancy test. Waiting for the results seemed to take forever. I sat on the patient table, too nervous to even make small talk with my husband. I felt like my period was coming any second and knew the test would be negative, but my mother's voice would not leave my head.

"Which way were you hoping this would go?" the nurse asked me as she came through the curtain. I jumped off the table and tried to see the test in her hand.

"Why?" was all I could exclaim, my heart pounding. Could it be possible that my mom's silly dream had been true, and that all of the signs she spoke of were actually real?

The nurse smiled and handed me the test. "You're pregnant!"

My infected tear duct burned painfully as tears sprang to my eyes, and I looked at the test in my hand. I was pregnant! Just three months before, I had suffered an early second-trimester miscarriage that had left me depressed and sad ever since.

Everyone at the front desk congratulated me as I waited for my prescription. The moment we walked out of the urgent care, I dialed my mother's number on the phone. She didn't answer with a hello or ask what was going on. Instead, I heard her voice tell me one more time excitedly, "You're pregnant!"

~Jill Keller

The Reluctant Astronaut

I still say, "Shoot for the moon; you might get there."
~Buzz Aldrin

It was 1955 and my family was vacationing in New York City where we visited the Hayden Planetarium. This fine institution still flourishes, and today, through modern technology, offers virtual trips through space and firsthand looks at a re-creation of the Big Bang start of the universe.

In those days, shows were mostly projections of the night sky on the overhead dome. After the show, we saw a stand with a large ledger in the lobby. Visitors could sign up for a trip to the moon when that became feasible. Only a few pages had been filled. My dad declined, but I signed up. My mother, I'm sure in the spirit of looking out for a family member, wrote her name under mine. There the matter rested for the next few years.

President Kennedy launched the space program, and the original seven astronauts were chosen. Like most Americans, I was fascinated, but my mom was secretly alarmed. She had gotten it into her head that the government planned to begin flights at once. A primary facet of mom's persona was that you absolutely had to do whatever you said you would do. Since she and I had put our names down on an official-looking document, our time to go into space would come soon. I told her that the Hayden Planetarium was not a branch of the government, much less NASA, and we were in no danger of being selected. She listened carefully, but in the end patted my arm as she had when I was small and told her about the tigers that lurked behind the neighbor's shrubbery.

"Yes, dear. I'm sure that's true, dear."

She was humoring me while not believing a word.

The tragedy of Apollo 1 on January 27, 1967, reinforced her notion that moon voyages were practically suicide missions. The fact that I was deploying for a year to Vietnam almost that same day caused her a lot more anxiety than I ever knew. Just before Christmas of 1968, I was home on leave from the Navy. My sister's husband worked for NASA in the training department at the Cape. Consequently, my family had front-row seats for the launch of Apollo 8, the first mission to orbit the moon.

That night, we gathered in my sister's yard, all of us staring up at the nearly full moon and talking about the men up there. My sister had let slip to her husband that my mom worried she and I were on some list for moon missions. Before I could stop him, he pretended to confirm this and offered to find out how long before we would be strapped in and sent off. I dragged him aside and, in no uncertain terms, informed him he would suffer dire consequences unless he confessed the whole thing was a joke. He confessed, but again my mother wasn't really convinced.

On the long car ride back to Alabama, she kept returning to the fact that he was in the NASA program. "But dear," she would say, "Glen works there. He must know how they are chosen."

"Mom, that was just his twisted idea of humor. He told you it wasn't so."

"He was just saying that to make me feel better."

Each Apollo mission, I would get a call from her, ostensibly just to chat, but with the fear that she and I were now three people closer to our turn. When my business required travel to New York, I offered to return to the planetarium and rip out the page with our names. My mom, who never broke a law in her life or even jaywalked, was horrified. To her, obligation was sacred, even though it involved what she thought was mortal danger. With the return of Apollo 17 in December 1972 and the announced end of the manned moon program, I hoped her anxiety would end. When the space shuttle program started up, I felt she might worry again, but if so, I didn't hear about it.

Years later, I was with her during her final illness. As she drifted in and out of sleep, I thought about the woman I had known all my life. Her life had begun during the horse-and-buggy era and ended in the space age. She came from grinding poverty as a girl to self-sufficiency through her own efforts. She had come through two world wars and the Great Depression. Later, she and my dad raised two kids on what would be poverty-level income today, but we never felt poor. There had to have been many times she had fears, but she conquered them. Now, her body seemed small and frail, but her gallant spirit had not gone. Her eyes fluttered open, and we chatted about things for a few minutes. Then, apropos of nothing, she said, "You know, in some ways I'm kind of sorry they never did call us for that moon trip." She gave a tiny, mischievous grin. "I would have been scared, but if I was called, I would have gone."

"I know you would have, Mom," I responded. "I never doubted it."

~Charlie Wyatt

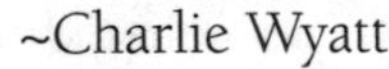

The Surprise Party

A smile starts on the lips, a grin spreads to the eyes, a chuckle comes from the belly, but a good laugh bursts forth from the soul, overflows, and bubbles all around.
~Carolyn Birmingham

The year my mother-in-law, Dorothy, was turning ninety, my husband Ted and his sister Crystal decided to throw a big party to celebrate. We would host the gathering, since it would be in August, and we had a pool that everyone could enjoy.

It wasn't going to be a surprise. Ted and Crystal thought that would be too hard to pull off, and their mother would certainly suspect something. So Dorothy was told ahead of time that everyone was coming to our house to celebrate her birthday and enjoy a backyard barbecue.

When the day arrived, our house exploded with friends and family, from babies on up. Kids ran around playing, while the adults cooled off in the pool or lounged on the deck. Crystal even joined some of the grandkids on the trampoline! Ted had set up a karaoke system outside so there was plenty of entertainment — good and bad!

The food was amazing. Everyone brought a variety of side dishes to go along with the standard hotdogs, hamburgers and barbecued ribs. My kitchen was littered with slow-cookers, casseroles, and desserts galore! We had chips and dips, baked goodies, salads, soups, corn on the cob, and baked beans. The aroma was wonderful!

It was delightful to see the joy on Dorothy's face as she watched her children, grandchildren and great-grandchildren enjoying a beautiful sunny day. Laughter could be heard from everywhere.

After many hours of good fun and good food, it was time to bring out the cake. Crystal and Ted handled the task of carrying the large sheet cake outside while I trailed behind with paper plates, forks, and napkins. The crowd erupted into a loud "Happy Birthday to You" song as they approached Dorothy sitting out on the deck. Dorothy smiled, and then made a wish and blew out the two candles—a "9" and a "0."

As Ted and Crystal placed the cake on the table, Dorothy said, "You know, I'm only turning eighty-nine this year." There was a stunned silence. Ted and Crystal looked confused and were clearly trying to do the math in their heads. Finally, Ted asked, "Why didn't you say something, Mom? Why didn't you tell us?"

To which Dorothy replied, "Because I wanted to have everyone together for the party. We don't get to do this often. I wanted to have the party!"

With that, everyone laughed and enjoyed the birthday cake. Later, we lit the tiki torches and had a bonfire, still laughing, realizing that we hadn't planned a surprise for Dorothy, but she had clearly surprised all of us.

~Lil Blosfield

The Lab Coat

Cleanliness is next to impossible.
~Author Unknown

During my childhood, the topic my mother and I most disagreed upon was the length of time an article of clothing could be worn before being washed. Mom thought a pair of jeans should only be worn for a maximum of eight hours before being consigned to the wash. I preferred to wear them till the back of my knees started itching.

In hindsight, I was probably responsible for her premature graying. But these differences of opinion were nothing compared to the time I brought my chemistry lab coat home. This garment had seen continuous service for over a year of weekly lab experiments. Standard treatment was to roll it up and stuff it into the locker, only to be unrolled the next week. It had never been cleaned. Assorted organic and inorganic chemicals were deposited on it, interspersed here and there with regular old-fashioned grime.

One day my locker door jammed so I had to take the lab coat home with me. My mother was appalled when she saw it. Initially, she refused to let that coat enter the house. She announced that she had not seen such levels of filthiness even in her oldest floor mops. Finally, after some cajoling, she allowed the offending garment into the house. The condition was that she be allowed to wash it. I tried to dissuade her, but to no avail.

So she went about her mission as diligently as she did anything she undertook. She brought all her (considerable) laundry skills to the task, soaking it multiple times in the strongest detergent she could find. She washed it by hand, not trusting a machine to do the job half as well. After a few hours, it was a tired but proud mother who brought the coat to me, nicely ironed, almost as white as it was the day it was bought.

The only problem was that there was only half a coat left. The bottom half was in tatters, and I realized that the multiple layers of grime had another function — that of binding the threads together. Without it, the threads had simply given up and dissolved. Even the pocket, with its double lining had a thumb-sized hole right through it.

The next day in the lab, I put on the coat, ruing my decision to take it home. The boy at the next table took one look at it and smirked. "Couldn't make it past your mom, could you?"

~Sandeep Sreedharan

My Mother, the Pistol

Some mothers are kissing mothers and some are scolding mothers, but it is love just the same, and most mothers kiss and scold together.
~Pearl S. Buck

I watched the scruffy stranger approach my elderly mother as I dropped her off at the entrance to the grocery store. He wore a grimy T-shirt with wording that bordered on obscene. I parked my car and rushed to check on my mother. By the time I got there, she already had her wallet in her hands. She was shelling out dollar bills, handing them to the man, one by one. Not wanting to show my alarm, I asked carefully, "Anything wrong, Mother?"

"Nothing's wrong." She rolled her eyes. "You always think something's wrong."

She started to walk away. Then she turned back to the man, whose name she had already learned. "And shame on you, Ed! Buy yourself a decent shirt, for Pete's sake," she admonished him. With a shake of her head, she handed him five dollars more.

I knew better than to lecture her about giving money to strangers. It wouldn't do any good.

My mother lived with my husband and me on and off. Her only income was from her lifelong savings and Social Security. So, usually she was careful about money.

I take that back. Sometimes, she was very extravagant. We just never knew. But I knew she could never turn down a person in need, like that shabby man outside the grocery store.

We did our shopping, and she waited for me at checkout. When the customer in front of us was collecting his change, he dropped a quarter on the floor. Knowing Mother, I could have predicted what was about to happen. Her foot slammed down on the coin as quick as a flash.

"Mine! It's mine!"

"Mother," I said. "Give the man his quarter."

Why did I bother? She gave me a dirty look.

"Mind your own business. It fell out of my pocketbook."

She picked up the coin and walked away.

Taking a quarter out of my purse, I handed it to the man.

"Sorry about that."

He smiled knowingly.

Mother was not like other mothers. Her life hadn't always been easy, living in a postwar, Communist Eastern European country and raising two children alone. She *had* to grow up tough. But she also had a heart of gold.

Our friends affectionately referred to her as, among other things, "Your mother, the Pistol."

I can't say it was always easy for me when she lived with us, but she and my husband Larry got along beautifully. Sometimes, I felt as if *he* was her real son, and I was the in-law.

She was feisty, and she was loving.

Many a day, my husband and I would come home from work to a house filled with the aroma of her European specialties, such as chicken paprikash or Wiener Schnitzel. Or maybe it would be a good old-fashioned American hamburger.

"Who wants the hamburger V.D.?" she'd ask innocently in her thick Slovak accent. She meant "well done." She got her Vs and Ws mixed up sometimes.

After dinner, the three of us would chat and laugh around the kitchen table. Sometimes, the playing cards came out. Mother had taught Larry a Slovak card game similar to gin rummy, but the rules changed as she saw fit.

She never cursed — until she was losing at cards. Then, watch out! Hopefully, there were no clergy or little kids around.

She never cheated either — until she was losing at cards. Then, if it was her turn to shuffle and deal, she'd make quarters, dimes, and nickels disappear in the blink of an eye. The magicians in Vegas would have been impressed. She'd cover the coins with the cards and her arms, and then gather everything toward her. As she'd shuffle, everyone's money would "accidentally" get mixed up with her own. When confronted, she would feign outrage.

"Whassa matter you?" she'd protest loudly. "You think I take a dime from you?"

We learned not to take a potty break when it was Mom's turn to shuffle. I believe she enjoyed cheating more than the card game.

Yes, she'd swindle her own flesh and blood and her beloved son-in-law out of small change. However, the next morning a few coins would appear mysteriously by our coffee cups.

"Oh, you dropped these last night."

We'd just smile.

But when Larry lost his job, I came home to find Mother at the kitchen table, hunched over her savings account passbook. Like many women her age, she had never learned to write a check. She had dealt with cash all her life. She kept the account in both our names.

"What are you trying to figure out, Mother?"

"I vant you to take out some money and give it to Larry. He doesn't have a job. How much do you think he needs? A thousand? Two? Take it out and give it to him."

When I told Larry, he was touched. He didn't need it. He didn't take it. But he was moved almost to tears to think that this woman on Social Security was offering some of her life savings to him, her son-in-law, a forty-something professional businessman.

Yet when a Very Important Person called Larry about a Very Important Position, and Mom was asked to take a message, she told him: "I can't now. I'm vatching *Veel of Fortune*."

The next day, we bought an answering machine.

Another time, I came home and found a strange man on his knees in my bathroom. He startled me half to death!

"Who are you, and what are you doing here?"

"Fixing your toilet, lady," he replied.

Mother rushed in. "Leave him alone! Can't you see he's busy?"

In the kitchen, I asked, "Who is he, Mother?"

"He's your new handyman," she announced calmly.

When I asked where she had found him, she replied, "On LBJ Freeway and Preston Road. He had a sign saying he was homeless and hungry."

"So you gave him our address? Tell me you didn't, Mother."

"Of course I didn't. Vat do you think, I'm crazy? I told him, 'Mister, if you vant some money, you have to work for it. Do I look like a millionaire?'"

"So how did he get into our bathroom?"

"I drove him here."

"You didn't!"

A woman in her seventies picking up men off the streets and driving them to her home! To *our* home. Scary!

But she must have been a pretty good judge of character because that man, Alfredo, was our handyman for the next ten years.

Yes, Mother was a pistol, a character, a magician, and a rascal with a spirit that was both tender and harsh. But I wouldn't have had it any other way. One thing she never was — Mother was *never* boring.

They didn't call her "The Pistol" for nothing!

~Eva Carter

Ready or Not

I am always ready to learn although I
do not always like being taught.
~Winston Churchill

Right before my twenty-eighth birthday, my mother announced she was leaving New York to move to a retirement community in Central Florida with her boyfriend. Mom and her partner decided to toss the majority of belongings accumulated from their separate lives, leaving most of it curbside.

A few days prior to their departure, I went to Mom's for a farewell/birthday dinner.

"I know how much you love my cat," Mom began, cutting nonchalantly into her chicken cutlet.

I knew where the conversation was headed. I did love our family pet, stoic black Sheba with her verdant eyes, but I was reluctant to accept her as a "gift."

"Um-hmm," I said, shoveling a mound of mashed potatoes into my mouth.

I was upset that my mother — my best friend — would be moving away, so having something as a daily reminder of our bond would be fantastic, but I wasn't yet ready to nurture another life.

Mom persisted: "You know, Steve is allergic to cats, so I was thinking..."

My fork picked up speed, now nervously galloping from plate to mouth.

Mom stopped and placed a warm hand on my arm. "Honey, are you okay?"

I dropped the utensil and swallowed hard.

"I could bring her to an animal shelter, but I didn't think you'd want that for her."

There it was. *The guilt.*

"Fine. I'll take her."

Mom pumped her fist in celebration of another item ticked off her "Things to Purge Before I Move" list.

Acquiring Sheba was no easy feat. The co-op I had just settled into didn't allow pets, which meant she would have to be smuggled in. This didn't hinder Mom's agenda. The woman I grew up with — a straight-laced role model who abided by every rule — was rolling up her shirtsleeves and concocting a scheme.

"We'll give her a mild sedative and sneak her in through the back entrance where the trash receptacles are," Mom said, pointing out of the window of my apartment. "And from there we'll bring her up in the freight elevator."

Still unsure, I glanced out of the glass casement, wondering if we'd really get away with it.

"Ready to do this?" Mom turned to me and smiled. I looked at her and gave a meek nod.

"Oh, and before I forget," Mom said, dipping into her purse. She pulled out a small envelope and handed it to me. "It's a gift card for Petco. I'll send you one every month. You know, to offset the costs of litter and food."

I studied the yellow card, my official golden ticket into cat-ladyhood, and shoved it into the back pocket of my jeans. "Come on, let's get this over with."

I held the door as MacGyver, I mean Mother, led the way out. In the back seat of our family sedan was Sheba, awake but tranquil, in the plastic carrier Mom had managed to secure her in. I stood back as my mother shimmied the case out of the car. When the cat let out a screeching howl, I jumped away, expecting Mom to do the same. Instead, she casually reached into the car and grabbed a blanket from the floor. I watched in wonderment as she draped it over the cage and hushed the animal back to a calm silence.

"Have you done this before? You're like the cat whisperer," I said, only half-joking.

"No, I'm a mom." She winked and then put a finger to her lips, signaling for quiet. I proceeded with caution.

As we approached the freight elevator, I jabbed a finger on the button and scanned the area for the nearest surveillance cameras. Luckily, they were aimed in the direction of the exit doors, out of view from where we stood.

"Geez, don't ever try to rob a bank," Mom said, and nudged me.

A loud, grinding noise followed by a thud of heavy metal echoed in the vestibule. Mom jerked open the door to the freight elevator and waved me inside. Slowly, the machine lifted us to the eighth floor. As we ascended, a black paw poked out from under the blanket and swatted at my leg. I swatted back. The cat did it again, but this time rested her paw on top of my hand.

"She's playing with you," Mom said with a grin.

"I know." I knelt down and rubbed the side of Sheba's head through the grate. She let out a vigorous purr, the vibrato of her throat tickling my fingers and, surprisingly, my heart.

The elevator jerked to a halt. The cat retracted into the carrier as Mom yanked at the door handle to free us. Mom eased down the hall and into my residence. Once we were inside, she set the holder on the carpet and let Sheba out. The cat's head darted in one direction and then the other. I was sure she was going to run and hide under furniture — either the sofa or the bed. I lowered myself and sat on the rug, cross-legged and curious, waiting to see which way she'd go. When she noticed me sitting there, she strutted over, stepped into the crook of my lap, arched her spine into a big stretch, and then nestled down into a big black ball of fuzz.

"You're a natural," Mom said.

I looked down at Sheba and petted her warm, velvety fur. We bonded, and I laughed at the realization that mothers really do know best once in a while.

~Dawn Turzio

The Jackpot

Most grandmas have a touch of the scallywag.
~Helen Thomson

In the summer of 1973, my new husband offered to help a co-worker by driving her '69 Lincoln from Los Angeles to its new owner in Las Vegas, in exchange for expenses. As we were newlyweds on the verge of broke, a free trip to Sin City sounded wonderful.

Grammy Lil lit up when she heard the plans. "A free ride to Las Vegas? Your Grandpa JoJo and I will come along."

But a family road trip wasn't what my husband and I had in mind. "Maybe not this time," I said.

She didn't hear me. "There's a little casino on the Strip with penny slots. Lots of jackpots. I can play all day for three dollars."

One more try. "It's going to be awfully hot in the desert, and I know how much you hate the heat." Grammy walked around with a damp washcloth behind her neck all summer because my grandfather refused to run the evaporative cooler in their tiny, post-war bungalow.

"Your big car won't have air conditioning?"

"Yes, I'm sure it'll have air conditioning, but…"

"If I can survive the summers in the Valley with your cheap grandfather, I can go on a little ride to Las Vegas in the fancy-schmancy car with the nice, modern air conditioning."

It was clear that my seventy-five-year-old grandmother, who had witnessed her family's execution by the Bolsheviks in the streets of Kiev, would not be denied her beloved penny slots by a little desert sunshine.

The trip began on a mid-August morning when my husband rolled up in the shiny black Lincoln to our rundown apartment building. The imposing vehicle looked more like the car of a local drug lord than that of an elementary school teacher.

As Grammy Lil and JoJo settled into the comfy back seat, I noticed wide compression bandages wrapped around Grammy's legs under her cotton, floral house dress.

She must have noticed my concern. "They're for the circulation. Not to worry," she said.

We stowed Grammy's aluminum walker in the spacious trunk and hit the road. The Lincoln was a sweet ride, with thick leather seats and an impressive stereo — the lap of luxury compared to the 1960 Impala handed down from my mother that I had been driving since high school. We rolled along in air-conditioned bliss, navigating the congested freeways of Los Angeles County, until we broke out of the traffic and onto the open highway heading into the desert.

After a couple hours of celebrating our good luck, we crapped out.

The hiss started low and slow, like a teakettle at the beginning of its boil, and I knew we were in trouble. As we climbed the grade outside Victorville, the nasty hiss became a loud whistle.

"Turn off the radio! Turn off the air!" JoJo ordered from the back seat.

Our driver complied, but the overheated engine complained even louder, sending up plumes of steam from under the handsome hood.

"I thought you said the car was in excellent condition," I yelled.

"That's what she told me," my husband yelled back. "But it's hot as hell out there. Maybe it can't take the climb with the air on."

"It's a Lincoln Continental, for God's sake. It's the size of a yacht. What do you mean 'maybe it can't take the climb'?"

Grammy intervened. "Yelling won't do any good. Let's pull over."

Luckily, I had packed a chest of ice, a Thermos of water, and a couple of washcloths. I wrapped some ice in a damp cloth and passed it over the seat for Grammy to put on the back of her neck.

The men opened the hood and watched the dragon spew its

contents. "We'll have to hitchhike into Victorville and get some help," JoJo said. After a short wait, a good Samaritan stopped to drive my husband and grandfather into town to call for roadside assistance.

Meanwhile, I was becoming more and more concerned about Grammy Lil. Even with open doors and windows, the black car already felt like an oven. To make matters worse, she wouldn't drink anything, insisting that the wet cloths would keep her cool like they did in her house.

"How about taking off the bandages," I said.

"No." The woman was stubborn, and there was no arguing. But fifteen minutes later, I began to feel panicky.

"Let's hitchhike," Grammy said.

"You're not serious."

"Get my walker," Grammy Lil commanded.

So, on a scorching afternoon, Grammy Lil, with bandaged legs, maneuvered her walker along a dusty shoulder of the desert highway and, without hesitation, stuck a thumb in the air. "Is this how you do it?"

We must have appeared an odd mirage to travelers speeding by—an old woman with a walker and her younger companion thumbing for a ride. Thankfully, an elderly gentleman picked us up after a few minutes. He had a shock of white hair and a George Hamilton tan.

Our handsome driver crammed Grammy's walker into the trunk of his compact car and gently helped her into the passenger's seat, while I stuffed myself into the back, sitting sideways in the minuscule compartment. The hot wind from the open windows burned my face while Grammy and our driver chatted and laughed up front.

After dropping us off at a Victorville diner, he said that he would get back on the highway and wait for the men by our disabled car to let them know where they could find us. I thanked him over and over for his kindness.

As Grammy Lil and I waited and sipped cold drinks, I leaned across the table and whispered, "Was that man trying to make time with you?"

"Maybe," Grammy grinned.

After spending the night in a cheap motel in Victorville, my grandparents called my aunt in Vegas for a pickup, while I called my parents in L.A. for a lift back to the city.

And every summer until she died, Grammy Lil loved to retell the adventure of hitchhiking through the desert with her granddaughter and making time with a handsome stranger — a jackpot more wonderful than three-of-a-kind on the penny slots in a little casino on the Strip in Las Vegas.

~Karen Gorback

Modest Mom

Dressing well is a form of good manners.
~Tom Ford

Out of breath from running, I tossed my schoolbooks on the kitchen table and raced downstairs to Mom's sewing room where I knew she was busy working on my gorgeous formal. Mom's willingness to sew "this" dress finally proved my mother wasn't such an old fuddy-duddy after all.

Earlier in the month, my boyfriend had invited me to a fall dance at his high school. We had lined my girlfriend up with his friend so that the four of us could go to the dance together. Once plans were set, my girlfriend wasted no time in buying herself an adorable halter dress to wear to the dance and suggested I do the same.

However, in my family, buying a formal gown was out of the question. My mother had always made our clothing, and I knew beyond a shadow of a doubt that Mom would never let me wear a backless, revealing dress, let alone sew one for me. After all, Mom had always been the queen of modesty.

Even though I knew the answer would be no, I finally gathered my courage and asked my mother if she could sew me a halter dress to wear to the dance, mentioning that my girlfriend had bought one. Surprisingly, Mom said yes.

During our trip to the fabric store, my mother found a bolt of slinky, royal blue material with tiny white stars on it, as well as a cute nautical-looking dress pattern. There was no question in my mind that

I'd have the most gorgeous gown at the dance. Mom's willingness to sew this dress completely transformed my opinion of her — she was now the coolest mom ever!

We spent hours in her sewing room while she took extra care to fit the pattern perfectly. Mom had an astonishing talent when it came to sewing. She could alter patterns or design her own as well as embellish her projects with ease. We were the best dressed kids on the block, and yet I never appreciated it at that time.

As Mom pinned the pattern to my front, she clipped some extra tissue paper and added it to the neckline. "What are you doing?" I asked. "This fits perfectly. I don't think we need it hiked up any higher."

"I don't want you tumbling out when you bend over," Mom mumbled as she pulled a pin from between her teeth and attached the piece.

Now I certainly didn't have all that much to expose, but figured I wouldn't argue with her. After all, I felt fortunate that she'd even agreed to make me this dress, and I didn't need her changing her mind.

However, the alterations didn't stop there. As the dress progressed, my mother extended the back of the dress up several inches. "This is almost up to my neck," I whined. "Besides, no one will see my back if that's what you're afraid of. My long hair will cover it."

This time, my mother remained silent.

The final blow came when Mom extended the underarm piece to an uncomfortable height. "Now what's the problem?" I asked.

"I don't want you exposed on the sides," Mom answered quietly.

Even with Mom's alterations, the gown was gorgeous! During the last dress fitting, Mom examined every inch of it, I'm sure to make certain that not a hint of flesh would accidentally slip out.

Finally, the evening of the dance arrived. Our dates took us to a fancy restaurant before the dance. While we were eating, I suddenly had a binding, painful feeling under my armpits. The dress hadn't felt this way at home. In fact, it had been quite comfortable. Yet, now with my every move, it pinched my flesh. Excusing myself, I hurried to the restroom to see what was amiss.

Lifting up my arms, I discovered that at some point between my final fitting and the dance, my mother had secretly added another section of material under my arms for good measure. At first, I felt annoyed that I'd now spend my night in misery, but that soon turned to laughter as I stared at the extra underarm piece and thought about my sneaky mother and what she'd done. Unfortunately for me, both my underarms remained red and chaffed for a week following that dance.

Of all the formals my mother made me over the years that dress went down in history as my favorite. It's safely tucked away and always brings a smile to my face when I think about my modest mom finally giving in and letting me wear a backless dress, but doing it on her terms. My mother and I still laugh about that gown today. And even though she somehow managed to fashion the most modest halter dress in the world, I still thought she was a pretty cool mom.

~Jill Burns

The Feather Duster

It may be that all games are silly.
But then, so are humans.
~Robert Lynd

"Mom, I just landed on you," I said with a fake apologetic look on my seven-year-old face. "And you know what that means."

Mom sighed. "And I was almost home, too." We were playing the board game *Trouble*, and everyone knows that if you land on another player's piece, he or she has to start all over.

I shrugged and apologized, although I wasn't really sorry.

Mom pushed down on the Pop-O-Matic device that the good people at the toy company designed to replace actually rolling a dice. "I never win when we play games," she said.

"But it's still fun, right?" my little sister, Mandy, asked.

"Yes, it's always fun spending time with you guys," she said. Her smile grew bigger. "You're my monsters." It might sound bad, but that was what she called my siblings and me. She said it with such love that we all knew it was a term of endearment, just the same as "honey" or "sweetie."

"If I roll a five, I win," my older brother, Mike, said. He pressed the Pop-O-Matic and up popped the five. "Yes!" he hissed, with a fist in the air.

"How could you have won already?" Mom asked. "I'm not even close."

"That's because we all landed on you and sent you back to Start," I said. "I think each of us sent you back at least once."

Mom pretended to pout. "How many times did you guys have to start over?"

"Not as many times as you did," Mike said with a grin.

"So who wants to play again?" I asked.

"Not me," Mom said. "If I don't win, it's no fun."

"That's not good sportsmanship."

Mom grinned. "I know. I'm only kidding. I can't play again because I've got housework to do."

My siblings and I reset the game while Mom got out the feather duster.

"Mom, will you please play with us again?" Mandy asked. "It's so much more fun when you play."

She pretended to think about it. "Will you make me go back to Start this time?"

"If we land on you, we will," I said pragmatically.

Mom wrinkled her nose. "Then I'm not playing." She turned and started dusting the lamps in the room.

"Please, Mom, won't you play?"

With no warning, Mom turned and started tickling us with the feather duster. "I told you, if I don't win, it's no fun!" she said, giggling.

We screamed and held up our hands to block the tickling. But the feather duster's long handle gave her the advantage. We jumped up and ran away from her. To our surprise — and delight — she chased us, still giggling and tickling whomever she could reach.

We ran around the house, laughing so hard it hurt, while Mom chased us. All the while, she was shouting, "If I don't win, it's no fun," which was eventually shortened to, "I no win, no fun."

I don't know how long the game lasted, but it felt like hours. I was breathless — both from running and from laughing — by the time Mom stopped chasing us and returned to using the feather duster for its intended purpose.

When my dad got home from work that night, we told him about our new game, which we'd dubbed, "I no win, no fun." Dad smiled and nodded, but we could tell he didn't get it. It just sounded strange for a thirty-something-year-old woman to be chasing her children around the house with a feather duster.

And maybe it was strange, but maybe that's what made it so wonderful. My mom was like everyone else's mom. She cooked our dinner and washed our clothes. She worked part-time in our local library. Chasing us around the house with a feather duster was out of character for her. It was so unexpected — in the most wonderfully crazy way.

When I was a kid, we took a family vacation every summer. Every year, Mom and Dad piled us into our station wagon — complete with wood paneling — and drove us from Indiana to one of America's must-see attractions. I've seen the Grand Canyon, Old Faithful, and Mount Rushmore. I've been to Washington, D.C., Hershey, Pennsylvania, and even the Vermont Teddy Bear Company factory. My parents went to a lot of effort to make these family vacations memorable for my siblings and me.

But strange as it may be, "I no win, no fun" is one of my fondest childhood memories.

To this day, more than thirty years later, I still vividly recall the look on her face and the sound of her laughter as she chased us.

Only my mom could take a feather duster and turn it into the best day ever.

~Diane Stark

The Battle of the Buckets

You will do foolish things, but
do them with enthusiasm.
~Colette

Our family lives on a small hobby farm, which is home to a wide diversity of talents and interests. Two of the major ones happen to be my horses and Mom's gardening.

Now, most of the time, Mom and I get along pretty well from our different worlds. We tolerate and respect each other's talents and even occasionally help each other. Her garden makes excellent horse treats, and my horses manufacture top-quality mulch for her gardens and flowerbeds. We get along quite well on the same farm.

There is one area of conflict, however: Buckets.

Now, buckets are great little creations. These seemingly unassuming little characters can buckle down and get a whole lot of work done that we never could do on our own. Set upside down, I can use them to reach the top shelves in my barn, or as a makeshift chair or mounting block. Right side up, I can carry feed and water in them, haul things in and out of the barn (namely carrots and apples stolen from Mom's gardens), and use them as wash tubs for my horse brushes… the list goes on and on. Mom has a similar list of the diverse uses for a bucket in her garden. Real workhorses, those buckets are.

I have several of these buckets in my barn—maybe twenty or so, to be precise. Mom also has twenty or thirty in her garden shed. We both know each and every one of our buckets by name, and if one goes missing, the two hundred feet of land between the barn and the garden shed turns into a war zone.

That was the reason I found myself one day crawling through tall grass and bushes to get to the garden shed without being noticed. A few of my buckets had mysteriously disappeared, and I had reason to believe that Mom had stolen them. The reason was that she had been accusing *me* the previous week of stealing *her* buckets. I argued that I would *never* steal her buckets—those new ones in my barn had just walked in on their own! I wouldn't dream of stealing my own mother's buckets!

So there I was, on a perilous secret to investigate the whereabouts of my precious buckets. I made it into the garden shed, shut the door firmly behind me, and took a look around. Aha! There, sitting innocently in the corner, were three buckets that clearly belonged to *me*. After a joyful reunion, I explained to my buckets that I would take them back to the barn to be with their friends. But I had a feeling the enemy was on the prowl, and we would need to be very quiet and nonchalant. We couldn't risk getting caught.

I was halfway to the barn and feeling pretty good about myself when the first missile came in. It landed inches from my feet and was cleverly disguised as a rotten strawberry. I broke into a casual trot, and then a run, as the enemy's voice rang out clearly: "Hey! What are you doing with my buckets? Those are mine! Stop, thief!"

I made it to the barn that time, but from then on, the location of the buckets became a constant battle. We started taking regular inventory of our buckets, and if one of them went missing in action, a desperate battle ensued. Accusations were hurled, ransoms were demanded, and once I even thought I saw my group of buckets huddled close together, squeezing their eyes shut and whimpering.

"This can't keep happening," I decided. So one day I met up with my mom and requested a parley. "The buckets and I are sick of all the strife, Mom. So I came up with a plan. How about if we say that all the buckets with handles are mine, and all the ones without are yours?"

This seemed perfectly reasonable to me, but the enemy was not impressed. Did I really think I could get away with that? Was this my idea of a joke? Did I not understand that *all* the buckets belonged to Mom, handles or no handles?

So we found ourselves at a stalemate. Neither of us would budge, and the war continued relentlessly. It still continues today; in fact, it may soon take the record for the longest lasting war. I need to look that one up. But first, I just saw Mom drive out the lane. I'd better go storm the garden shed and bring home the prisoners of war. While I'm out there, I might just take a few captives of my own.

~Hannah Yoder

The Separation

Mothers and fathers do really crazy things with the best of intentions.
~Rosalind Wiseman

When I graduated from college and moved to the other side of the state, Mom was downhearted. The next year, when my sister graduated from college and moved across the country, Mom was dejected. And when neither of us got home to visit for the next year, Mom was downright miserable.

So, I wasn't surprised when Mom called me the weekend before Thanksgiving to complain.

"It's not right," Mom grumbled. "Neither you nor your sister came home for any holidays this year—not Christmas, not Easter, not even Groundhog Day."

"Why would we come home for Groundhog Day?" I asked.

"I have no idea," Mom replied. "But it would have been nice."

"I told you I just can't make it home right now," I said.

"Then I guess I should break the news to you now," Mom sighed. "Your father and I have decided on a separation."

This couldn't be happening. Not my parents! I hadn't even known anything was wrong, but obviously it had been a while since I'd been home.

Shortly after hanging up with Mom, I received a series of frantic texts from my sister. She'd heard the news, too.

I rushed to my laptop and scheduled a last-minute flight home on Wednesday in time to meet my sister when she arrived at the airport. We planned to share a rental car to my parents' house.

Wednesday evening, my sister and I shared a long hug at the airport when she disembarked from her flight. Her arrival had been delayed due to bad weather in the Midwest, so I'd had plenty of time to claim my luggage and pick up the rental car before she arrived.

"What's going on?" my sister asked. "Mom called me nonchalantly mentioning a separation."

"Same for me," I replied as we climbed into the car. "I thought everything was fine."

Forty minutes later, we reached our parents' colonial, suburban home. The windows were brightly lit, and pumpkins lined the front steps.

"Hello," called my sister, rapping on the back door as we stepped into the kitchen. "Mom? Dad?"

"What are you doing here?" answered Mom. She was at the sink washing dishes in her apron. She grabbed us in a hug. "The kids are home!" she called to our father.

Dad emerged from the den, smiling. "What a surprise," he said, hugging us.

"You shouldn't be surprised," I responded, taking off my coat, "especially after Mom's phone call."

"What phone call?" asked Dad.

"The call about the separation," answered my sister.

"Oh, brother." Dad tucked his hands in his pockets and began walking back toward the den.

"Hold it," said my sister, folding her arms. "What's going on?"

Dad shook his head. "Your mother told me to mind my own business, or she wouldn't make pumpkin pie. And I want pumpkin pie." He disappeared into the den.

"Yes, about the separation…" Mom said as she scooped her Thanksgiving-themed salt-and-pepper shakers off the stove and handed one to each of us. "I'm giving you these."

I got the Mr. Pilgrim saltshaker; he stood at attention in his buckle hat with a musket in one arm and a turkey in the other. My sister got the Mrs. Pilgrim peppershaker; she wore a bonnet and held a pumpkin.

"What's this?" inquired my sister.

"Like I told you," Mom said, "your father and I decided on a separation — of the pilgrim salt-and-pepper shakers."

"No, no, no!" I pointed at Mom. "You said 'separation,' but you never said 'salt-and-pepper-shakers.' We thought you and Dad were getting a separation."

Mom held up her hands, laughing. "Your father and I have been married for twenty-six years," she said. "We can't separate! Your father could never survive on his own."

"I can hear you!" Dad shouted from the den.

"And you know it's true," answered Mom. She motioned to my sister and me. "Sit, relax. I'll make tea."

"Mom, you lied to us," said my sister.

Mom shook her head. "No, you misunderstood. That's all right, we'll have plenty of room at the table tomorrow." Mom put the kettle on the stove, and then shrugged her shoulders. "All I know is that I no longer have pilgrim salt-and-pepper-shakers, but my children, who haven't been home in ages, are here for Thanksgiving."

"This is unbelievable," I said to my sister. "We were outsmarted by our mother and a pair of ceramic pilgrims."

"I guess the important point is that children should come home on a regular basis," said Mom. "That way, they'll know for sure what's happening with their family."

"What are we supposed to do with half a set of shakers?" asked my sister.

"They're a nice memento." Mom grinned. "A reminder to visit home more often."

When I got home that Sunday, I placed Mr. Pilgrim on my nightstand — a token of my lesson learned. My sister keeps Mrs. Pilgrim on her desk at work.

I know Mom has a set of Mr. and Mrs. Santa Claus salt-and-pepper-shakers, so if I stay away from home too long, another separation announcement might be imminent. Just to be on the safe side, my sister and I now make sure to visit our parents as often as possible.

~David Hull

My Very Unpredictable Mom

Prudence keeps life safe, but does not often make it happy.
~Samuel Johnson

We never knew what my mom would do next. She was adventurous, impulsive, and unpredictable, and she never worried about what our family—or anyone else—thought about her.

We were not wealthy, but my mother loved to travel. She reveled in saving nickels and dimes, little by little, to take short trips. Every time she went out the door on another short venture, the neighbors would laugh at her and say, "There goes Mary again—with her suitcase and her five dollars." She didn't care. Mom was on her way to another new experience.

One year, she even managed to get to the New York World's Fair. When she arrived there with her friends, they suddenly decided to stay in the hotel and not venture out at all—after traveling from Pennsylvania! Mom wasn't about to miss that huge World's Fair, so she went to it by herself, and came home with glowing reports, showering us with loads of brochures about our exciting future. I don't think she missed a single exhibit.

My mother was also ingenious. Her own mother was extremely ill when Mom was a child. That forced my mother to quit school in the sixth grade to be her mother's caregiver. But my mom's mind was sharp and inquisitive, and she absorbed facts like a sponge. When she grew up, she and my father were raising our family on my dad's income. As our expenses rapidly increased, Mom wanted to work, but she had no office skills and could not type — so she became a waitress.

While working at the Press Club in our city, she soon learned that if a person got their favorite drink, the tips were higher. So wherever she traveled, she'd learn the favorite drink of that city, and memorize how that drink was made. When reporters would come into the Press Club and want a drink not known to our city, she'd take their order, go to the bar, and from her remarkable memory, she would teach the bartender how to make it — which glass to use, salted rim or not, the exact ingredients — and gain another very satisfied customer, plus a nice tip.

She became so good at her job that she eventually became the head supervisor of a posh country club's dining room.

My mother was also impetuous. When my husband and I moved to California, she came out for a visit. There was a vineyard next to our tract of new homes. Our neighbor next door built small motorcycles. Always curious to learn something new, Mom went over to his garage to watch his progress. Soon the air was filled with the blasting roar of an engine tearing through the rows in the vineyard!

Thinking my neighbor was testing one of his newest creations, I glanced out, and was horrified to see my mother, astride a motorcycle, tearing up and down through the rows of grapevines and laughing as she bounced over one dirt hump after another!

We were terrified that she'd crash and injure herself, but she managed her ride just fine, pulled in, clicked off the engine, and came back to our house beaming, saying what tremendous fun it was.

On another California visit, I took her to the Los Angeles County Fair, which was known as the largest in the world. She was like a little child, eagerly inspecting one exhibit after another and enjoying all the new and interesting items.

A feature at the fair was the Monorail, which rode underneath the rail to give fairgoers an airborne look at the expansive grounds.

Of course, my mother wanted to ride, but we got so busy looking at exhibits that by the time we got to its entrance, it was late. The Monorail ride had closed.

The next day, we went back to the fair so Mom could get that ride. But lightning began to flash, the clouds opened up, and rain began to pour. Because the Monorail ran on electricity, it was immediately shut down — with the passengers still inside!

Fire trucks were rapidly called into play. One by one, the passengers began to be removed, brought safely down a ladder to the ground.

As we watched, a distressed look formed on Mom's usually happy face. "Gosh, I wish I were up there on that Monorail," she said, as she eagerly watched all the exciting action.

"Don't worry," I assured her. "The fair runs four more days. We can still come back for you to get that ride."

"Oh, no, that's not the problem!" she said. "Just think! If I were up there now as a passenger, I too would have to be helped down that ladder by a fireman, and what an outstanding experience that would be!" That was my mom, the adventurer.

She could also be a prankster. One year, during one of her California visits, we took her to the famed Farmers Market in Los Angeles. It's a unique place where Hollywood celebrities often shop. While we saw no celebrities, Mom had a wonderful time exploring all the unique foods and other items, and buying gifts to take to the family back home.

A few weeks later, I was talking to my aunt, Mom's sister, by phone. We were discussing all the interesting things Mom had done during her visit with us.

"And how did you enjoy all the unique goodies Mom brought back from the Farmers Market?" I asked.

"Oh, they were all fine," she said, "but your mother was up to her usual tricks."

Probing further, I asked, "What are you talking about?"

"Well," she said, "she invited us all over to tell us about her exciting visit, and to give us the gifts she bought at the Farmers Market. Everything was fine, except for one item. Your mother served each of us some special chocolate-covered delicacies that she had bought there, and they were quite delicious."

"Well, what was wrong with that?" I questioned.

"The chocolate was fine," she said, "but it wasn't until we had each eaten all of ours that she told us we had just eaten — chocolate-covered grasshoppers!"

I howled with laughter at that one.

But Mom also used her ingenuity for good. Whenever she felt that a city law was harmful — especially to the elderly — she would check the laws as they were written, do some homework, and then go down to the City Hall meetings to appeal for change. Since she always had her facts down pat, she sometimes got those laws revised. My sixth-grade-educated mother was never afraid to stand up to anyone, even the honorable City Council and Mayor.

My children have often told me that I'm just like my mother, which I consider to be a wonderful honor. I feel that I've definitely inherited her intense love of travel, adventure, ingenuity, curiosity about new things, and yes, even her quirkiness. I'm extremely proud — and grateful — that I had her for my mom.

~Kay Presto

Recipes for Life

A recipe has no soul; you as the cook
must bring soul to the recipe.
~Thomas Keller

A Suitcase Full of Love

Food is symbolic of love when words are inadequate.
~Alan D. Wolfelt

The early April breeze was chillier than I expected as I walked anxiously toward the front entrance of the Holiday Inn at Union Square in San Francisco. With every step I took, I heard my mother's words: "Johnny, I am all packed and looking forward to seeing you!" She had sounded so excited when we talked over the phone a few days earlier.

After five years of trying to get a visa to the United States to visit me, she finally succeeded on the third attempt. The tedious process, while at times heartbreaking and emotionally draining for both of us, could not dissuade my mom from her desire to make the trip. Despite being only five feet, three inches tall, Mom had always been the pillar of the Tan family. Her ingenious solutions to the visa challenge proved once again that no obstacle was a match for Mom's steadfast determination and love for her family—in this case, me!

Although excited, I was extremely nervous. Mom and I had not seen each other in more than eight years, since I left Malaysia at eighteen to attend college in the U.S. Due to a glitch in the federal immigration system, my application for permanent residency was in limbo. In spite of being gainfully employed and a homeowner, I could not leave the country until my paperwork was resolved.

In the beginning, our only source of communication was through letters. Later, it evolved to lengthy phone conversations. Much had happened during the eight years while I was absent. My father passed away a year after I went abroad. Our family dog died five months later. Observing our Chinese tradition, my sister and her fiancé waited until a couple of months after the anniversary of Dad's death to get married. Eventually, my mom became a grandmother. These were all the things I missed back home while becoming a young adult working in corporate America.

By this point, Mom was an accomplished globetrotter, exploring countries near and far. From Thailand to Australia, Egypt, Turkey, Japan, and New Zealand, she had experienced many cultures firsthand with her traveling buddies. However, the United States would be her farthest journey yet.

During the months preceding her U.S. trip, I tried to prepare my mom regarding what she needed to pack. We planned for her to stay with me for four months, during which time we would be traveling throughout the United States. Her reply was always, "Don't you worry about me. I know what I need. How about you? What would you like me to bring you from Malaysia?" My answer never wavered. All I wanted was a couple bags of authentic curry powder and two bags of chili powder from our hometown of Melaka, as I was running low on these treasured spices.

I had started cooking in my sophomore year while living off campus due to my tight budget and a yearning for my favorite Malaysian dishes. Upon request, Mom eagerly would send me the curry and chili powder. Finally, after all these years, I was looking forward to eating my mom's cooking once again!

The timing couldn't have been more perfect. A tour bus pulled up right in front of the hotel as I made my way to the main door. Intuitively, I sensed Mom was on the bus. I stood nervously in anticipation. One by one, passengers exited the bus. Suddenly, I saw a woman who looked like my mom stepping off. She was not the same person I left behind in Malaysia, but an older version of herself, seemingly smaller in size. Perhaps I had grown taller and more muscular, and she was viewing me the same way—as an older version of myself. We made eye contact, and immediately I saw tears in her eyes followed by that familiar loving smile.

As I walked toward her, I felt numb. No words could express my happiness, so I gave her a very long bear hug. Much to my surprise, she hugged me back. Hugging was not the norm for us in Asian culture, but I had assimilated to American customs by then. Soon, a curious and friendly crowd was upon us. Apparently, Mom had told her traveling group that her time with them would end in San Francisco upon a reunion with her son. That night, we dined in Chinatown, talking about family and celebrating our long-awaited time together.

The next morning, we were up bright and early for our 7:00 a.m. flight to Louisiana. I helped Mom check in her ample luggage, amazed that she had managed it this far by herself. She was obviously well packed for the trip with a heavy, oversized suitcase, carry-on luggage, and an extra-large shoulder bag. Perhaps I had over-prepared her for the trip!

It was late afternoon by the time we reached my house in Baton Rouge. I gave Mom a quick tour of my garden home. She was pleased with what I had accomplished in eight years. As she sat down on her bed to rest, I offered to bring her luggage upstairs. She quickly directed me to bring only the carry-on and shoulder bags, and to leave the largest suitcase downstairs. Mom mentioned casually that there was no clothing in that suitcase, just items she had brought for me.

How could she have packed all her clothes for four months in just two small bags? In disbelief, I hurried downstairs and opened the huge suitcase. Inside, I discovered bags of curry and chili powder, bags of wet Malaysian satay spice mix, dried herbs, special Asian herb plants packed with ice, dried anchovies and Chinese sausage, pastries, cooking utensils, and home-decor items she and my sister had bought as housewarming gifts. Although the ice had melted down, the herb plants with roots looked fresh and healthy. Overwhelmed with her gesture of love, I realized my mom had planned for this trip better than I did. For weeks, she had painstakingly gathered these gifts and methodically secured each item to endure the long, arduous trip.

I asked Mom how she managed to carry these contraband items through U.S. customs. She said, "I knew I was taking a big risk, but the worst that could have happened was the officials would take everything and throw it away. I prayed as I was walking through the checkpoint and did not look anyone in the eye. When the final officer smiled at me, I smiled back. Since she did not stop me, I calmly walked toward our tour group leader who was waiting by the exit door."

As I sat beside Mom, my thoughts drifted to the contents of the suitcase downstairs. They were no longer food, spices, and gifts, but rather love itself… the unconditional motherly love that transcends time and distance. I rose and smiled at Mom, saying, "Well, okay then, I look forward to gaining a few pounds eating all your delicious cooking over the next few months and learning some new recipes along the way." I left her to unpack and recuperate for a while before dinner, which we would prepare with the ingredients she had brought from Malaysia. I could not think of a more perfect way to commemorate our first meal together in my kitchen!

~Johnny Tan

Sweet Balls of Dough

If baking is any labor at all, it's a labor of love. A love that gets passed from generation to generation.
~Regina Brett

My mom taught me many things while I was growing up—certainly, among them, the basic art of cooking. Most would agree it is a survival skill—we have to eat. But watching Mom all those years slicing and spicing, broiling and braising, blending and baking, I realized cooking was more than a survival task for my mother.

My mother loved to bake, especially her traditional Italian cookies. Whether it was for a birthday party, a holiday gathering, a club meeting, or a new neighbor, Mom would don her red flowered apron and start rolling dozens and dozens of sweet balls of dough. And that custom continued well into Mom's nineties.

I lived about an hour away, but I visited my mother often, especially when she turned ninety. Even though my brother and I had felt it was time for Mom to move in with one of us, or switch to an assisted-living residence, she wouldn't hear of it. She said assisted living was for old people. And as matriarch of an extended family living nearby, she insisted on staying in her own home. My brother and I acquiesced, but we strategically scheduled many family members and friends to stop by when we couldn't be there.

I remember one of my visits as if it were yesterday. Mom was ninety-six years old, and she had insisted on baking cookies for her great-grandson's birthday party. I had offered to make them for her, but she dismissed the thought. Even though she had advanced arthritis in her knees and couldn't stand for long periods of time, she wouldn't entertain the idea that she couldn't bake anymore. Mom was proud of her signature batch of sweetness decorated with confectionary sugar frosting and rainbow sprinkles. And she wanted to contribute to the birthday party's menu, just like she always had.

Mom had decided to bake first thing the following morning. I had suggested she wait until I arrived that next day, but she said she would be fine. So when I went grocery shopping, I made sure Mom had all the basic ingredients for her morning undertaking. I placed them on the kitchen counter, except for the milk and eggs, and gathered her yellow ceramic bowl, measuring spoons and cups, cookie pans, cooling racks, and her favorite mixing spoon. And since it had been a handful of months since Mom had made her cookies, I decided to write the recipe out again. The original was pretty worn and stained, and I wasn't sure she would still remember all the ingredients and measurements. Before I left for home, I set the oven temperature to 350 degrees. All she had to do was turn it on in the morning after she mixed and rolled.

When I arrived the next morning, a sweet scent filled the rooms. I walked down the hallway to the living room, through the dining room, and into the kitchen. Mom was sitting at the table with ice packs on her knees, a regular after-breakfast ritual. And her cookies were cooling in rows on wire racks. She had accomplished quite a lot that morning, and it was only nine o'clock.

However, Mom wasn't happy. She told me the cookies didn't rise like they were supposed to, and they tasted awful — her exact words.

I blamed myself for not insisting that we bake them together, but I had never talked to my mom as if she was a child, and I wasn't going to start then. When she couldn't golf anymore at the age of ninety, she had adjusted. When Mom couldn't drive anymore at the age of ninety-three, she had adjusted to that as well. But to not be able to bake her cookies anymore? The disappointment on her face made it quite clear that Mom felt defeated, as if she had lost her purpose at the age of ninety-six.

I looked at the cookies. They did appear flatter than usual, but still presentable. Mom had always been the master baker and definitive taste tester, and she was right again. The cookies tasted awful. I assumed she had probably left out some ingredients. Maybe she didn't read the recipe correctly. She told me she had used up the rest of the bottle of vanilla, but that confused me. The recipe only called for 1½ teaspoons.

After drinking her coffee, Mom slowly went upstairs to get dressed. While she was bathing, I washed and dried her dishes and utensils, and hung the rewritten recipe on the refrigerator for easier access. Then something caught my eye. The recipe called for 1½ teaspoons of vanilla. But it also listed three teaspoons of vanilla further down the list.

No wonder Mom used up all of the vanilla. And no wonder her cookies didn't rise much. The list should have read three teaspoons of baking powder, not more vanilla.

In my haste to get back on the highway to avoid commuter traffic heading north the day before, I had made a mistake writing out the recipe. I couldn't wait to tell Mom, although I felt like a kid again, confessing to a misdemeanor.

When Mom came back downstairs, she asked me what I was laughing about, and I told her. At first, she couldn't believe it. She sat down at the kitchen table. "It was you?" She paused. "Not me?"

I nodded as Mom's eyes widened, and her smile returned. It was as if she had won the lottery that day. She decided right then and there to bake a fresh batch of cookies that afternoon. I quickly corrected the mistake on the recipe and dashed out to buy another bottle of vanilla. After lunch, I sat and watched Mom in all her glory don her red flowered apron, just like she always did.

I find myself each and every day doing things like my mother. Why not? She was my first teacher, passing on what she had learned from her own mother and grandmother. And she taught me well — not only about cooking, but also about caring and sharing. When Mom passed away less than a year later, I took down her yellow ceramic bowl, now in my kitchen cupboard, and made dozens and dozens of sweet balls of dough. The wake wouldn't have felt like a family gathering without Mom's Italian cookies.

~Elaine D'Alessandro

Johanna's Recipes

The same way one tells a recipe, one tells a family history. Each one of us has our past locked inside.
~Laura Esquivel

When I was small, maybe eight or nine years old, I asked my great-grandma, Johanna, to share her recipes with me because she was the best cook I had ever known. She spoke only German, which I had been discouraged from speaking, so I learned by watching her as she cooked at her daughter's stove. I followed her every movement as I scribbled notes on index cards.

She was baffled by my need for precision in measurement. I was, even then, a scientist at heart and in manner.

"It's an art," she said, shaking her head.

"But how much nutmeg goes in?" I asked with a child's need for certainty. "A quarter teaspoon? Should I list it by weight in grams?"

"This much will do." She showed me some spice in the well of her palm.

"But how much is that?" I asked again, frustrated by the ambiguity of her answers.

"It's different every time," she said. "You'll just know."

As a child, I did not understand about the potency of herbs and spices. Nuts, seeds, stems, leaves, flowers, and roots varied from plant to plant, batch to batch, year after year, and species to species. Use a little more if it's been sitting a while. Use a little less if it's freshly ground. It was all done by feel, smell and taste. No dish could ever be recreated precisely. Each dish was a separate work of art, uniquely her own. Every recipe was an approximation of what she might make on any other day, in any other place, with any other products.

While I was cleaning this week, I opened the lid of the old wooden box that holds those recipe cards. I came across one — for her applesauce cake — that I had placed in the back and never used, deeming it indecipherable. I read the notes I had made as a child and I finally understood all that ambiguity and uncertainty I saw in the ingredients and quantities. I saw Johanna's wisdom, resilience, and foresight in all the wiggle room she built into her recipes.

She left room to account for temperature, humidity, the type of baking pan, the source of heat for the oven — did she once use wood stoves? Coal? Gas?

She accounted for the type of apples — was it a good year with sweet apples? Were they tart? Were they dry? If so, add honey and molasses for moisture. If not, use powdered sugars.

She accounted for economics — she'd been able to afford butter once, but she'd escaped to the States during a war. She could make due if only oil was available. And even if she only had oil, she made sure that her family had cake.

On that recipe card, I saw so much of Johanna's life, and I realized that I would never be able to replicate her cake. Hers was gone. Her art, intangible and fleeting, was her own. And I knew that any cake I made using her recipe would be my own, my own art.

So I made her apple cake, honoring her memory as best I could. I used organic cinnamon applesauce from new apple varieties she had never known. Organic Vermont butter with less fat content than the German pastry butter she would have recognized. Organic white flour and cane sugar without the bleaching she would have expected. Organic dark raisins, plumped as she had shown me. The cake rose and turned golden, as it should. And it tasted an awful lot like a memory.

~Beth Krone-Downes

Flake and Bake

The greatest weapon against stress is our ability to choose one thought over another.
~William James

I walked briskly around the track at the YMCA. My pace was firm, my teeth were clenched, and my eyes were fixed on nothing in particular. That meant it would be a productive walk, because I was managing my stress. That morning, as I balanced my checkbook, there was little doubt that my expenses were higher and my income was lower. I had taxes to pay, past-due medical bills, and repairs needed on the house. My stress level warranted a bucket full of tears, but Mom had taught me well.

"Don't work yourself into a tizzy during a crisis. Provide yourself with a distraction — something you like to do that doesn't take much thought. While your mind becomes distanced from frustration, let your head work on the problem." Then she would dive into baking something wonderful, and the aroma from her kitchen soothed any frazzled nerves. She had a gift of baking, sure, but baking was also her way of dealing with a tragic or difficult situation.

I learned many things from my mother for which I'm grateful, but overcoming stress by distraction is the one I use most. My older brother inherited Mom's calm spirit, but my emotional state was quite the opposite. Given any crisis or challenge, I let my blood pressure rise and my face get red.

During my adolescent years, I watched Mom's reactions when she wrecked the car, caught the stove on fire, stalled the car in four feet of water, and burned a hole in her silk dress with a hot iron. There were never angry outbursts, screaming or tears. Instead, she would heave a big sigh and say, "No problem, I'll think of something," or "How did that happen?" Then, she'd march off to the kitchen and bake something delicious.

Years later, I would realize that an enormous number of problems were solved as Mom kneaded, mixed, and measured, all the time working out her frustrations and finding solutions.

Childrearing is full of problems. Take the time when I wrecked my first car, or the numerous fights I had with my brother, some of which even drew blood. And then there was the time I decided to be a dressmaker and cut off my new dress because I thought it was too long. Another time, my brother took his brand-new Ford apart in an effort to customize it by modifying the suspension and adding dual pipes.

Mom's reaction was always the same. In a firm but low voice, she dished out punishment, something like grounding us for weeks, and then left the room to tackle sugar, flour and butter. She did the same thing when she lost her purse with all her credit cards and cash in it, and when the basement flooded, ruining everything in it.

As I grew older and realized Mom handled stress and crises differently from my friends' mothers, I asked her a question. "Why don't you yell, scream, and get angry like other people?"

She gave me an answer that has guided me ever since: "Nothing productive comes from anger. In a crisis, what's done is done, and I can't change that. If you can't laugh or make light of a situation, I've found it is better to hesitate and distance yourself from the problem a while before acting on it. It works well for me. My advice to you is when you experience anger or fear at something or someone, indulge in a distraction of some sort to get your mind off the emotional side and focus on a solution. For me, that distraction is baking. You'll find whatever works best for you."

Later, when I was an adult and raising my own family, I met with several challenges, and my first distress call was always to Mom. I'd stand in the middle of the room, hands on hips, and murmur,

"Distraction, my eye. I need to vent and maybe even scream a bit." Then I'd pace and grab the phone. "Mom? I've got a problem. Can I come over for a chat?"

An intoxicating smell would greet me. Yeast combined with flour, cinnamon and sugar wafted through the air. Now, I know she used baking not only for her own problems, but mine as well. We talked through a lot of problems during these sessions.

I'm happy to report I've finally learned how to use Mom's lesson. I don't bake, but I found my own distractions: yoga and walking. So today, I'm walking around the track with head held high, sorting out possible solutions to my current economic problem. Occasionally, I'll look upward and say, "Thanks, Mom, for your lesson in distraction. You're right. It is much better than anger." Sometimes, I fail, and I get frustrated and angry, but then I remember, and grab my jacket, cell phone, and house key for a trip to the track. There, I'll talk myself through the current crisis one step at a time.

~Arlene Rains Graber

Reconnecting

Context and memory play powerful roles
in all the truly great meals in one's life.
~Anthony Bourdain

Not long after my mother died, I turned to the bookstore to start the grieving and healing process. I could always depend on *Chicken Soup for the Soul* books to get me through a tough time, whether it was when I was a teenager and having boy problems, or when I was an adult needing a bit of inspiration. Now here I was, at the age of thirty, looking for some comfort beyond what I could get from friends and family. I needed to read stories by people who were in the same situation as me.

I had lost my grandfather while I was in high school, but this was different. This was my mother. And unfortunately, I had regrets—unfinished business with her, unsaid words and stories.

The funeral was over, and I was supposed to go back to "normal life" without her in it. The pain was raw and sometimes unbearable.

I bought *Chicken Soup for the Soul: Grieving and Recovery*. The stories of loss and pain made my cry, but at the same time it was comforting to know I wasn't alone. I was reading stories that were much like my own, that I could relate to. One story that really helped was "My Mother's Recipe Box" by Sally Schwartz Friedman. The title caught my attention immediately because my mother loved cooking, watching cooking channels, and keeping record of recipes in all her notebooks. Toward the end of her life, when she was in and out of the hospital, those recipes and cooking shows kept her entertained.

That story inspired me to gather up all five of my mother's recipe notebooks and put them together to make a cookbook. There were so many great recipes that I wanted to share with my friends and family. Since Mom never got to make most of the recipes, I would! I knew I had to do this for her. Although many of the recipes were not her own and had not been passed down through the family, they had obviously meant something to her, and it would be a shame for them to just sit in a box in the closet.

I decided to put Mom's handwritten recipe on one side of the page and the typed version of it on the other. There's something very comforting about her handwritten notes. I can hear her voice reading those recipes to me, and she doesn't seem so far away. I just wish she could be here to taste the recipes that she never got to try. But you know what, Mom? I will eat enough for both of us.

~Angelena Shepard

Christmas Our Way

The heart of every family tradition
is a meaningful experience.
~Author Unknown

I come from a long line of Puerto Ricans who celebrate American traditions and holidays like everyone else. At Christmastime, we follow the customs of decorating, trimming a tree, and baking. However, what sets us apart from most families is our Annual Pastele-Making Day.

Pasteles are a tamale-like dish that encompasses various ingredients, including potatoes, taro root, squash, plantains, green bananas, and yucca for the masa. The inside of the shell is a slow-simmered beef stew seasoned with red achiote powder mixed with cooking oil, for color and taste. Pasteles are an acquired taste due to the sour tang of the vegetables. To most of our guests, it is unpleasant, but for those of us who grew up eating this dish, it is wonderful.

Making this recipe is an arduous task that requires excellent leadership, organization, and tenacity. Only one person in our household fit that job description—my maternal grandmother. Mama had a shiny gray bob, never spoke English, never wore pants (only skirts and dresses), never drove, and never divorced my grandfather—who abandoned her decades ago. She always wore jewelry, hummed, and loved to read her Bible. She even had the resolve to return to school when she was in her forties to obtain her high-school diploma.

Mama loved to cook, and pasteles were her Mona Lisa, the pièce de résistance in her culinary repertoire. She was the master, and many people told her so.

Growing up, I remember Mama standing by the front door of the house with her handbag, waiting for someone to drive her to the market. Whoever drove Mama knew that the journey would consist of numerous stops at meat markets and small Latino grocery stores, all for the choicest ingredients. My brother, who could never speak a word of Spanish, usually "volunteered" for the job after Mama slipped him a twenty-dollar bill.

When Mama returned home with numerous bags of groceries, she instructed all of us to wash our hands and await further instructions. She then covered the dining-room table with newspapers, set out bowls on the table, and heaped all of the vegetables into the dishes for peeling and chopping. From there, she moved to set up station two, which consisted of meat preparation with sharp knives, heavy pots, spices, and mounds of the reddest ground chuck available.

When Mama nodded, we manned our stations. My sister and I peeled and chopped, and my mother prepped the stew. In the final position, Mama set up a food mill that attached with a clamp to the cutting board we pulled out from underneath our counter. There, my father would churn the cut vegetables to a smooth masa. Mama would assist him by adding warm milk and the achiote oil to the batter to form orange goo.

We were a finely-tuned machine. When things were going well, Mama would sing Christmas carols in her beautiful operatic voice. If things were moving too slowly, she would look at us sternly and tell us exactly what she thought. There were no excuses for doing a lousy job.

When the stew settled, and the masa mill stopped, it was time to assemble the packages. Mama replaced all the soggy newspaper and covered the dining-room table with an old tablecloth. Three chairs made up the assembly station, which encompassed a pot of masa, a pot of stew, a bowl of the red achiote oil, and three rolls of parchment paper. (While many Puerto Ricans swear by fresh banana leaves to encase the pasteles, Mama pooh-poohed the idea, stating that the banana leaves distracted from the taste.)

Mama sat down like a concert pianist ready to charm us with her talents. My mother and father sat on either side of her. Finally, Mama unrolled a cylinder of parchment paper, dunked her spoon in the red oil, and made a bull's eye right in the center of the sheet. My parents quickly followed suit on their parchment rolls. With a quick slap, the masa landed in the middle of the achiote, and the swirling continued, this time to make room for the stew. The yummy smell of garlic and onion from the meat hit our nostrils. We all longed for big, beefy pasteles, but she would have nothing to do with it.

To Mama, the determination of success was in the numbers. If she made fewer than 100 pasteles, she failed. If she mustered more than 100, it was a good day.

My older sister and I waited patiently to participate. When a stack of packages was ready, my sister and I went to work on tying bundles. We pulled the string from the roll, measured eighteen inches, and cut. On and on we would tug, measure, cut and then set aside 100 strings. When done, we dutifully bound two packages together and set them aside for counting.

As the years went by, we longed for promotion to assembly. My sister and I tired of cutting thread and bundling packages. Finally, when we were in our twenties, Mama promoted us to Assistant Pasteles Assemblers because she thought our parents were too slow.

We did this for years and grew to enjoy our special day with her. Years later, the doctor diagnosed Mama with Alzheimer's. She moved slower, forgot the achiote, and even stood in the kitchen staring into the open refrigerator. The year we placed her in a home, we quietly peeled our bananas, stirred the beef, and milled the orange goo. Tears rolled down our cheeks as we stretched the *masa* thin to make 100 bundles, just as she had.

It's been ten years since Mama passed, and we miss her. Although making Christmas pasteles is a laborious process, we still do it to honor her memory.

Even so, we changed a few things. My father retired the little food grinder for a state-of-the-art food processor, and we buy the meat already cubed. My niece now joins us on Pasteles Day. Although

I highly object to my mother allowing her to skip string cutting and move straight to assembly, I'm glad we can pass down the tradition to her. My niece may not make pasteles for her family, but she will always have a story about Mama to tell her children.

~Lizette Vega

Those Gentle Hands

Pie is a symbol of something bigger than
Mom and her way with desserts.
~Pascale Le Draoulec

My mother makes the best apple pie. Her apples are perfectly spiced, not too soggy, yet never undercooked. And her piecrusts are golden, flaky bursts of delight sprinkled with delicate cinnamon spice. My mother's apple pie has always been an important part of my family's holiday dinners.

My mother grew up helping my grandmother, who was confined to a wheelchair, with the care of the younger siblings, the cooking, and the household chores. My grandmother did teach my mother how to make piecrusts, and my mother took it from there and became the pie maker in the family. She was one of seven children on a farm in upstate New York, a farm her father had bought after the Depression. He was an engineer, educated at Pratt Institute, and very wise. He knew that the farm could sustain his family and allow them to be self-sufficient in a financially unstable world. My grandfather grew fruits and vegetables, and raised cows and chickens for milk and eggs. Pigs, cows, and chickens were slaughtered for their meals.

Pie turned out to be the most economical dessert to make. It was cheaper than making cake and didn't use the farm's supply of eggs and milk. Many of the fruits my mother used were grown on the farm. And it would give my grandmother a moment's peace; she would send her children scampering off to hunt for fruit. My mother made wild raspberry pies and strawberry rhubarb pies for her family, but the favorite, by far, was her apple pie.

It comes as no surprise then that one of my mother's favorite childhood memories was baking pies in 4-H. Her group leader would host a pie-making contest every year, and all of the 4-Hers in her group would participate. All kinds of pies and various levels of pie-making abilities were represented in this contest. The 4-H leader's son, who lived next door to my mother on a small farm, was always the judge of the contest. My mother had quite the crush on him, and when he voted her pie the best, she swooned.

My mother's apple pie has become legendary in our family. Her pies accessorize every holiday table. Her grandsons are especially fond of her pies, so she bakes extras for them to take away with them after family events. She makes apple pies to celebrate when someone is happy, and apple pies to comfort when someone is sad.

My mother has tried to teach me how to make her apple pie without success. The problem was she tossed a handful or two of flour into the bowl, added a shake or two of salt, and threw in a few scoops of Crisco. She crumbled it all together, added a few sprinkles of ice water, and the pie dough was magically formed. I had a notebook and pen ready to write down the exact measurements but I couldn't keep up. When I asked my mother how many cups of flour, she remarked, "Oh, about this much," as she held out her slender hands. The same thing occurred when I tried to figure out how much of the other ingredients she used. Needless to say, I did not inherit the apple-pie-making gene.

My mother's hands accomplished a great deal in this world; never were they idle. She was invaluable to my grandmother, and then she raised three daughters, caring for them with a loving heart and gentle hands. My mother was a talented artist, but she only considered painting a hobby. Her hands were skilled at nursing, and her elderly patients loved her. As a teacher, she tied shoes, and tended to scrapes and bruises. She turned the pages of a beloved book and acted out the songs she sang. And she baked apple pies.

This aging woman became legally blind a few years ago. I cannot imagine how difficult it must be for her to live in a world of shadows and blurry grays, unable to be as independent as she wants to be, no longer painting or able to do many of the things she loves. Miraculously, she still lives alone. She is a beloved friend, mother, grandmother, and great-grandmother.

My mother still insists on making her apple pies for every holiday. She can no longer see well enough to peel and slice the apples. So, this Thanksgiving season, I offered to help her and told her it was because I wanted to try to learn how to make her pastry crust again. My memories took me back to the first time she tried to teach me. I was a new mother then, realizing the love I had for my precious daughter was as vast and as powerful as my mother's was for me.

She sat in her kitchen that day and used her hands to guide her as we peeled apples together. She never even bothered to look down; instead, she seemed preoccupied, maybe thinking of years gone by. She struggled. I snuck my fingers back into the bowl, cleaning up the red splashes of peels she left behind and the speckle of seeds residing there.

But her hands, so thin and work-worn, still made magic with a handful or two of flour, a scoop of Crisco, and a splash of water. The fragrance of cinnamon, apples and pastry baking filled the air, and the latticework on her pies was like ribbons of love woven into my heart.

~Katherine Mabb

The Secret of the Gravy

Eating is a necessity, but cooking is an art.
~Gesine Lemcke

"Decrease the expensive ingredients and increase the cheaper ones." That was my grandma's philosophy when it came to cooking. She created all sorts of vile concoctions. There was her mock veal (breadcrumbs and tomato paste) and her macaroni and cheese (noodles floating on top of cheddar-flavored water).

Grandma prided herself on being frugal. She purchased dented cans of expired products and insisted that grocery stores with automatic doors sold overpriced merchandise. Grandma disapproved of her daughter-in-law's "extravagant" spending, especially when it came to cooking.

My mom happened to be an excellent cook. She was proud of her family's history of baking. Her great-grandfather had owned a bakery in St. Louis. The glass cake platter from this family-owned business had a place of honor in our china cabinet. There was also a family cookbook bursting with recipes, from my maternal grandmother's German waffles to my great-aunt's peanut-butter cookies.

Grandma's horrible meals, on the other hand, were always a source of entertainment in the household. We often joked about how our dog refused to eat the scraps that we tossed under the table.

My family often tried to figure out some of the more unique flavors that we had to endure in Grandma's cooking. One of the worst things she made was her gravy. It had a very bitter aftertaste, and we guessed that the tiny black specks in it were from Grandma burning the bottom of the saucepan.

But then one day, we learned the truth. My mom was preparing dinner — pot roast served with potatoes, plus a delicious cherry cheesecake for dessert. My aunts and uncle, cousins and, yes, my grandma, were all invited. Instead of socializing, Grandma chose to sit in the kitchen. She felt it was her duty to monitor her daughter-in-law's wastefulness. Occasionally, Grandma would let out a *tsk tsk* of disapproval. She clearly did not agree with Mom's purchase of pot roast.

"What's the point of buying beef?" Grandma demanded. "All you can do is eat it. You should do what I do. I find a nice, fatty piece of ham. That way I can render the fat and save it to cook with later." She frowned and crossed her arms. "And why must you use all those expensive ingredients?" Grandma nodded toward the skillet that sat on the stove. "Why don't you just use what I use to darken the gravy?"

Mom suddenly stopped whisking. *So the black specks weren't tiny, charred flakes?*

"What do you use?" Mom asked casually. She was doing her best to sound nonchalant. "What do you use to darken your gravy?"

Mom tried to anticipate the answer. *Pepper? Yes, that must be it, nothing more than lots and lots of pepper.* She took a sip of water, still trying to act casual.

Grandma tilted her chin up as if anticipating a battle.

"Coffee grounds," she answered defiantly. And my mom, who was normally so good about dealing with her mother-in-law's over-the-top frugalness, spit out her drink.

~Crissy Martin

The Five-Second Rule

Be master of your petty annoyances and conserve
your energies for the big, worthwhile things.
~Robert Service

My mom was many things in her life—a daughter, sister, wife, mom, grandmother, teacher, psychologist, university professor, author, and lecturer. But she was *not* a baker. She was a great cook, and she enjoyed cooking, but she did not bake. Ever! The running joke in our family was that I was a deprived child from a deprived home because my mother did not bake cookies for me. Never. My father tried baking… once. Once was enough. We always had cakes, cookies and sweets in our house, but either my grandmothers baked them or they were store-bought.

In her role as a university professor, my mom had to entertain other professors and people from the university a few times a year. She would plan these parties carefully, making sure to take care of every detail pertaining to the appetizers, salad and main course. But she bought the dessert from the neighborhood bakery.

My husband and I remember these parties very well. For many years, my mom asked us to help her host. We mingled and sat at the table and ate with the guests, but we also helped her serve and clean up. The parties always ran smoothly because of the time and attention to detail that my mom put into them.

Except one time… It started out just like all the other parties.

In the afternoon, Mom got things ready. She set the table, got out the dishes, prepped the food, and figured out when she had to put in the roast to have it ready to serve at 8:00 p.m. She seasoned it perfectly and popped it in the preheated oven at exactly the right time.

The guests arrived. We had drinks and appetizers. All went well. We sat down at the table to enjoy the salad and rolls. Mom was sitting at one end of the table, and my dad was at the other end. My husband and I were somewhere in the middle. Sitting to the right of Mom, in a place of honor, was one of the most respected professors in the psychology department at the university... a well-known name in his field around the world.

This man immediately tucked his napkin into his collar rather than putting it in his lap. It was a good thing too, because he was stuffing food into his mouth and dropping it all over the place, including on himself and on Mom. Mom just sat there smiling and nodding at whatever he was saying and never lost her composure. Not even once. Very subtly, she picked lettuce and cucumbers off her sleeve and the table. Not once did she look like she was shocked. On the other hand, I sat there staring.

The professor was very intent when speaking to my mom. In the middle of spraying his food on her, he grabbed her hand and held it as if to really make his point. There wasn't anything romantic about it; he was just so wrapped up in what he was saying that he wanted to emphasize his words. The only problem was my mom was right-handed. The professor was holding her right hand. She couldn't eat. So she did the only thing she could do in this situation—she started eating her salad with her left hand!

Finally, the salad was finished, and it was time for the main course to be served. Mom and I excused ourselves from the table, went into the kitchen and closed the door. Mom whipped the potatoes, and I stirred the vegetables. Both were steaming hot and put into serving dishes, just waiting to be carried out to the dining room. Mom was ready to take the roast out of the oven. She opened the oven door carefully, got the potholders ready and pulled the oven rack out a little. That roast looked so perfect. Cooked to perfection. And it smelled delicious. Mom carefully lifted the roaster out of the oven and turned toward the kitchen counter where the cutting board was. We could never figure out what happened next. It was like the world started turning in slow motion as the roaster tipped ever so slightly, and the beautiful roast fell right on the floor. *Plop!*

I gasped, but Mom didn't blink. Just as she had before, when she was having food sprayed on her while having her hand held, she reacted with poise and grace. She quickly picked up the roast from the floor, brushed it off and put it on the cutting board. She sliced it and artfully spread the slices on the serving platter, spooning a little of the au jus over the meat. She even sprinkled parsley on it for garnish!

Then she looked at me. I looked at her. We shrugged, smiled, opened the door to the dining room, carried in the food, and served dinner to the guests. People raved, as they always did, about Mom's cooking. Mom and I ate the roast along with everyone else as if nothing had happened and never said a word. It was delicious!

At that dinner, Mom taught me something I will never forget — the importance of the five-second rule. It sure came in handy later when I had three sons!

~Barbara LoMonaco

Snapping Beans

Grandmothers always have time to talk and make you feel special.
~Catherine Pulsifer

I remember sitting at a big wooden table as Elvis Presley played from a small cassette player on the kitchen counter. It was late summer, and the air was heavy. Somewhere, a box fan was blowing from a windowsill, bringing in more of that heavy, warm air. Yet, there she was, not a care in the world, humming along to the music and gathering the items she was about to bring to that big wooden table.

I couldn't have been more than six years old at the time. On most days, I could be found running wild through her rosebushes, digging in the dirt to make mud pies, or waiting patiently for the ice-cream truck to pass by her house. But not that day. That day, I got to sit beside my grandma and snap beans.

There was a rhythm to snapping those green beans. First, she grabbed one from the rolled-up grocery sack, snapped off both ends, discarded them, and then snapped the remaining bean into three pieces. She was able to snap ten beans to my measly three. Looking back, she could have finished snapping beans for the entire week in less than a half-hour if she had done it herself. However, she sat there for sometimes an hour or longer, letting me snap them with her. Being that young, our conversations while snapping revolved around trivial things like what I found on my latest treasure hunt or how I got my skinned knee.

As I got older, I anticipated the days when Grandma would pick the green beans from the garden. The snapping never changed, but the conversations did. I learned about the hardships she had endured while growing up in Kentucky. I learned about how she met my grandfather and knew he was "the one." I learned how to tell when the soil was fertile enough for planting beans and what to do if a late Indiana frost threatened the seeds. We could snap a pile of beans in record time, but we sat talking for hours after the last bean had been snapped.

I valued the time I had my grandma to myself. At that point in time, I had fifteen or so cousins who enjoyed their time with her as well. So when I could steal her for myself, I always would. She had the ability to calm all my fears, ease my anxieties, and lift me up when I felt defeated.

At twenty years old, I still found myself driving across town to sit at that wooden table, snap beans, and swap stories with my grandma. Only now, my pile would get snapped quickly, and hers would take longer to snap. But just as she was patient with me, I sat there happily for hours as she snapped and talked. It was never really about the beans, even though they were absolutely delicious. It was about the time spent with this beautiful, kind, gentle woman whom I was so fortunate to have in my life.

I knew my days at the table with her were not guaranteed. The cancer was slowly taking her strength, and a goodbye was on the horizon. In the end, we didn't get to sit around a table and cover new chapters of her life story. However, I did get to hold her hand and tell her all about the wedding I was planning. I wanted her to know all the details: the colors, the flowers, and the music. I wanted her to know those things because she wouldn't make it to my wedding the following year.

It's been eight years since my grandma passed away. There's a new table now. Only this time, it's in my house. On any given day, you will find a little three-year-old girl with the most beautiful brown eyes sitting at that table, slowly snapping beans with me. She calls me Mommy. We talk about butterflies, cupcakes, and everything pink.

And somewhere under the laughs and giggles and the sound of the beans snapping, you'll hear an old box fan blowing from a distant windowsill, bringing in the heavy summer air. In those moments, I find my grandma once again.

~Natasha Basinger

My Grandmother's Kitchen

Grandmas never run out of hugs or cookies.
~Author Unknown

Each time I bake, fond memories of my maternal grandmother float around my kitchen much like the aroma of her freshly baked bread. Vivid images of my grandmother baking cakes, cookies, and Irish shortbread appear when I close my eyes. And then I smile. Spending time with my grandmother in her kitchen was always an adventure and no matter how badly I failed at my own attempts to emulate her perfectly baked goods, she would always find the positive.

As a young girl, I was given the essential role of the helper—the "getter," as my grandmother called it. She would say, "I need you to get the flour from the cupboard," or "Can you get me a whisk?" I was happy to comply; I was an excellent getter and my reward was usually to lick the spoon, which was covered in cake batter or creamy fudge.

As the years passed, I learned about the art of baking from my grandmother. I studied her recipes, each one handwritten and stored in an old wooden recipe box. Her measurements for various ingredients always baffled me. Words like "smidgen, pinch, dash, dollop, and tad" were commonly used in her directions.

My cookies never looked as good as hers—hers were perfectly shaped, thick, and evenly sprinkled; mine were misshapen, flat, and sometimes burned. But instead of criticizing me, she made a game of identifying the not-so-perfect cookies, and if they did not pass our inspection, we would be forced to eat them ourselves. We both had an insatiable sweet tooth. Oh, how my belly would ache by the end of the day from laughing and eating so many sweets. It was no surprise I was a chubby girl throughout my adolescence.

Presentation was a valuable lesson. When it came to bake sales, my grandmother's baked goods were always the first to disappear. Her logic was simple: "If it doesn't look good, it doesn't taste good." It didn't matter how wonderful someone's baked goods tasted if they were not festively decorated and packaged well. Spreading chocolate frosting on a cupcake with a butter knife was not up to snuff in my grandmother's opinion, and usually those were the cupcakes still sitting on the table at the PTA bake sale at the end of the day. Her sugar cookies always had colorful sprinkles on them; peanut butter cookies always had a cross-hatched fork imprint; chocolate chip cookies always had extra chips placed strategically on the top before baking.

We would often visit the local church bake sales and she would point out the items she predicted would sell first—and she was usually right. Cookies in a decorative plastic bag with a ribbon were popular; conversely, cookies on a white paper plate covered with cellophane were the leftovers. Customers might never know how good your baked goods tasted if you didn't entice them to purchase them—the presentation alone could sell the item.

My grandmother's love for baking never faltered over the years, but as human nature would have it, she became forgetful in her old age. One time, she admitted sprinkling poultry seasoning atop the coffee cake instead of cinnamon. Upon realizing her mistake, she remade the coffee cake—and then accidentally used the poultry seasoning again. Occasionally, she would call me at home, frantic that she had not remembered to mix the eggs into the cookie dough before she added the flour. I asked her if she had checked the wastebasket for any broken eggshells. "Oh, I guess I did remember the eggs," she would say, and we would laugh about it.

On one occasion, she was asked to bring a half-sheet cake for her senior citizen luncheon and she had forgotten to bake the cake the night before. Not having the ingredients on hand to make one from scratch that morning, she borrowed a boxed cake mix from a neighbor.

She called me as the cake was cooling on a rack and told me she had seen a coupon in the dry cake mix, but she could not remember whether or not she had removed the coupon before mixing the batter. With only one hour before the luncheon, she was forced to frost the cake without knowing if the coupon was baked inside. I suggested not bringing the cake to her luncheon, but she said, "Let me give you some good advice, honey. Never let your friends down when it comes to dessert — they're counting on you." And so, she began to formulate a plan in her head as we spoke.

As I mentioned, my grandmother had a way of making a negative into a positive and this was her plan: If the coupon had not been baked into the cake, no one would be the wiser; if the coupon had indeed been baked inside the cake and someone bit into it, she would announce that he or she had won a prize! As it turned out, there had been no prizewinner that day, but remembering my grandmother's back-up plan still makes me chuckle.

Although she has passed on, I still display her box of handwritten recipes in my own kitchen and keep them close to my heart, as baking will always be a hobby and a passion for me. She not only taught me about the art of baking, but how to look for the positive in any situation, even if it takes a little improvising.

This year would have been my grandmother's 100th birthday. I miss her terribly, but her teachings and the fond memories we shared in my grandmother's kitchen will live on.

~Suzan Teall Headley

Chapter 5

My Amazing Mom

My Role Model

If I have done anything in life worth attention, I feel sure that I inherited the disposition from my mother.
~Booker T. Washington

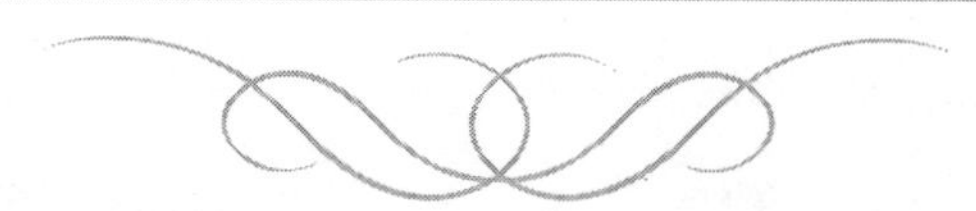

Hurricane Betty

A strong woman understands that the gifts such as logic, decisiveness, and strength are just as feminine as intuition and emotional connection. She values and uses all of her gifts.
~Nancy Rathburn

My incredible mom, Betty, gave birth to my younger brother when she was forty-one years old. Her role became that of the devoted and tireless round-the-clock caretaker right up through her early sixties. By the time my brother finally left the nest for medical school, and my thoroughly exhausted dad had reached mandatory retirement age, money was very tight. Mom was forced to go out into the workforce for the first time since her days as a cosmetics salesperson some forty-five years earlier.

I don't know where she found the strength or the courage to re-enter a competitive "new-age" employment environment. But, then again, my mother was always one to do what had to be done in the name of her family.

Armed with only a high-school diploma, a decent feel for numbers, and a boatload of moxie, Betty applied for a job at the preeminent New York department store at the time, Abraham & Straus. The position? Executive Assistant to the Senior Buyer for Abraham & Straus's men's apparel department. Aware that her résumé was not competitive with that of most of the other applicants, she offered to work the first month for free. The head of the department saw something special in her and hired my then sixty-five-year-old mom rather than some young upstart with actual bookkeeping experience.

How'd she do? Well, I recently uncovered a 1986 employee evaluation written by her boss. It reads as follows:

> *Betty is an expert with the most complete knowledge base possible. She is not only a role model for her peers, but for the assistant buyers here as well. She is truly the most important cog in the running of this office!*

The success and respect that Mom enjoyed in the workforce during those years gave her the confidence to tackle even more daunting challenges in the years to come.

When Betty turned seventy, she had to quit her job at the department store in order to take on a new career… that of round-the-clock caregiver for my father. My dad, who had already been suffering from severe Parkinson's disease, now was being further victimized by heart disease, and then a stroke that brought with it immobility, incontinence, dementia, and drastic mood swings.

I often wondered, during that period, how on earth she could keep going day after day, year after gloomy year. To say her life had become lonely, robotic, and exhausting would be an understatement.

When my dad passed on, my mother, then in her mid-seventies, could have taken one of two roads. She could have given in to the toll of physical, mental, and emotional exhaustion she was experiencing, and withdrawn from life. Or she could look at this as the start of yet another great adventure, a bold new challenge! Thankfully, my "warrior" of a mom, Betty Stein, was not the type to live out the rest of her days hibernating in a comfort zone of sadness and regret. Instead, she made the courageous decision to embrace the road rarely traveled and return to school after a sixty-year hiatus! She enrolled at Kingsborough Community College with a major in Media Studies. I remember her saying to me at the time, "You know, Gary, I probably can't compete with these young people today. My goal is just to pass my courses and keep my mind stimulated."

Well, she wound up doing a lot more than just passing her courses! She graduated Phi Beta Kappa and was the only Media Studies major to make the Dean's List that year! And today, hanging in the narrow hallway of my apartment, you'll see a framed transcript with all her course grades on it. My miraculous mother had achieved a perfect 4.0! Well, almost perfect...

It seems one professor had it in for my mom. He gave her an A-minus. Maybe she reminded him of the mother who had abandoned him when he was two. Maybe he believed old folks should spend their days playing mahjong and shuffleboard instead of going to college. Or maybe, perish the thought, she didn't deserve an A in the course. But my mom believed otherwise, and so, not all that surprisingly, Hurricane Betty blew into the professor's office that day and slammed the door behind her. I don't know what transpired in that professor's office, but suffice it to say, when my mom left she had her A... and that perfect 4.0.

At age eighty, Betty joined her apartment complex's creative-writing class and wrote... and wrote... and wrote. Over the subsequent decade, she authored a substantial volume of high-quality columns, poems, and personal stories — enough to fill several books. A few years ago, I compiled what I felt were some of the best and published them in a paperback entitled; *The Golden Years Can Kiss My Ass!* (On the cover, my mom is dressed, biker-style, in leather, chains, tattoos and dark glasses.) A year later, we went into a second printing due to the unexpectedly high demand.

In 2013, the amazing woman whom I was blessed to call my mother finally met her match — that heretofore undefeated opponent known as Father Time. She was ninety-five. But just a few days prior to falling into a coma, my mom whispered something to me that seemed, at least at first, totally out of character for the "force of nature" I'd had the privilege of knowing and loving for fifty-seven years.

"Gary, I don't want to lie in bed all day being fed through a tube. I just want to go to sleep and die," she said in a voice that was as sturdy as it was certain.

A week later, she was gone. And you know what? When I think back now, Hurricane Betty had once again made clear, even in how she approached her own death, that she was ready to step outside yet another comfort zone and venture bravely into the great unknown.

~Gary Stein

The Greatest Blessing

We should certainly count our blessings, but we should also make our blessings count.
~Neil A. Maxwell

I was raised by a single mother who often worked several jobs just to make ends meet. When I was fifteen, she started dating the man who is now my stepfather, and things began to get easier financially. There was no longer a question as to whether she'd be able to afford groceries for the week.

The following spring, when I was sixteen, a new family began attending our church. The wife, Melissa, quickly befriended my mom, and the children, though younger than I, became my pals. They lived within walking distance from us, and once school let out for the summer, I would trek over to their house to watch Disney movies while my mom was at work.

One afternoon, I was at their house during lunchtime, and they were gracious enough to include me in the meal. Their daughter, ten at the time, requested a glass of milk with her food. Melissa stated, "We're out of milk, and we don't have any more money for groceries this week." She suddenly realized I was present and explained with a defeated look, "Money has been really tight."

The family had recently moved to Central Pennsylvania from California because Melissa had been offered a good job. The position hadn't worked out, and her husband had to take the first job he could find. They had uprooted their children and moved across the country, leaving behind family and friends, only to end up in a bind. I thought about our own circumstances just a year earlier.

Later, I trudged home with a heavy heart as I reflected on their hardship. I told my Mom about the rough time Melissa and her family were experiencing. "Do you think we could help them?" I asked. In response, she immediately flung open the cupboard doors and started pulling out food. We ransacked each cabinet, grabbing bag after bag, can after can — cereal, peanut butter, spaghetti sauce, and more. Then we tackled the canning shelf where Mom's precious homemade goods were stored. We found a sizable box and packed it full. Then off we went to the grocery store where we picked up perishables such as milk and eggs. We drove to our friends' house, made our way to the door with our box and bags, and knocked eagerly.

When they opened the door, all four of them were there, clearly surprised by our visit. As we stepped inside the kitchen, their eyes found the box, and the parents' jaws dropped. Handing the items over to them, Mom said, "We just wanted to bless you." They were speechless. Melissa then grasped Mom in a tight embrace and started to sob. Tears began to roll down my mother's face as she held onto her friend, feeling her pain, fear and frustration, understanding how devastating it can be to struggle to provide for your family. I felt my eyes moisten and throat tighten with emotion as I watched my mother. Then I looked over at the children. Their son was beaming, and their daughter was sniffing away tears.

My gaze shifted back to my mom, and I was proud to be the daughter of this incredible woman. She was the one who had worked so hard to pay for the groceries that she didn't hesitate to give to those in need. Because of her, we were able to share this amazing experience. What a great example she set for me that day! Though our intentions were to bless our friends, thirteen years later I still feel like I'm the one who received the greatest blessing: one of my most cherished memories with my mom.

~Savannah D. Cassel

A Bowl of Raspberries

Grandparents and grandchildren, together they create a chain of love linking the past with the future. The chain may lengthen, but it will never part.
~Author Unknown

I was nine years old when my parents put me on a train in Chicago. Dad slipped the porter a few dollars to keep an eye on me until I reached Rock Island, Illinois. When the train pulled into the Rock Island station, wheels grinding, puffs of steam coming from the engine, I slid to the edge of my seat and peered out the window at the people waiting outside. Excitement, then fear moved in because I didn't see a familiar face.

The porter bent down and said, "C'mon, miss, this is where you get off. Your grandma be waitin' for you."

I slid off the soft upholstered seat and followed the man down the aisle. The porter smiled broadly as he helped me down the two steps to the ground, and before I could look around, my grandmother appeared. She nodded her thanks to the porter, accepted the small suitcase he handed her, and clasped my hand in hers.

Grandma was tall, slim and serious. No hugs and kisses. She wore her long gray hair in a braid that wound around the top of her head, and her rimless glasses gleamed in the sunlight. She walked fast, her laced-up black oxfords keeping a steady beat. My little legs had to work overtime to keep up with her.

We marched for several blocks at this smart pace when Grandma stopped so suddenly I nearly fell on my face. She pulled me into a small neighborhood grocery shop and let go of my hand as she picked up a wooden box of red raspberries. A smile lit up her usually sober face.

"We'll have these," she told the clerk as she handed him the box of raspberries and some money.

Back on the sidewalk, we passed houses that were old and not very well kept. Some lawns were neat and tidy, while others were overrun with weeds and tall grass. Finally, we reached a big, yellow house with a fence around it. Grandma opened the gate and climbed the front steps, pulling me with her. "This is the rooming house where we're staying," she said as she opened the screen door.

I wasn't sure why my mother and father had sent me here. I knew Grandma lived in Arizona now, not here in Rock Island with Grandpa. I didn't like the narrow hall with a steep stairway rising to the unknown. I didn't like the smell of old food that seeped into my nose and stayed there.

We climbed the steps and went down another hallway to a small bedroom. "This is where I sleep—you'll stay here with me," Grandma said.

She laid her pocketbook and my suitcase on the bed, and then led the way to a tiny kitchen that held all the necessary equipment. A small, square table sat under a sloped ceiling, a red geranium perched on the windowsill, while white curtains fluttered in the open window. A calendar picture on the wall showed a calm, blue lake with August 1948 printed underneath.

Grandma washed the raspberries, divided them into two green glass bowls and poured heavy cream over them.

Placing them on the table with two spoons, she said, "Now, sit down and have your raspberries. They're only good if you use real cream on them."

And they were good—both sweet and tangy, and covered in the smooth, cold cream. They were so good that I think of the day Grandma introduced me to this wonderful fruit every time I see them. And I know they need "real cream" to taste their very best.

When we'd spooned up the last bit, Grandma said Grandpa was

waiting for me. My hand tightened around my spoon, and I wished there were more berries in the bowl to delay the visit. My mother said he was sick and asked to see me. *Was that why Grandma was here? Was she taking care of him?* My friends' grandparents lived together. Mine did not. I didn't know why.

We moved down the long hallway to a small bedroom that smelled stuffy and like medicine. This room had a sloped ceiling, too, something I'd never seen. I studied it carefully so I didn't have to look at the bed right away. Finally, I moved to the side of the bed where my grandfather lay. He didn't look like the grandpa who came to visit us. He didn't look like the grandpa who brought me a cigar box filled with pennies he'd saved for me.

This grandpa looked thin and pale, with deep circles under his eyes. His silver-white hair was combed neatly, but there was a bit of stubble on his face. His hand trembled as he reached out to me. Grandma nudged me, and I moved closer and took Grandpa's hand.

"How long have you been here?" he asked in a quivery voice. Not like Grandpa at all.

I looked up at Grandma, not sure what the answer was.

She said, "About an hour."

Grandpa chuckled. "If that had been your mother when she was your age, she'd have known everyone in town by now."

This was the grandpa I knew, and seeing him released the knot of strangeness and fear in me. I chattered on about my mother and father, my little brother, the train, the raspberries—whatever came into my mind. Grandpa listened to every word. Finally, Grandma told me we'd better leave.

I slept that night with Grandma in a bed meant for one person. The next morning, I reached up to touch her cheek. Her skin looked so soft. She put her hand around mine and squeezed it ever so gently.

Our days went on, with short visits to Grandpa. Once, Grandma made me wait in the little kitchen while she gave Grandpa a bath and shaved him. When she was done, she came to get me, and I moved quickly through the narrow, dark hallway. Grandpa asked me questions about school and my friends. Sometimes, he closed his eyes and lay there quietly, but I knew he wasn't asleep. He was sick, but no one told me what was wrong. When I was sick, I got well in a few days, but somehow I knew Grandpa wasn't ever going to get well. Not even with Grandma taking care of him.

***

It was only weeks later when my mother got the call that made her cry.

She hugged me close as she wiped her tears. "The last thing my dad asked was to see you one more time, and he got his wish before he died."

I didn't fully understand then, but many years later I realized what it must have meant to him, and I understood what my grandmother had done. Even though they'd lived apart for so many years, she spent those last weeks by his side caring for him. Though she'd never said a word about what she was doing, I learned something about duty, loyalty and, yes, love from this serious grandmother who also taught me the joy of a bowl of raspberries swimming in cream.

~Nancy Julien Kopp

Washday Worries

Keep your chin up, trust in God, and
believe in good things to come.
~Jeffrey R. Holland

Dad's words bounced off the cellar walls: "This old thing is shot for good, and that's all there is to it."

"Say it isn't so," Mom whispered, as she contemplated trekking to the laundromat during the heat of summer to keep up with the wash for our family of seven. That meant several loads of wash in a shopping cart along with an entourage of kids toting coloring books and crayons.

"What are you looking for?" my mother asked as I sat on the back porch that evening staring up at the sky.

"I'm looking for a lucky star so I can wish on it and get us a new washing machine."

"You go right ahead, Annie, but it will do you no harm to whisper in God's ear while you're at it. We need all the help we can get."

To my mom, good luck was a gift God reserved for those who kept in regular contact with him. Mom hopped on prayer duty the moment Dad declared the old washer beyond resuscitation.

I didn't want to take any chances, so I found a shining star, declared it lucky, made my wish, and slipped a few humble words in God's ear about how much my mom needed a new washing machine.

Every day, I awoke hoping I'd witness a washing machine floating down from the clouds. After all, Mom was praying like mad, and I had wished on a lucky star. It was just a matter of time.

Meanwhile, we toted the dirty laundry to the laundromat every few days as predicted. When we weren't coloring, Mom kept my sister Marie and me busy sorting and folding clothes to distract us from making racecars out of the wash baskets on wheels.

Though Mom had full faith that God would answer our prayers, she cautioned me not to count on a spectacle. She believed God would shoot a good-luck beam in our direction through the subtle path of the classified ads as opposed to my theory of a parachuting household appliance.

That goes to show just how smart moms are. About three weeks into our ordeal, she spied an ad in the local paper. A nearby apartment house was replacing its washers and dryers. The ad said their current appliances were all in working order and available "for cheap" — no price mentioned.

Mom called right away and learned that for twenty dollars we could stop dragging our wash to the laundromat. She'd have to cut corners to come up with the money, but it was worth it. To top off our good-luck streak, the building manager owned a pickup truck and was willing to deliver for no extra charge.

When he arrived the next morning, Mom practically skipped to the front door with a crisp twenty-dollar bill in her hand. This certainly was a red-letter day for the Tait family.

Imagine her surprise when asked if she wanted "the pair of them" brought through the front door or the back.

"Pair of them?" she said. "I only bought one washing machine."

"That's right, lady," he replied. "You bought one washing machine and one dryer."

"There must be some misunderstanding. I only have twenty dollars for the washer."

"It's twenty dollars for the set. Do we have a deal?"

From the look on her face, I didn't know if she was going to faint or kiss him. She did neither, but when he raised an eyebrow at Mom's freshly baked chocolate-chip cookies cooling in the kitchen, she made sure he left with a sackful.

We had walked through the valley of no washing machine and emerged with bragging rights to a genuine clothes dryer in the bargain. Talk about lucky!

After Dad hooked up the washer, our whole family went down to the cellar to check it out. The sparkling pale pink machine stood proudly in the spot where, just three weeks prior, the carcass of our old, dilapidated washer slumped in ruins. It was a sight to behold.

It wasn't until we were all admiring the washer that I noticed it had a coin slot just like the ones at the Laundromat. What a novelty! When we slid the quarter into the coin slot on this one, Dad fixed it so that it returned to us — every single time. Nobody else on our block could boast of owning a coin-operated washer, let alone one that actually returned the quarter.

A few days later, Dad installed the dryer. But even after it was operational, Mom only used it when bad weather prevented her from hanging the clothes outside on the line. She always said that owning a dryer was no excuse for wasting gas and electricity when the sun shines right outside the door for free.

Whenever we were in a fix, Mom always led the way with a good sense of humor and a whisper in God's ear to lend a hand. I think this is the most valuable lesson Mom never set out to teach me, but I learned it just the same.

~Annmarie B. Tait

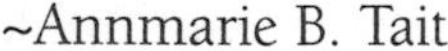

Barefoot

Our mothers are our first teachers, and we teach others the same lessons we learn from them.
~Caroline Kennedy

My mom was a dedicated churchwoman whose favorite story from her childhood during the Great Depression had to do with the county supplying her big family with shoes one winter, since the children were going to school barefoot. Mom was a good student, but she was embarrassed that the big, clunky shoes screamed "county issue." She was relieved when the final bell rang, and she went to pick up her little sister. She found a crowd of jeering students laughing and pointing at the child who sat on the steps with a beaming smile, hugging her new shoes to her heart and loudly thanking Jesus and the county for them. My mother always ended the story by saying she was grateful for the shoes, but she never forgot her classmates' cruelty.

Mom had a unique perspective on being charitable that I didn't really appreciate until one cold, winter day when we picked up my brothers at school.

"Who is that child?" Mom peered through the windshield as a skinny, greasy-haired angry-looking girl herded a crew of raggedy children across the street. "They don't even have coats. It's freezing!"

"That's Becky Ingler. She always looks mad like that," I replied.

My mother eyed the straggly group as they moved along the

sidewalk. My brothers jumped into the back seat as Mom eased away from the curb.

"Where are we going?" I asked as she inched along the street, keeping pace about a half-block behind the Inglers.

They entered a crumbling, old storefront. "They live here?" Mom mumbled, then looked at me. "Tell me about them."

I didn't know much, but my brothers did, including that the Inglers didn't have a father, and sometimes they smelled funny and everybody laughed at them. My mother nodded thoughtfully. Something was up, and it made me a little nervous. "I think I'll visit them tomorrow," she mused, turning to me, "and I want you to come with me."

"What?" I exclaimed. "I don't want my friends to see me go into that place!" Mom shot me a look. "I mean, you know, it's not that I don't like them or anything, but they're just… you know."

My mother nodded and replied softly, "Yes… I know."

The next day, I followed Mom as she made her way across the cracked concrete to the Inglers' front door. A tiny, exhausted-looking woman appeared, and Mom smiled and offered her hand. "Hello, Mrs. Ingler. I'm Mrs. Tovey from the church. I'm just visiting some of our neighbors to get acquainted." Once inside, my mother studied each of the children surrounding a scowling Becky, who was reading from a tattered book. She rudely ignored my nod.

A rusty coal stove in the middle of the room emitted a thin, grayish film that floated through the air. A big, messy bed sat in one corner where a toddler napped, thumb in mouth. Mrs. Ingler listened to my mother discuss some of the church programs, then smiled politely, thanking us for our visit. As we left, Mom told Mrs. Ingler she sincerely hoped she would see her again soon.

I couldn't get out of there fast enough, almost choking on the despair that hung in the air as thick as the coal residue. I could not fathom why my mother was so interested in the Inglers, but I soon learned.

Mom's old sewing machine whirred for two days and nights as she collected coats from the church donation barrels, local second-hand stores and our own closets, patching, taking in and letting out seams. My mother was a talented seamstress, and I admired the way she turned the shabby hand-me-downs into stylishly tailored winter coats. I said as much, still feeling guilty about how I had criticized the Inglers for… well, for nothing at all, really, just for being less fortunate than we were. "I'm glad you approve," she remarked, "because I need your help to deliver these coats to the Inglers this afternoon. But we need to do this carefully."

"Wow!" I said. "They're lucky to get these."

"No," said Mom as she faced me. "We're the lucky ones to be able to help them, but that's all it is, just luck. We could just as easily be in their shoes, or in no shoes at all, and then we'd be the ones needing help. We want to make sure these coats are given freely, without the Inglers having to pay a price for them." I didn't understand, and she continued, "I don't want these coats to cost them their pride or dignity. We aren't able to help them because we are somehow better than they are. We're just luckier right now."

I thought about Becky. She had a rotten attitude, but she also had a lot of responsibility, caring for her siblings and helping her frail mother in really bad living conditions. I knew the kids at school gave her a hard time because of how she and her family looked on the outside, without ever really seeing what was inside — a girl who was doing her best to keep her head up while living through a nightmare.

Later that day we went to the Inglers' again. "I hope we haven't come at a bad time," my mother apologized as we entered the smoky, little room.

The kids were all on the bed, watching a little television set perched on a nightstand. "I know this might be an imposition, and I hope you won't mind," Mom smiled at Mrs. Ingler, "but we have some winter coats here that are in decent condition from the church, and I just wondered if you might know of children who could use them. It seems a shame to let them sit in the donation barrel during this cold and maybe you know some kids in the neighborhood who could use them. Maybe even your own might like them. It was just a thought, so…" My mother lifted a blue girl's coat out of the bag.

Mrs. Ingler gazed at the coat, and then glanced at Becky, who was eying the garment with interest. "I'd be happy to help." Mrs. Ingler gave my mother a knowing look. "And I appreciate you thinking of me for this. Thank you."

"Oh, please, don't thank me. You're doing us a favor," my mother laughed.

As we left, I glanced at Becky, who was examining the coats. She smiled, and her face was transformed into a Becky I hadn't seen before. I smiled back.

Over the years, I thought about how my mom accomplished this act of kindness, and about her gift for caring about people. She cared about the whole person in everyone—the outside, which might be poor or sick or homeless or barefoot, as well as the inside, which might be frightened or desperate or overwhelmed.

My mother is gone now, but her legacy lives. The lessons I learned from her have helped me many times to remember that it's important to see the whole person and to relate one to one, reaching out in love, not judging, and remembering that everyone can end up barefoot sometimes.

~Luanne Tovey Zuccari

In Her Footsteps

We are not put on earth for ourselves, but are placed here for each other. If you are there always for others, then in time of need, someone will be there for you.
~Jeff Warner

My ninety-year-old mother had come to stay with me. Every day, I watched as her arthritic fingers adeptly tied the laces of her favorite white sneakers. I marveled at her strong will to be self-sufficient. Whenever I asked if she needed help, she simply looked up at me and smiled, saying, "Remember, I'm the one who taught you."

In spite of my mother's strength and her will to survive, her heart weakened. Soon, she became bedridden. All the while, under the dust ruffle of her bed, her sneakers waited for her.

As I watched her strength diminish, I began to think: *No one can fill your shoes.* I recalled a lifetime of friends and family members she had healed and assisted. She had cared for her husband with heart disease and subsequently faced forty years of widowhood. Her mother received her personal attention until a fatal stroke. Her World War II war-hero brother, battle weary from a war with cancer, had stayed in her home until he required hospice at the veterans' hospital. After her first daughter died she had raised her six grandchildren. When an estranged son-in-law was dying of emphysema, she took him in and cared for him until the end. When she was eighty-five, her Russian-born childhood friend came to her home, where he was helped until his illness worsened and he required hospitalization.

She had an enormous heart and had acted as caregiver for so many people, taking them into her home. I wondered why. What was the catalyst that created this beneficent behavior? What triggers the selflessness of being a healer?

After my mother's death, I traveled to her home to sort through her belongings. There, hidden in a box in her bedroom closet, I found the answer. Wrapped in tissue paper was a twelve- by fifteen-inch professional photograph that I had not seen since my childhood. I recalled the rainy day when I had stumbled upon it while playing in the attic. I had asked my mother about it, but she offered no explanation. From that time until the day I returned to my mother's home, the photograph had disappeared. That picture showed a young child in a casket. Perhaps she thought that it was too disturbing for me to see, for the child was three years old, dressed in a white dress with a white veil, laid out in a white casket.

Later, at my mother's wake, I heard the story. The child's name was Janina. My mother had been her godmother and aunt. Janina's family lived above the neighborhood grocery store, and she had been the prize of the family, a Shirley Temple look-alike with a sparkling personality. At that time, there were no vaccines for childhood diseases and Janina contracted diphtheria. Back then, if you kept a sick child at home, the public-health authorities were authorized to quarantine your home, and if you had a business attached to it that would be quarantined too. If Janina stayed home the grocery store would have to be closed and her whole family would lose its livelihood. So Janina was sent to the hospital.

Visiting hours were limited but my mother and her sister went by trolley and visited as much as they could. Nevertheless, Janina declined and died. The hospital nurses said that she died of a broken heart. My mother and aunt had felt that if only Janina had been able to stay at home, she would have rallied and survived. My heartbroken mother decided that she would never let that happen again. She would care for the people she loved so they would never die alone with broken hearts like Janina.

With the passing of my mother, the legacy of caring for others was passed onto me. Her lesson was so simple: take care of others. No one can completely fill her shoes, but I try to walk in her footsteps every day.

~Lorraine Allison

Just Like Mom

If you're always trying to be normal you will never know how amazing you can be.
~Maya Angelou

When I was in high school, people would give me a weird look when they found out my mom rode motorcycles. I would beg her to let me off her motorcycle a block away from school, so as not to be spotted riding on the back. Although it embarrassed me a little in my teen years, Mom's passion for riding eventually became an inspiration to me.

In her day, it wasn't as common for women to ride their own bikes. Mom didn't care about what was "normal." She took a small-engine repair class to learn more about motorcycles and was featured in the local paper.

Despite my teenage embarrassment, I secretly admired Mom for pursuing her passion. She looked great in her leather gear with her long brown hair blowing in the wind. Heads would turn when she rode by on her bike in the little Northern California town where we lived.

Twenty years later, I got the bug, and I confided in Mom. I had mentioned the idea to a couple of friends, but they thought it was silly, so I kept future discussions to myself. I planned to take the Motorcycle Safety Foundation class with another girl, but she backed out. I was so nervous I signed up three times before I finally went through with the class.

Learning to ride a motorcycle was a total boost to my self-confidence, and it fed my independent side. As a former motorcycle magazine editor, I'm often asked about motorcycles and how to get started riding. The best advice I can offer is this: "Take a Motorcycle Safety Foundation class and learn the proper techniques from the start. It is much easier than trying to break bad habits later."

Living on opposite coasts has proved challenging for Mom and me. We never really had the chance to ride together on our own bikes. But, a few years ago, while attending a rally in North Carolina, I was able to show Mom the beautiful Ladies' Edition Kawasaki Vulcan 900 loaned to me by bike builder Scott Britt. It occurred to me then that this was the first time she'd seen me ride my own motorcycle.

As I reflect on my journey, I must give credit to Mom for setting me on the path to a wonderful and exciting life. Mom has since hung up her helmet and given her riding gear to me. It's never too late to learn. You might even surprise yourself and have a great time like I did.

I am, in fact, my mother's daughter.

~Teri Anne Conrad

Treasures in Trash

Ours is a culture and a time immensely
rich in trash as it is in treasures.
~Ray Bradbury, Zen in the Art of Writing

My mother's inspiration didn't come from traditional places. In fact, most of her masterpieces started out as someone's trash. Literally.

As Mom would drive us through the neighborhood, we'd hear the screeching sound of brakes stopping the big green monster (the fifteen-passenger van my mom drove until the wheels fell off). We'd pull up to a house. If we were lucky, one of our friends didn't live there.

All eight of us would close our eyes and pretend to be asleep. "Okay, we're here!" my mom would exclaim, as if she owned the home we had just pulled up to. "If we all work together, we'll have this stuff moved in fifteen minutes."

Everything with my mom consisted of "fifteen minutes." As in, "I'm almost there; I'll be there in fifteen minutes," or, "If you took fifteen minutes to [insert activity that will probably better your future or you as a person], you wouldn't be dealing with this."

We would continue "sleeping," hoping to avoid trash duty. The next thing we knew, our silence was met with "Well, I thought we'd go to the pool tomorrow, but I see no one wants to go..." Ah, yes, the pool. The Southfield Civic Center was where we spent our hot Michigan summers. Now we were fighting to get out of the van. It didn't matter if friends saw us absconding with their trash, there was swimming at stake.

We'd pile tables, chairs, and old pictures in the van. We grabbed whatever caught my mother's eye. The funny thing is, my mother could have easily afforded to buy these things brand-new, but I believe the artist in her liked the challenge of the hunt and turning trash into treasure. And that's exactly what she did.

Boring tables would be beautiful after she put her touch on them. Bookshelves would get new paint, and chairs would get refurbished and reupholstered. Our garage sales were always a hit. I remember thinking to myself, *If only these people knew they were buying back some of their old stuff!*

As an adult, I attribute my love of thrifting to learning at an early age that one person's trash truly is another person's treasure. My mother and I still enjoy thrifting to this day. Thankfully, we now do our thrifting in stores. The key to thrifting is to not look at what things are, but to look at what things can become.

~Candace L. Parker

Small But Mighty

Setting an example is not the main means of influencing others; it is the only means.
~Albert Einstein

My mother, Isabel Gaynor, was a petite, pretty, and shy Hungarian woman. She was a stay-at-home mom, like most other moms in the 1940s and '50s, and so heavily dependent on my father's ability to deal with the world outside our home that she didn't even drive a car.

She lavished on me all the love and attention she would have given to a whole houseful of kids had she been able to have them. I am thankful to her for so many things that I can barely list them. But if I were asked to thank her for one specific action she took in my childhood, it would be the way she handled herself in the face of injustice many years ago.

In 1951, when I was six years old, the wealthiest family in our suburban New York neighborhood employed a black nanny named Harriet to care for their young son, Vince. My mom struck up an acquaintance with Harriet, who had a quick sense of humor. Sometimes, on hot summer days, we joined them at a nearby brook to cool off in the water. Vince was five, a small, shy boy. He and I played happily together, splashing and shrieking. My mom, who'd never learned to swim, sat on a stump on the bank of the brook, chatting with Harriet.

One day, two half-grown boys with sneering faces rushed up to us, and for reasons I didn't understand then, called Harriet a word I'd never heard before, and then began pelting her with ripe tomatoes.

I don't remember what Vince and I said or did when that happened — or what Harriet said or did either. I can't say if she stood frozen with shock at the attack, or if she showed anger or fear or outrage at the hateful behavior. But what I do remember, clearly, all these years later, was my polite, timid mother's exclamation of disgust directed at those boys — before she stepped, deliberately, between the nanny and the tomatoes.

I can still see the blotchy red stains on Harriet's starched white uniform and on my mother's white arm.

Thanks, Mom, for the life lesson in courage, fairness, and good, old-fashioned decency. Your behavior that day not only made me proud of you, but it shaped me into a woman who doesn't hesitate to speak out against injustice and oppression.

~Lynn Sunday

The Trash Guys

Charity begins at home, and justice starts next door.
~Charles Dickens

My mother taught her eight children to be mindful of two important things: First, gratitude, because in reality we had it better than most people. And second, the importance of treating people with dignity. She didn't talk about these lessons much; instead, she lived them, and we watched and learned.

As a young child, I remember our station wagon packed with clothes and quilts barreling into migrant-worker camps. Before my mother had even turned off the ignition, all the doors were opened and the unloading began. It was almost a waste of time to turn off the car as it was emptied so quickly. There was no conversation as we didn't speak Spanish. But as we cruised out of sight on the dusty dirt roads, we understood what we heard the workers calling to us: "*Gracias! Gracias!*"

When the federal Head Start program began, my mom volunteered for years. Then she worked at her church's food pantry, choosing to take menial tasks rather than being in charge of making the tough decisions about who got food and who didn't.

As teenagers, we would lobby hard to go to poverty projects around the country or overseas with mission groups to serve people who were suffering and oppressed. Her answer was always a terse, "Charity begins at home." Then she would mention that Widow Johnson's lawn needed mowing or suggest some other need right in our community.

One of my most profound memories of my mother's charity occurred one frightfully hot summer day when my children and I were visiting her. When we got up the first morning, she informed me that none of *her* grandchildren would be going outside that day as the temperature would be close to 100 degrees. "Grandma rules," so my kids played quietly inside all day.

After lunch, I was helping Mom clean up the kitchen. She stopped in the center of the kitchen. "I hear them," she said. "Get out my cut-glass tea set." I knew better than to argue, as she was obviously on one of her missions. Quickly, she filled the glasses from a plastic pitcher of lemonade in the refrigerator and added ice. Then she filled the matching glass pitcher and arranged everything on the glass tray.

With that, she opened the back door, gesturing to me. "Go! They will be around the corner and at the driveway in less than two minutes." I was confused, but carrying the tray, I started out the door and onto the asphalt. The heat was oppressive. The thermometer on the side of the house read 105 degrees. I was instantly nauseated, but I made my way to the street. As I got there, a trash truck swung around the. Two guys were in the cab, and two were hanging off the back. They stopped right in front of our trashcan. A wave of awful stench wafted in the air around me. In the moment, I remembered visiting those migrant camps of my childhood.

The trash guys approached me. "My mom told me to bring you something cold to drink because it's so hot out." The men didn't speak at first. I noticed their faces were totally black with grime, and sweat made their bodies glisten like prizefighters. Time seemed to stand still. I was getting woozy from the heat and the attack on my senses.

Finally, one of the men spoke, "Your mother is so good to us." I noticed then there were little rivers streaming down; lines of white in the grime on their faces. It wasn't sweat. These men were silently crying. They were all visibly moved. One man was actually trembling with emotion as he stepped forward to take the heavy tray from me. "We can't stop right now — not until the end of the block for lunch — but we'll bring this back as soon as we are done."

I nodded as the men hopped back on their truck after emptying our trashcan. When I got back into the house, Mom was playing quietly with the grandkids. There would be no explanation; there never was. In due time, the trash truck was back, as indicated by a long, blaring horn blast. Outside again in the oppressive heat, I found the trash guys smiling and almost revived. "Tell your mom thanks," said one of the men as he handed me the glass set. They all waved, and the truck vanished around the corner.

I took the beautiful, fragile glassware back into the house, carefully washed each piece and put it away. It was as if nothing had happened when I finished and closed the china cupboard door.

Later, I would find out from friends and neighbors that my mom was known for her gracious behavior. Although people didn't always agree with her, they admired her for reaching out to others and giving them dignity.

To her credit, her children quietly reach out to developmentally disabled adults, homeless folks needing a warm breakfast, and mentally challenged children, and work in food ministries just to let others know they are an important part of our planet. My mother never forced her beliefs on people; she just set a great example.

~Pamela Gilsenan

The Question I Didn't Need to Ask

The art and science of asking questions
is the source of all knowledge.
~Thomas Berger

My first word was probably "Why?" My toddler questions weren't the usual ones like "Why is the sky blue?" or "Why does a cat have whiskers?" Instead, they leaned more toward "Why can't I have another cookie? I'm still hungry." Or one of my constant favorites, even today, "Why do I have to go to bed? I'm not sleepy."

Yes, I was a classic strong-willed child with an inquiring mind. Mom knew how to handle me from the start. When she finished an explanation, she'd often pat me on the back and say, "It's always okay to ask questions; it's one of the best ways to learn."

That was my signal that it was time off from questions. If I persisted, she'd reply with a short response and then lead my interest elsewhere by asking me about the games I played with my dolls.

When I started elementary school, my questions didn't end, nor did my mother's responses. I learned she had three adages about questions: 1) There is no such thing as a dumb question. 2) You won't learn unless you ask questions. 3) You may not always like the answer to your question.

Working on a papier-mâché sarcophagus for history class, I could not get the hang of how much paste to use, which resulted in more paper sticking on me than on the sarcophagus. In utter frustration, I whined, "Mom, I can't do this!"

She replied softly and simply, "Why not?"

"Because I can't" wasn't an acceptable answer for her.

Together, we worked on completing my project. She asked details about what needed to be done and let me find the answers on my own. Something else happened as well: Our bond as mother and daughter grew. Mom shared with me some of her own experiences in growing up and being frustrated over similar school projects.

Mom had the patience of a saint with all my questions. School was a totally different situation. Some teachers wearied of my inquiries that slowed their lessons down, so they ignored my hand in the air. Others had fun with my queries and answered back with questions of their own.

As a high-school student, I believed I could figure out things on my own and didn't need my mom's help anymore. Or so I thought until I broke up with my first real boyfriend. I came home from school that day, ran into my room and shut the door. Knowing something was wrong, she knocked gently on my door and then walked in. When she saw me crying on the bed, she brushed her hand over my hair. "What's wrong, honey?"

Between sobs, I replied, "It's Drew. We broke up. He said he wants to be with Rosemary and not me."

"I'm so sorry this happened. It's hard growing up and learning people may disappoint and betray you. This storm in your life will pass, and things will get better. Remember, believe in yourself and know you are special in God's eyes."

"How would you know about getting hurt?" I asked as I wiped away my tears. "You and Dad have been married forever."

Mom chuckled. "I know it's hard to believe, but Dad wasn't my first love. Jimmy was the one who broke my heart. And if he hadn't, I probably wouldn't have met your dad. See, things do get better."

My college choice was out of state. Now the questions were coming from my mother, asking about my classes and my new friends. During semester breaks, we got back to our in-person Q&A. My favorite discussions were about my broadcast-media class, where I co-anchored a talk show for a local cable TV channel. Mom loved watching the tapes I brought home. Her questions about the show always entailed "Why this?" or "Why that?" This gave us both a laugh as we realized the tables had turned, and now she was the one asking all the questions.

After college, I married and learned there were matters beyond my experience. Once again, I was drawn to ask Mom questions such as: How do you make love last? How do you make a budget and stick to it? Mom showed me how to live by asking me leading questions so I could find the answers that worked for me.

Mom has since passed on, and my husband now bears the burden of my many questions. He often refers to me as "She Who Questions Much." He's come to understand that if he makes a statement and I respond with, "Really?" I'm not doubting the veracity of what he said. It's merely my way of beginning the five Ws—who, what, where, when and, my personal favorite, why. In return, I've come to accept his rolling eyes, which means, "Can't we just get past all the questions?"

I'm still practicing Mom's three favorite adages about asking questions and receiving answers. When I'm at a business seminar, I'm always the first to have my hand up. The same goes for town hall meetings. When the discussion opens for questions, I'm ready with the first one. No matter where I am, if something catches my attention, I make sure to take the time to inquire about the details.

And it all started when I was a child, when Mom said, "Do you have any questions you'd like to ask?" She taught me it was always okay to ask and seek out answers. However, there was one question I never had to ask her—"Mom, do you love me?" She always showed it in her encouraging ways. Thanks, Mom, for being such a great role model of love.

~Christine L. Henderson

The Sacrifices She Made

An effort made for the happiness of
others lifts us above ourselves.
~Lydia M. Child

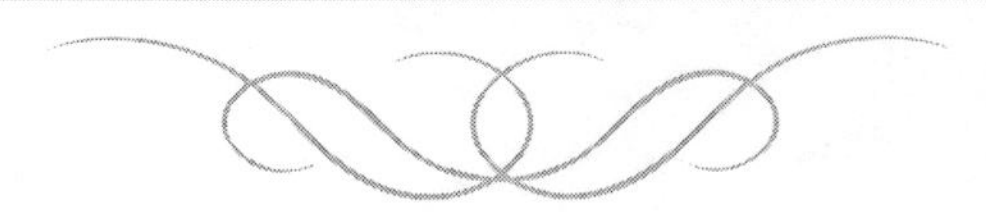

Home Is Where My Mom Lives

First my Mother, forever my Friend.
~Author Unknown

My mom and I are having lunch with her friend, Wanda, a woman I've just met, when talk turns to updates about Wanda's family. "Wanda is so lucky," says my mom. "All her children and grandchildren live nearby, and she gets to see them often." She says it matter-of-factly, not to make me feel guilty for living far away, but I can hear the wistfulness in her voice, the recognition that she lacks that particular kind of luck.

I nod and continue to half-listen to the conversation, but part of me is thinking about that long-ago day when I told my mom I wanted to move to Oregon from our small town in Louisiana. I had met someone, and he lived in Portland. My heart told me he was the one, the man I would make a life with. But my head told me I had to live close enough to know for sure. I was twenty-five then, full of restless energy and enamored with the possibility of embarking on a grand adventure.

The trouble was, that adventure meant leaving my mom.

At the time, we were living almost as roommates, cleaving to each other for support during what was a difficult time for both of us. Recently divorced, my mom was known in the 1980s as a "displaced homemaker," someone who had spent most of her adult life raising four children, putting three meals on the table day after day, and making sure the household ran smoothly. After my dad left, she attended vocational school to train in secretarial skills, and then found a low-paying job at a construction company. I, in turn, struggled to find a stable job after graduating from college during tough economic times.

We both went out with our separate friends, but we also spent time together, seeing movies or getting a scoop of ice cream to bolster our spirits after a rough day. We were buddies, pooling our resources, facing challenges, and shoring each other up.

"I need to talk to you," I said when I could no longer delay telling her about my plan to move. "Can we sit down at the kitchen table?"

If we had created a sanctuary for ourselves in the house we shared, the kitchen table was its altar. There, we read our morning newspaper while sipping coffee and eating breakfast. We watched TV there in the evenings while keeping our hands busy crocheting, peeling pecans, or painting ceramic pieces. We sat there with friends and family who came to visit, stopping by to chat and check how we were getting along.

I don't remember how I expected her to react. Maybe I thought she'd cry and ask me to stay. Maybe I thought she would get angry and forbid me to go. Technically an adult, I was still her child, and I believe she knew I would stay if she asked me to. Instead, she wanted to know when I planned to go and how I would get there. Then she fell silent. After a few minutes, she got up, walked into her bedroom, and sat at her sewing machine, picking up a project in progress. As the needle whirred up and down, I remained at the kitchen table, uncertain whether I should rush in and tell her I changed my mind or let myself feel giddy about the possibilities in my new life.

In reality, I couldn't have made the move without my mom's help and support. She lent me part of her meager savings so I would have money to fall back on until I got settled. She helped me decide what to bring, and she chose basics from her own kitchen cupboards and linen closet so I could set up an apartment. She helped me plan a driving route and pack the car. And, barely two weeks after our kitchen-table conversation, when I drove out of our driveway, she sat in the passenger seat next to me, with freshly baked banana bread in her lap.

For eight days, we acted like tourists, stopping at the Painted Desert, the Grand Canyon, Las Vegas, Yosemite National Park, and San Francisco. We drove next to giant redwoods and dipped our toes in the Pacific Ocean for the first time. Eventually, we made it to Portland and found the place I would stay while I looked for a job and an apartment. She met the man I had decided to uproot my life for, and she asked him to keep me safe.

Then it was time for her to go.

"One of the hardest things I ever had to do," she tells me sometimes when we talk about my move, "was to leave you in Portland and get on that airplane by myself to come home."

She may have hoped it wouldn't last. In some way, I may have hoped that too. Instead, decades have slipped by as I have built a good life away from my mom with the man who became my husband and the father of our two daughters. Her life among friends and family has been rich as well. Still, we have felt the loss of living far away from each other.

Now that I am about the age she was back then, with daughters about the age I was, I realize even more clearly the sacrifice she made by letting me go while assuring me she would be okay. One day, maybe soon, I may have to help my own daughters move away. If that day comes, I hope I can be strong like my mom, supporting whatever path they choose, even when it leads away from me.

We are lucky, my mom and me, that despite the miles between our everyday lives, we are close in every other way. We talk on the phone often and visit each other as much as we can. I confide in her, listen to her advice, and trade recipes with her.

When I visit her these days, and she introduces me to people I haven't met, she often says, "This is my daughter from Oregon. She's lived there thirty years."

It's a statement of fact that recognizes our loss as well as the full lives we have lived in spite of it.

"That's a long time to be away from home," people often reply.

"It's been more than half my life," I say, "so I guess I can call Oregon home now." But the truth is, I know that home for me will always be where my mom lives.

~Cindy Hudson

A Special Place in Heaven

A woman is the full circle. Within her is the power to create, nurture and transform.
~Diane Mariechild

"You are a wonderful mother." I would tell my mother that often. At age ninety-five, when she reflected back on her life, that's what was most important to her. Over a cup of coffee, she would often muse, "I hope I was a good mother. I wanted to be the sort of person that my own mother was. They didn't come any better than that."

My mother was the oldest daughter still at home when her mother's longstanding heart condition worsened. She was forced to drop out of school in tenth grade and watch her dream of becoming a nurse evaporate as she helped her mother with the younger children.

When I was a child and we visited my mother's family I would watch her withdraw when her younger sisters talked about their nursing careers. Her bright blue eyes would reflect her sadness, which I didn't understand at the time.

She had wanted to be a nurse. But instead, she helped raise her siblings and then she raised her three.

She had wanted to be a teacher, too, but instead spent hours at the dining-room table helping her siblings and then her children with homework or science projects. She wanted to be a veterinarian, but instead spent long, sleepless nights trying to ease the suffering of our dog dying from congestive heart failure, and bottle-feeding kittens that were abandoned when their mother was struck by a car. She wanted to be a missionary and help children in another country, but instead spent many hours sewing nightgowns and pajamas for the Red Cross.

She wanted to be a hairdresser, but instead spent her time creating ringlets for school photos. I have struggled with stubborn hair my entire life, but when I look at old family photos, I am amazed at her talent.

She wanted to be able to provide for us in a way that her parents could not always provide for her or her siblings. During times when my dad's business did not have a favourable year, she would stay up late at night and knit new outfits for my dolls so I would always have presents for my birthday.

She became the "go-to mother" for kids whose parents worked. A child with a skinned knee, or just someone needing a cookie and a hug, would find her way to our house. She loved them all and they loved her back.

She wanted to travel the world, but instead bought me a suitcase for my graduation and encouraged me to "travel while you are still young." I remember how excited she was when they left me at the airport for my first trip to Europe. And I remember seeing the relieved smile when she saw me walk out of the airport upon my safe return.

She was quiet and unassuming. She always looked for the good in everyone, even when it was harder to find in some people than others. She loved my father in a way that can only be described as a match made in heaven, and he loved her with equal intensity. She was kind, caring, and devoted, and always thanked God for the life she was blessed with.

At the end, she reflected back on her life and realized that she did achieve what was truly important. A framed poster on her wall said simply, "There is a special place in Heaven for the mother of three girls." It was worth more to her than any of the degrees she so coveted as a young woman.

To me, it makes no difference. When I looked at her I saw a nurse, teacher, veterinarian, motivator, wife, friend and, most importantly, the best mother ever.

~Brenda Leppington

Through a Storm

A mother understands what a child does not say.
~Jewish Proverb

I was eleven, and I liked thunderstorms. They filled me with awe. I usually stood right by the window to watch the power of nature.

But today I was filled with fear because I had never been through a storm like this one. The sound, the fury, the darkness… and the rain, falling in sheets so heavy I couldn't see the houses on the other side of the street.

And the worst part was, I was alone. Well, except for the baby. How she slept through it, I will never understand, but she did. I was grateful because I kept thinking that if the phone rang, I would jump out of my skin! I was so terrified that all I could do was sit on my hands on the sofa, staring out the big picture window and praying that the phone wouldn't ring.

I was babysitting, and I'd never babysat at this home before. It was the middle of the day, and everything should have been fine, but it wasn't. I was sure the baby's mom and dad would call any minute to find out how things were going in this storm.

So, alone with my terror, I sat as still as death. As the thunder roared, I watched the rain get heavier… was that even possible? I couldn't see anything at all!

And then, suddenly, a shape started to form out of the downpour. Whatever it was, it was moving fast! It was a person….

It was my mom! We lived about ten houses away, so I knew how far she'd come in this downpour. Without waiting to put on a raincoat or even pick up an umbrella, she had rushed out the door and hustled up the street. Seeing her, I was no longer afraid to move. In fact, I jumped up and ran to the door to let her in.

What a reunion we had! She was soaking wet, but I hugged her hard and didn't mind at all.

She told me she knew I would be afraid of this storm. How did she know?

Because great mothers always do! And they will toss aside all thoughts of danger to themselves and think only about comforting their children when things go wrong. They feel our tears; they "hear" our fervent prayers; they sense when the bravest of us is looking fear in the face.

Mothers know.

~Christine McCleod

The Dress

Every girl deserves to be treated like a princess.
~Heidi Montag

"There it is, honey. That box there," my frail mother softly said. I reached under the bed and pulled out a dusty, old wooden box. Sitting next to her, I brushed off the lid and opened it carefully.

"Oh, Mom, how long have you had this?" I asked as I shuffled through her keepsakes. I saw elementary-school report cards, high school and college diplomas, and letters my daughters had written in their crooked, little-girl penmanship. Then something in the bottom of the box caught my eye. It was a letter addressed to my mom in my handwriting. As I carefully opened it and began to read, my eyes filled with tears.

***

My mother was the daughter of a humble mechanic and a stay-at-home mom. Summer visits to my grandparents' house were filled with fond memories. In my mind's eye, I can see Grandpa in his old, dusty garage tinkering away and Grandma puttering busily in their tiny kitchen, making cookies that tasted like heaven on earth.

Mom carried with her into adulthood that same moderation her parents fostered in her as a youth. Dad preached in small churches in farming communities. He played the piano on Sunday morning, and she harmonized on the organ. When I came along, they were living happily on a shoestring. Upon graduating from the nursery, they sat me in the second row next to the center aisle where I sat perched each Sunday morning with my feet dangling haphazardly and strict instructions to "Behave!"

As a child, I didn't realize how little we had. Mom made my clothes, and I always had a new dress for Easter and Christmas. This tradition endured into my teen years. Upon entering my adolescence, I resented our meager lifestyle. We couldn't buy the expensive clothes the other kids wore. When my friends started driving their own cars to school, I suffered riding the bus. Shy and awkward, I did my best to be invisible.

Invisible, that is, until my senior year of high school. My friends and I were sitting in the cafeteria eating lunch one snowy December afternoon, waiting for an announcement about the upcoming Christmas Ball. Who would be the Prince and Princess for the Ball?

When the principal came on over the loudspeaker, announcing the result of the student-body vote, we expected the Princess to be from the same group of girls who always won, girls who we didn't like much. Then I heard my name. *WHAT?* I looked over at my friends. Their mouths were open as they looked back at me.

Later that day, one of the boys from our class sat next to me and explained. He said that a number of boys had gotten together and decided to pool their votes. "We wanted a nice girl to win this time," he explained.

Racing home from the bus that day, I was ecstatic to share the news with Mom and Dad. There were hugs and whoops and, of course, they said they weren't surprised because they "always knew I was princess material." After wading through a sea of satin and lace in a few of the shops the other girls had talked about, Mom and I quickly came to the conclusion that we were out of our league. Mom stated simply, "I will make your dress!"

She quickly went to work. Never wavering in her efforts to create a dress that would make every head turn at the Christmas Ball, she would smile and say, "After all, I'm sewing for a princess!" She truly was my fairy godmother. However, I did not have high hopes for the rapidly approaching event. I was certain that I would not look as pretty as the other girls when they appeared in their extravagant store-bought dresses.

Surprisingly, when the dress was complete, I was delighted with it. My mother had poured her heart into every stitch.

Then she surprised me more. "We're going shopping!" Shopping trips were very rare at our house.

Mom hung my dress over the back seat of the car, and off we went to hunt for treasures to complete my ensemble. We found a necklace and earrings dripping with fake diamonds and rubies to match my red dress. "Perfect!" she exclaimed. We had shoes dyed bright red and found a red satin slip to wear under my dress. "Gorgeous!" she announced. It was an afternoon I would never forget.

We couldn't afford any of what Mom bought me that wintry afternoon. But for my special night, she pulled out all the stops. My frugal mom went all out for her daughter who had the chance at a once-in-a-lifetime dream. Doing what only moms can do, she fully understood what mattered to my heart.

I showed up at my Christmas Ball looking every bit as lovely as any other girl in the room. It was a magical night. I danced. I laughed. I sparkled. At the end of the evening, I was crowned queen.

Years later, I was shopping for my own daughter's school dance. In my mind's eye, I wandered back to that cold December afternoon of shopping with my mom. That evening, I sat down and wrote my mom a letter.

Dear Mom,

Thank you so much for all of the sacrifices you made for my dance. Thank you for understanding me and making my dreams yours, even though they were far removed from what you grew up with. That was one of the few times I ever felt beautiful. It is my hope to be the mother for my girls that you have been for me.

***

I'm a grandma now. Many years have passed since that Christmas Ball, and my own girls are now buying Christmas dresses for their daughters. My incredible, unstoppable mother was finally stopped, by cancer.

The letter I wrote is in my own box of keepsakes now. It is a constant reminder of my frugal mother, who poured out extravagant love for her daughter. I hope I can be the mother and grandmother that she was, and that my daughters will someday remember that I loved them with the same extravagant love.

~Cindy Morris

The Gift of Motherhood

One of the most courageous things you can do is identify yourself, know who you are, what you believe in and where you want to go.
~Sheila Murray Bethel

Tears streamed down my face as I sat holding the greatest gift anyone had ever given me. However, my joy at becoming a mother was mixed with sorrow for the one who gave her to me.

A young woman made the final, heart-wrenching decision to place her baby girl up for adoption. Then she chose my husband and me to be her parents.

For three days, we spent time in the hospital with our daughter's birth family. Each of us took turns cuddling, feeding, and changing our baby girl. We shared meals, conversations, lots of tears, and even laughter. I never imagined my quest to become a mother through adoption would be bittersweet.

I remember that final day in the hospital. We met the social worker in the lobby. She seemed excited for us. And while I was excited for myself, my thoughts were also on the pain that another family was experiencing.

We went up to the hospital room with a little gift for the birth mom. Sobbing, I handed it to her, saying something about how it paled in comparison to the gift she was giving us.

I handed her a necklace, and she handed me her child. It still gets me every time I think about it that way. What love she must have had for her little girl. What amazing strength and courage she had to follow through with her decision.

It's been ten years, and those three days are still etched in my mind. I remember how we all walked out of the hospital together — my daughter's birth mother, her parents, our daughter, and us. We loaded our baby girl into the car and drove away.

We cried with joy over finally becoming parents, but were also thinking of the pain of our daughter's birth mother. I don't think I'll ever understand how she was able to go through with it. All I know is that I'm so thankful she did.

There are many mothers in my life, including my own, who have taught me so much. But there is a special place in my heart for the woman whose decision made me a mother.

She lovingly cared for our daughter for nine months as she carried her in her womb. She took care of her body, ate healthy, got proper medical care, and took needed supplements. She spent time talking with counselors about what would be best for her daughter's future. She bonded with her baby before turning her over to us.

Ultimately, in love, she chose what she felt would be the best decision for her daughter. The courage and selflessness it took for her to go through with her decision is greater than any I've ever seen. When I think of her, I am challenged to be a better mother.

~Michelle Armbrust

A Ragged Nightgown

My mother gave me life and never asked for anything in return. That is her secret, you know, always giving without any expectations.
~Author Unknown

Near the end of my ninth-grade school year, my twin sister and I were invited to a party at the home of a high-school classmate. We were new kids at the local school, and the party was to be at the home of a rather affluent family, so it was an exciting event for us.

I will never forget the party or the evening — not because of any extraordinary social setting or the fun with new friends, but because of what transpired when we returned home.

My sister, Eleanor, and I had both worn beautiful dresses that were certainly fit for a late spring evening in the Deep South. Mother had worked for several days making them. I still remember how pretty those dresses were, and the amount of time that went into making them. Mine was a rosy pink patterned with tiny flowers, while Eleanor's dress was identical in design, only greenish-hued in color. We knew we looked great, and we were quietly confident as one of our aunts dropped us off at the party.

Another aunt drove us home after the party and we hurried in to tell Mother all about it.

The image is still vivid to me.... I was standing in the hallway beside my parents' bedroom. Mother was standing near the foot of her bed, dressed for sleep but without her bathrobe. Her flimsy nightgown had torn at the shoulder and been mended; from about the knees down, the gown had gaps, tears and pulls. I realized that I had never seen that nightgown before, as it was always hidden beneath the old robe that she wore.

I looked at my lovely dress and then at her ragged nightgown. We all said goodnight, and the party was over — in more ways than one.

Lying in bed that night, I revisited all the times my mother had sacrificed for us. I remembered the beach party at the end of seventh grade. We couldn't go because we didn't have swimsuits. Eleanor and I had accepted the fact and told the teacher we would not be able to go. "Of course, you are going!" Mother had insisted.

The night before the beach trip, she sat up all night long making swimsuits! She found a pattern, bought material for the suit and lining, and by the next morning she had two swimsuits lying on the sofa in the front room. Mother did not have her own swimsuit, yet she had produced suits for my sister and me.

Then there was the slumber party when we were twelve. Out came the trusty old sewing machine, and within two days we were sporting brand-new pajamas that would fit right in at the party.

As I lay in bed that night, more and more scenes from the past flooded my mind. I recalled time after time when Mother sacrificed for us, never thinking of herself and her own needs. I recalled how she went to work at a neighborhood launderette to earn a few dollars a week — not for her own personal use, but for us.

I remembered The Bike.

Our brother, Alan, was two years younger than us. We lived in a neighborhood teeming with children about our age, and all of his friends had bicycles. Occasionally, they would let him ride, but more often than not he would sit on the front steps and stare wistfully at the other boys as they rode up and down the street. Then came that Saturday morning.

As was her custom, Mother walked to town to do the grocery shopping. (Daddy had the car, of course, and "had things to do" in his life that rarely included us.) And, as was her custom, she returned from the local A&P in a taxi. We were sitting out on the front steps waiting for her. (That was our custom — we knew she would bring us each one piece of candy!)

This time, something was different — the trunk of the taxi was not shut all the way. The cabdriver got out and removed a shiny new red-and-white bicycle! Alan's eyes were like saucers, and we were deliriously happy for him. While our little brother soared down the street to join his friends, we learned that Mother had taken her pay from the launderette and gone to Western Auto, made a down payment, and signed a note to pay five dollars a week until the bike was paid off.

My mother never said the words, "I love you" out loud. But she showed us her love through a life of personal sacrifice. We got new shoes while she re-soled her own and re-tapped her heels; we got coats and jackets while she wore the same coat year after year.

My only regret is that it took seeing that ragged nightgown for me to fully understand my mother's love.

~Elaine Herrin Onley

A Salute to the Mothers of Freedom

A hero is an ordinary individual who finds the strength to persevere and endure in spite of overwhelming obstacles.
~Christopher Reeve

My mother was a military wife. She moved our family twenty-two times in thirty-one years, over three continents, through three wars. Dad was the one who wore the uniform; Mom was the one who wore the brave smile. She served her country every bit as much as her husband did, and she did so with no hesitation, no complaints, and no regret. Mom was the wife of a warrior. She kept the home fires burning while Dad put his life on the line to protect his family and country.

I realize now that Mom put her life on the line, too. She was just twenty-two years old when she boarded a ship in San Francisco and spent the next twenty-one days horribly seasick sailing to the Philippines to join my father. She stayed up on deck much of the time, carrying her nine-month-old baby (me) in her arms, trying desperately to calm her queasy stomach. Over the years, she always said how grateful she was for the kindness of sailors and strangers who helped care for me during her miserable voyage across the Pacific.

Just a few months after we arrived in the Philippines, the Korean War broke out. Dad was sent to Japan, leaving his young family behind.

Mom would sometimes stand on the front porch of our house on base with her toddler on her hip and a gun in her other hand. She could hear the Hukbalahap insurgents fighting just a mile up the road, and at night she could see the flashes of gunfire in the nearby mountains. It would be six long months before she was allowed to join my father in Japan.

It couldn't have been easy for a young mother to be alone with her baby in a foreign country, with a civil war nearby. But when my mother tells the story now, she always makes it sound like a great adventure rather than a terrifying war zone. That's Mom — always putting a positive spin on things.

A few years later, after short stints in Montana, Texas, Los Angeles, and Sacramento, we were transferred to Virginia for six months where Dad attended the Armed Forces Staff College in Norfolk.

In 1959, we shipped out to Germany, where we had our longest tour of duty — four and a half years — during which we moved three times. Dad often joked that just when Mom got a place fixed up the way she liked it, we had to move again. Mom always laughed, but I'm not sure she really thought it was funny.

We were stationed in West Germany when the Cold War began. The Berlin Wall went up and so did the tension in the air — even we kids could feel it. We never knew if war was going to break out and our dads would be called to fight. Everyone lived in a constant state of alert, wondering and waiting to see if families would have to be evacuated back to the States. My parents never talked about their fear of a potential World War III, but kids are intuitive and smart — we could sense that something ominous was looming.

My high-school years were spent in Illinois, followed by our second tour of duty in Germany. Then Dad was off to War College again, this time in Montgomery, Alabama. From there, it was north to Dover, Delaware, for a couple years, then south to Puerto Rico. Next was Thailand for Dad, while Mom remained stateside in San Diego so my brother Roger could finish high school.

And so it went over the years — from base to base, state to state, country to country — my mom hauling her kids and boxes of belongings (and sometimes a cat or dog) from one assignment to the next. She was a military mom, and that's just what they do — get their marching orders and report for duty.

Every day, month after month, year in and year out, in wartime and in peacetime, millions of American women serve their country with honor. They provide support to their military husbands, while raising their children in the shadow of the fortress. These women often do long stints as single moms, while their husbands are deployed overseas for extended periods — months, even years.

There are no medals for bravery awarded to the wives of warriors, but there should be. These remarkable women deserve their own "Mother of Freedom" medal.

On Mother's Day this year, remember the military moms. Seek them out in your neighborhood, workplace, church and local school. They are the unsung heroes — the patriot moms who serve our country with selfless love and loyalty. Salute them. Thank them. Hug them. Honor them. They are the Mothers of Freedom.

~BJ Gallagher

Love that Spans the Ocean

There is an endearing tenderness in the love of
a mother to a son that transcends all
other affections of the heart.
~Washington Irving

I stopped dead in my tracks in my small kitchen and looked up at my son. "What did you say?" I asked.

I listened as my twelve-year-old son repeated calmly, "You can take the mom from the kid, but you can't take the kid from the mom." He stirred his melting chocolate on top of the stove and smiled his toothy grin at me.

My young, budding chef clearly had no idea how profound the words were that had spilled from his mouth.

As a transcultural family, we strive to keep our son attached to his Filipino roots, both in tangible and intangible ways. Adopted at the age of five and a half from the Philippines, our son's memory of his birth mother is limited. The one thing I want him to always, always hold onto is that she loved him.

One year on Mother's Day, we launched a balloon in honor of his birth mother. At the age of ten, he understood that the balloon would not travel overseas, but this symbolic act of love to honor the woman who gave him life characterized the love that spans the ocean.

His handwritten words across the Happy Mother's Day balloon read: *Thank you. I love you.*

A mother's love goes deep. Sometimes, the greatest sacrifice a mother can make is to know that she is unable to provide the life she desires for her child. She makes the heart-wrenching decision to release her child into the heart and home of another mother.

To me, that is a courageous act of love.

You can take the mother from the kid, but you can't take the kid from the mother.

I will never meet this woman, this mother who birthed my child, but I know she loved him. She came to his orphanage to make sure he was safe and okay. She chose not to see him, the pain too deep, too real, too close, but she loved him and needed to know he would be taken care of.

Now, almost eight years later, this son of hers is thriving. And he knows he is loved, not just by one mother, but by two. Somewhere, miles across the ocean, he knows a woman dearly loves him and thinks about him.

Because you can't take the kid from the mom… he lives on in her heart. And for that, as my son's mother, I am forever grateful to the sacrifice of his precious birth mother, who has filled my heart with my dream to be a mother to a precious boy.

~Tammy Allison

Chapter 7

My Amazing Mom

Special Memories

Creating memories is a priceless gift. Memories will last a lifetime; things only a short period of time.
~Alyice Edrich

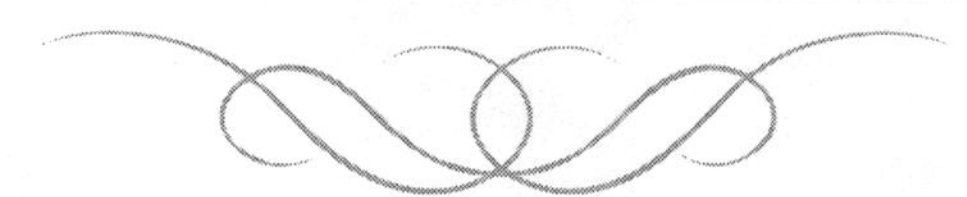

Knit One, Purl Two

Youth fades; love droops; the leaves of friendship fall;
A mother's secret hope outlives them all.
~Oliver Wendell Holmes

"Knit one, purl two. You're doing great!" I heard my mom say in a soft, gentle voice. I was in the kitchen as I listened to my mom instruct a neighbor's young daughter, Yolanda, on how to knit a scarf. I peered around the corner to catch a glimpse of the two of them talking over a huge ball of red yarn. Yolanda looked so interested and smiled often as my mother helped her along. Mom was so patient. I was about fourteen at the time, and the furthest thing from my mind was learning how to knit or crochet. "Come on over and sit with us," my mother encouraged me.

My answer was always the same, "I'm busy." I was a teen after all, and I had better things to do. I had friends to call, music to listen to, and boys to daydream about. Why would I want to learn how to knit?

Our tiny apartment was always filled with brightly colored yarn, knitting needles, and crochet hooks. Our sofa was piled with unfinished knitting and crochet projects. Quilts, hats, scarves, sweaters and slippers were stacked high. When a project was completed, my mother would give it away to anyone who asked, or she would surprise friends with a warm quilt or sweater. Back then, although I loved her work and was in awe of her talent and kindness, I would never wear one of the sweaters. Being a teen, I thought they weren't fashionable or "cool enough." My mom would laugh with a gleam in her eye and say, "One day, you will wear one of these sweaters!"

In my early twenties, I got engaged. My mother surprised me with an engagement party. When it was time to open all the gifts, I noticed one huge box that was left toward the back of the room. I received the usual gifts every young bride-to-be would want. I got a coffee maker, dishes, and a blender that had been on my wish list. Lastly, I opened the huge box, a gift from my mother. I couldn't imagine what it could be. As I lifted the box top, I could see multi-colored patterns through the white tissue paper. Lifting the paper, I saw she had crocheted a granny-square quilt to fit the queen-sized bed my husband-to-be and I had planned to buy. "Don't unfold it now!" my mom insisted. "I had a hard time fitting it into that box."

After the party, we brought all the gifts to my future mother-in-law's house. Her house had a lot more space than my apartment. We would keep the gifts there until after we got married and had our own apartment. The next summer, we said our "I do's" and settled into our apartment. I stored the big box that contained the quilt my mother made in our closet to use once the cooler weather arrived.

One chilly November evening, I unfurled the quilt and something fell to the floor. Looking down, I saw something bright purple. When I picked it up, I let out a roaring laugh. "Oh mom, you're crazy!" I laughed even harder. In my hands was the most colorful purple cardigan sweater I had ever seen. I called her up as fast as my fingers could dial. We laughed until we almost cried about her prank.

"I knew you'd get a kick out of that color!" my mom said between giggles.

That night, I hung my purple sweater in the closet. It certainly was a bright spot against all my dark clothing.

A few years passed.

When I had my daughters, my mother lovingly crocheted each baby a coming-home blanket, sweater set, bonnet and booties. "I'm glad they're not bright purple," I joked each time.

"Don't tempt me!" she shot back, laughing.

When my youngest daughter was just a few months old, my

mom came for a weekend visit. She brought a few skeins of yarn, along with crochet hooks and knitting needles. While the girls went down for a nap, my mom asked, "Are you ready to learn how to knit or crochet now?"

I was ready. In the middle of the afternoon, my mom taught me to knit. "Knit one, purl two," she said, as she showed me the simple technique. It brought me back to the time many years prior when I was a teen and watched her teach Yolanda. She had the same gentle voice and patience as she had back then. I had a newfound hobby: knitting.

Not long after I learned to knit, I settled down one cool night to knit a scarf for my three-year-old daughter, Heather.

I went upstairs to get a blanket from the closet, but the purple sweater caught my eye instead. *Why not?* I thought to myself. It was the first time that I put it on. It fit perfectly, and was so soft and warm. Most of all, it was cozy.

That night, I called my mom. "You're not going to believe this, but I wore the purple sweater while knitting!" That made two things I thought I would never do — knit and wear that sweater!

"See, I told you that one day you would wear one of my sweaters!" We both had a good laugh at that.

My mom passed away a few years later. I still have the sweater. Whenever I wear it on cool nights, I feel like I'm getting a warm hug from her. I look down at the bright purple that has hardly faded with time, and I can't help but smile.

~Dorann Weber

My Mother's Hands

The hand that rocks the cradle is the
hand that rocks the world.
~William Ross Wallace

I always loved my mother's hands. They weren't particularly beautiful, but I always envied her long, thin fingers and oval fingernails filed smooth. We used to joke that I somehow inherited my father's hands instead, with fingers that were meaty and masculine in their shape.

When I think of holding my mother's hand, I always recall a memory of when I was about five or six. It was summer, and a heavy rainstorm had left steam rising off the sidewalk.

"Let's go for a walk with no shoes or socks on," my mother said.

She held my hand as we walked down our street. Always yearning for me to use my senses to embrace the beauty of nature, my mother called my attention to the warm, wet concrete on the soles of my feet. I marveled how she didn't seem bothered by the small pebbles that occasionally pierced the bottom of my foot. My mother's hand felt warm that day, although usually her hands were cold, a condition she jokingly blamed on poor circulation.

My childhood memories of my mother frequently include her hands. I'd often fall asleep to the sound of her in the next room, typing on a typewriter, the clicking of the keys lulling me to sleep. When she wasn't working, she'd inevitably be outside in the garden, digging in the dirt and planting her tomatoes. She'd come inside, dripping with sweat, and I'd notice the black dust around her fingers, with more of it caked under her nails. When she'd drive me places, I always stared at her hands curled around the steering wheel. When she got older, she would occasionally flex her fingers while driving to keep them from feeling too stiff and arthritic.

As an adult, I've become addicted to weekly manicures. I do what I can to make my hands look prettier, and more frankly I simply enjoy the thirty minutes of relaxation while someone dotes on my hands.

My mother always took care of her hands by filing her nails herself. I believe the only manicure she had in her whole life was the day before my wedding, when I insisted she come to my neighborhood manicure salon. I know she enjoyed the experience, and although she had the means to continue to treat herself each week, she never went to another nail salon again. I suppose she thought her in-home manicures were sufficient and didn't crave the spa-like escape like I did.

Shortly before her seventy-fifth birthday, when she was battling pancreatic cancer, she landed in the ICU, the chemotherapy wreaking havoc on her insides. Each day I visited her, trying to make her as comfortable as possible, in the same way I would nurture my own kids when they weren't feeling well. I'd offer her water or food that I snuck in from the outside, but usually she was in too much discomfort to want anything. But one day, she had a question: "Do you have a nail file with you by any chance?"

I didn't, but that night I went straight to the drugstore and bought her a two-pack, which I brought back with me to the hospital the next day. I watched her file her nails in her hospital bed, seemingly content that she could make them smooth and oval, the way she liked them. I smiled at the absurdity of what made her happy at the time, but it made me happy, too.

When my mother passed away a few weeks later, I lay my head sideways on her chest and grasped both her hands, which felt the way they always did: graceful, strong, and cold. I stayed that way for several minutes, until my father told me gently that it was time for us to say goodbye. I stood up and took one last look at her still body. I didn't want to look too closely at her face because I wanted to remember her smiling. So, I looked down at her hands and did my best to memorize them, knowing their image would continue to bring me comfort and beautiful memories.

~Emily H. Cappo

Our Mother's Heart

A mother's love for her child is like no other love. To be able to put that feeling aside because you want the best for your child is the most unselfish thing I know.
~Mary, American Adoptions Birth Mother

In 1962, my mother experienced a heart-wrenching betrayal. She clutched me, a one-year-old baby, in her arms, and crossed the shabby apartment to face my callous biological father. "I'm pregnant with our second child."

He shook his head in disgust. "Give both kids to the orphanage. I don't want anything to do with them."

Heartbroken, she told her doctor the news during her next prenatal check-up.

"I've taken care of you and your family for years," the doctor said. "I'd like to share a story with you."

The doctor told Mom about a childless couple he knew. "They'd do anything for a baby. They're wonderful people and would give your little one a good life. The baby would be loved and protected. Your child would have a secure future."

Alone and unable to support two children, Mom made the agonizing decision to let the couple adopt her soon-to-be-born baby.

After giving birth, the hospital staff refused to let Mom hold her newborn girl. "It's for the best, dear," a nurse said, and whisked the infant away.

Mom struggled to her feet and crept down the cheerless hospital corridor. She found a secondary nursery tucked off a back hallway. Babies filled the unmarked cribs. Heartsick, she left the hospital never knowing which child belonged to her.

Along with the baby girl, Mom left a piece of her heart behind.

Soon after, Mom moved out of state for a fresh start. Years passed, and Mom met the hard-working, loyal man who would become my new father.

They went on to have three sons. And with each birth, Mom thought about the precious little girl she'd given up, praying the child remained loved and safe with her adoptive family.

My brothers and I grew up and had children of our own. None of us knew the private grief Mom still carried in her heart.

Meanwhile, Mom's old doctor had proven true to his word. His ecstatic friends had adopted the baby and named her Annie. They showered her with love.

Annie grew up in a large, exuberant family, filled with aunts, uncles, and cousins. Laughter marked every celebration.

Many years passed, and two of Annie's friends, also adopted, began searching for their birth mothers. Sadly, both mothers had passed away.

"What am I waiting for?" Annie wondered. Her friends' lost opportunities motivated Annie to seek out her own birth mother. Two years of searching ensued.

On July 20, 2016, my parents' phone rang. Dad answered with his trademark good-natured, "Hel-lo?"

"Hi, is Nancy there?"

My father, used to screening numerous sales calls, asked, "Why do you want to talk with her?"

Annie hesitated, unwilling to open old wounds or reveal secrets if her existence remained unknown. She said, "I'm doing genealogical research, and I believe Nancy and I may be related."

Dad heard "research," mistook Annie for a telemarketer, and hung up.

Annie spent an uneasy night, apprehensive but determined to make contact. The next morning, she prayed and called again.

My mother answered, and Annie blurted out, "Does the date

October 1, 1962, mean anything to you?"

Mom clutched the phone with a shaking hand. "Yes. Yes, it does."

"I'm the person associated with that date."

Mom slumped against her living-room wall. Tears of joy streamed down her face. "Oh, honey, you finally found me!"

A two-hour conversation ensued. Annie talked about her loving parents and happy upbringing. Mom shared family history and the reasons she'd given Annie up for adoption.

After they hung up, Mom blasted off an e-mail to our family. The subject line read: *Joyous and for most of you shocking news.*

Mom wrote: *In 1962 before I moved here, I gave my little baby girl up for adoption. Birth records are now unsealed and she was able to locate me. Annie called today and we had a wonderful visit.*

I read the e-mail and called Mom immediately. "Are you okay? How are you feeling?"

Mom's joy bubbled through the phone line. "I've prayed for her all these years, hoping I'd done the right thing, but never truly knowing. Annie told me she has a terrific life. Now I finally have peace."

For Mom, learning that her sacrifice hadn't been in vain healed the hidden ache she'd dealt with for so long. The missing piece was again in place.

After fifty-three years, our mother's heart was finally whole.

~Jean Jones

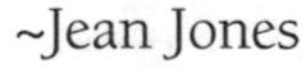

Dancing from the Heart

Great dancers are not great because of their technique,
they are great because of their passion.
~Martha Graham

Now, I'm the first to admit that I'm not the greatest dancer in the world. In fact, the phrase "two left feet" might have been coined specifically for me. But I never miss a chance to dance when the music starts playing because of something I learned from my mom: If you're going to dance, do it from your heart.

I'd always thought of my mom as a great person. She loved life and enjoyed every moment of it. She knew hard work and want for most of her life, but it never seemed to get in the way of her understanding that we're also here to enjoy this life, and to do what we can to help others enjoy it, too. I just never realized how big that feeling was inside of her until I saw it come out one day.

We had gone to live with my grandpa shortly after my mom and dad divorced, and the transition was anything but smooth. My grandpa was a stoic man, and though he was kind enough to offer us a place to live, it was easy to see that having three grandchildren constantly underfoot wasn't an easy thing for him. We were constantly disrupting the peace and quiet he was used to, and we thought of him as this stuffy old man whom we didn't really know well. It was tough going at first.

Mom and Grandpa had a tense relationship following the divorce. Back then, people didn't divorce without a lot of repercussion, and

Grandpa didn't think it was a good idea that she did it, but he took us in anyway. Mom took care of the house in exchange for Grandpa putting a roof over our heads, but I never saw them really comfortable around each other. Moving back in with a parent isn't always an easy fit.

Music had always been a big part of Grandpa's life. He had played the trumpet, trombone and accordion as a young man, and being Polish meant he was always playing polka music on the old phonograph in the den. The den was a large room with a beautiful chandelier that had once been used for parties and visits from family when my grandma was alive. But the room was largely unused the days we lived with Grandpa. He liked it quiet in the house, except for the polka music coming from the phonograph.

Mom used to do dance steps as she dusted and cleaned the house, but very quietly, so as not to disturb Grandpa. I knew she had gone to dances as a girl, and whenever any music played, her feet would start moving of their own accord. But I had never seen her really dance, and I admit I began to think she might become as quiet and withdrawn as Grandpa.

How wrong I was.

One afternoon, my brother, sister and I were put to work moving furniture in the large den. We moved chairs to the side, rolled up the big carpet, and made sure there was lots of space in the center of the room. Mom brought out Grandpa's old accordion case and laid the accordion on the table next to a filled punch bowl. I had never seen the instrument before, and I was baffled at how it worked. I didn't have to wait long to find out.

Mom told us it was Grandma's birthday, and even though she had passed away a few years before, Grandpa had decided to throw a party in her honor. I thought maybe Mom had a hand in suggesting this, and in inviting all my uncles and aunts and cousins to attend the party. It felt like something she would do.

Soon, people I had never seen before filled the house, and instead of listening to the phonograph, several of our relatives brought their guitars, or fiddles, or whatever other instruments they could play. Grandpa took his accordion and fingered the many buttons on its side.

I saw a smile break out on his face as music started to fill the room.

Then my mom began to dance. I watched as this often quiet, hard-working woman appeared in a flowing red dress and took the center of the floor. Grandpa and our other relatives began to play, and my mom began to twirl, dancing and laughing as I had never seen before. I saw her not just as my mother, but as a distinct person, a woman who danced with joy and talent I didn't know she possessed.

Then she grabbed my hand and pulled me out onto the floor. I tried to pull away, to remind her I didn't know how to dance, but her smile was infectious. She twirled me around, took my hands in hers, and whispered, "Don't worry; just dance from your heart!"

Suddenly, my feet were moving. I danced around with my mom, then with my cousins and sister, laughing and whirling across the floor. I knew I must look silly, flailing and spinning without any idea of what to do, but I felt so free, wonderful, and full of joy. I saw that expression reflected in my mom's eyes and knew she had given me something wonderful I would treasure for the rest of my life.

Now, whenever I get the chance, and the music starts to play, I remember the image of my mom — a young, vibrant woman dancing and whirling for the sheer joy of being alive. I get up and start my clumsy version of dancing. I move unafraid, free of inhibition, feeling alive and full of joy, because my mom taught me it's all right to dance, and to always do it from the heart.

~John P. Buentello

Still My Mother

Where we love is home, home that our feet may leave, but not our hearts.
~Oliver Wendell Holmes

A winter storm was moving in, and I was anxious to get back to my warm home and family. My list of tasks and errands was almost complete. I had just one last stop to deliver supplies to the assisted-living cottage where my mother lived.

As usual, the day had been full of responsibilities, and I was beginning to get a headache. Keeping up with four teenaged boys, a busy husband, and a mother with dementia was taking its toll on my own wellbeing.

I keyed in the door code and the cozy country décor of the foyer welcomed me as I blew through the door. Soft strains of old-time music wafted from invisible speakers, but no one was in sight. It was still late afternoon, but with eight women to bathe and get to bed, the caregivers tended to get an early start on their bedtime routines.

The cottage was nearly as familiar as my own home. I was delighted to have my mother living in my hometown after being apart for nearly thirty years. Dad's recent death and Mom's progressing dementia had led us to find a place for her to live nearby. The atmosphere and the caregivers of Cottage Seven were all I could have desired, and I truly loved spending time there.

I planned to quickly drop off this bag of supplies and get going.

It was too late to stay and visit, and I really wanted to go home and unwind.

With a cheerful knock, I entered my mother's room, which was mostly dark with just the otherworldly glow of a small old-fashioned table lamp. The sweet fragrance of lavender bath soap added to the ambience.

Bathed in the twilight softness, I saw my mother, Grace, and her roommate, Ruth. Side by side in their rocking chairs, their faces turned toward me in unison. My heart nearly filled my entire chest.

My mom, in her long, flowing pink nightgown, and Ruth, in her aqua one, were the most beautiful sight I had ever seen. Soft white curls crowned each head. Their faces, lined with decades of smiles and tears, were angelic. Their skin seemed translucent, and they each had perfectly polished scarlet fingernails. Their eyes lit up, and they smiled when they saw me.

Despite the cruelty of dementia, the scene before me on that stormy evening radiated joy and satisfaction. But there was something more. The atmosphere glowed with a deep serenity, that elusive quality which all crave, but few attain. Serenity wrapped its arms around these two angels in the twilight of the day, in the twilight of their lives.

I dropped to the edge of the bed and drank in the blessing, which poured silently from Grace and Ruth. The serenity I had prayed for was all around me. I would carry this sense of peace home with me.

"Have you come to sleep with us?" Mom asked.

I was sorely tempted.

"Oh, no, Mom, I can't sleep here. There isn't enough room. You only have two beds."

"That's not a problem," Ruth said. "If you'll help us, we'll just push our beds together, and you can sleep in the middle."

How many times had my mom crawled into my childhood bed and cuddled me to sleep? Surely Ruth had done the same with her child. What would it be like to feel the arms of these sweet mothers enfold me as I drifted off to dreamland?

Two angels in the twilight, one in pink and one in aqua, smiled invitingly at me. I felt all my responsibilities melt and slide off my shoulders. In this unlikely place, with a snowstorm on its way, it became clear to me that God had not abandoned these two women. They smiled contentedly, almost mystically, at one another, and awaited my reply.

"I would so love to stay here with you, but remember, I have a husband and four boys waiting for me at home. They're hungry, and I have groceries in the car. I need to go home and cook supper."

Understanding dawned on the angels' faces. Of course! They knew the importance of cooking supper for hungry families. Dementia had not stripped them of their motherhood — they would remain mothers to the core right to the end.

"Well, then, you'd best get going. We can manage here. After all, we have each other." Grace and Ruth nodded reassuringly at each other.

With a renewed lightness in my step, I pulled on my jacket and prepared to bid the ladies farewell.

For some time, I had doubted whether my mother still recognized me as her daughter. Yet now I waited for the motherly question with which she always sent me on my way. She asked, "Do you know your way home?"

With my usual delighted laugh, I assured her that I knew my way home.

Yes, Mom, thanks to you, I always know where home is. Of course, it is in a nearby house with my wonderful family, but I know that I also have a home here in Cottage Seven, where two angels in the twilight, one in pink and one in aqua, will welcome me and fill my entire being with serenity.

~Cynthia Siems Carlson

The Heart Remembers

In my life I find that memories of the spirit linger and sweeten long after memories of the brain have faded.
~Harry Connick Jr.

I punched in the security code and walked through the gate. I was used to the quick turns and corners to get into the facility. I had been coming here for months. I could manage the turns, but it was more difficult for the residents. That is why the turns were there. No dash for escape through an open gate.

Escape was probably the wrong word to use. They weren't prisoners here. They were patients — specifically, Alzheimer's patients. I had come to see my mother as I did almost every day. The fences and security gates helped to keep the patients from wandering. They could be outside in the yard, but not go too far from their cottages. My mother had her own room in a cottage with others at about the same stage as her. For my mom now, that meant End Stage. This would be the last place my mother lived, and she didn't even know where that was.

When my sisters and I first placed her here, she did know. She had been diagnosed six years prior. During that time, my father had cared for her. She had gone through the various stages, such as misplacing things, frustration, and then anger at everyone. The anger was based a lot on her fear about the situation as well as the uncontrollable emotions that come with this kind of illness.

My father had been confused when she asked about a purse she had never owned. Maybe it was a purse she had owned in high school, but her brain didn't know that the purse no longer existed. Or when she lost her purse, and they had to cancel all the credit cards. Dad filled her wallet with old, expired membership cards, and she never noticed.

They had to leave the security alarm of the house turned off after the police showed up for the third time when she opened the front door in the middle of the night. My father had to be aware at all times.

Then my father got sick. Actually, he had already been sick. His doctor gave him six months to live. At this point, we knew we had to find a place for Mom. Luckily, my family is good about planning. My sisters and I had been researching and checking out different places for a year. Once my father said it was time, we told him we had a place. The morning we placed her, he held her hand and merely said, "Fifty-three years." They had celebrated their anniversary just a couple weeks prior. He knew it would be the last time they saw each other.

That was more than a year ago. Now my father was gone, and my mom didn't even remember she was married. I had learned how to relate to her in this new way. I didn't ask her to remember things I talked about. I asked her questions and never knew what kind of answer I would get.

My favorite answer was to the question of who her best friend was. I knew the names of her various good friends throughout her life, so I asked her who her best friend was. Would she pull a name from her childhood? Or perhaps a friend from later in life? Maybe she would call up a name of one of the staff or other residents in her cottage. Instead, she surprised me with her answer. She looked at me with just a hint of confusion before she replied, "I thought you were." It took a lot of strength not to break into tears of love and joy for that one simple statement. Instead, I managed a deep breath and agreed that I was her best friend.

My mom had no idea what my name was. She didn't know I was her daughter. Some days, I came to visit, and she thought I was her sister. One time, I was introduced around as her roommate from college who had traveled a great distance to visit her. I just went along with it. Trying to redirect or correct Alzheimer's patients only confuses them more. When she asked me a question, I answered honestly and as simply as possible. I did my best not to confuse her.

I came at lunch and fed my mother. She had forgotten how to use a fork. As the disease progresses, things we've learned are forgotten. How to tie shoes, feed yourself, use the toilet and get dressed all fade away. Alzheimer's is often referred to as a return to childhood because everything we know how to do is forgotten.

This small, frail woman had raised me with intense love. During this time, I did my best to make her happy and comfortable. One day, she fell asleep on my shoulder. When she woke up, she apologized for drooling on me. I merely said it was okay, and I was sure I had done worse to her.

As she got closer to the end, I spent more time with her. I stroked her hair as she had stroked mine when I was sick. When she was scared, I held her as she had held me. I sang to her the song she sang to me many times as a child. She commented that it was a pretty song as if she had never heard it before.

I never knew what to expect each day. We were on a new adventure together. I valued each moment we got to share. I painted her nails and sang and danced for her. On her last day, my sisters and I played her Christmas music and told stories. We surrounded her with a feeling of love.

I will always miss my mother, but will always have her love. She forgot my name and that I was her daughter, but she was always glad to see me when she saw me. She wanted me with her even if she didn't know exactly why. Her heart remembered even if her mind didn't—and in the end, that's what really mattered.

~Traci E. Langston

Morning Donuts

Happy is the son whose faith in his mother remains unchallenged.
~Louisa May Alcott

When I was little, my mom always went to the store on Saturday mornings. My sisters and I would wake up to find five little plates of powdered donuts, one for each of us.

One Saturday morning, I woke up earlier than the rest of the children. Being the selfish, chubby, little man that I was, I quickly finished my plate and wanted more. My mom told me that I could have the others as long as I finished them all and destroyed the evidence; it would be our secret. So that morning, while the other children slept, I got to spend all morning with the entirety of the donuts—and the entirety of my mom's attention.

I am not exaggerating when I say that I woke myself up early every Saturday from age seven to twelve, eating all the donuts I wanted and getting time with my mom all to myself. We ate donuts, watched cartoons, played games, and read books—just the two of us.

When I was twenty-seven, I mentioned this to my sisters in passing, sure that my mom had told them at some point in later years. Well into their thirties, they were furious; they had always wondered what happened to all those donuts and why I was always up so early. My mom had never made a peep.

The donuts were tasty, but they were honestly just an excuse. I woke up early not because, as the youngest of five, I didn't have to share donuts. I did it because, for a little while, I didn't have to share my mom.

~James Kinneen

Bedtime Stories

Children will not remember you for the material
things you provided, but for the feeling
that you cherished them.
~Richard L. Evans

Nights in bed with my mother
Stories flowed through the dark—
Red fairgrounds, blue seashores, green-wet, shimmering parks,
And the images rainbowed and spread arcs of dreams,
As her life ran in to me in pictureful streams.

I'd listen enrapt
As they'd bloom in my head,
Great gardens of moments come alive in the bed,
And I'd see her the heroine win what in life
Had eluded her when she became someone's wife.

Each night a new tale,
Then, a favourite of old
But the warmth and the smell of her skin always told
Of days at Cavehill, or the nights when she sang
And I'd long in my young heart for times auld lang syne.

In the dark we'd explore
Wild musical fairs,
And I'd watch from the edge of her dreams as her hair
Curled in and through candy-floss memories so sweet
'Til at last I was found by sleep's secret police.

She's been gone twenty years
But these stories still spark
Like stars on cold nights, pinprick holes in the dark
And I've learned in the end, what I knew at the start
All my life is her story, a dream of her heart.

~Carolyn McCartney

A Gift from My Mother

What a lot we lost when we stopped writing letters. You can't reread a phone call.
~Liz Carpenter

My mother always said, "The greatest gift I ever gave you girls is each other." My four sisters and I know how true that is.

But in terms of concrete gifts, what I appreciate most is something I found while cleaning Mom's house after she passed away. It was a box full of her letters.

We are five sisters with twelve years between the oldest and youngest. Every few years, Mom wrote a description of each of us. It's a bit disconcerting to read about my eight-year-old self as "a bit lazy about making her bed," but how wonderful to read that Mom thought I was "happy and thoughtful and so good with the baby" at the same age. It's fun to read Mom's thoughts about my sisters, as well. It always leads us to a "Mom always liked me best" competition—and we can point to the truth in her very own handwriting.

The box also contains letters from my dad during World War II. He describes Italy with such passion that I wish he could have revisited a place he seemed to love in spite of the war.

There are diaries that detail trips my parents took. I can see the sheep pastures in Ireland, taste the bangers and mash in London, and smell the fish market in San Francisco as my mom experienced them.

She saved letters from friends and relatives that contain bits of stories I wish I knew enough to ask about while there was still time. I think she kept every letter I wrote to her from college and postcards from trips I took. I relive my own long-forgotten experiences in my own words.

Mom has letters dating back to the 1940s from her aunt in Key West and her cousins in County Cork. She has the telegram that arrived when her sister eloped, programs from class plays, and yellowed newspaper photos depicting friends experiencing their fifteen minutes of fame.

Hundreds of pages introduce me to so many sides of my mom that I love learning about. I am going to savor it all, slowly.

I feel sorry for the next generation. With all their tweeting and texting, they will never find a treasure such as this.

~Eileen Melia Hession

Laying My Mother's Day Cards on the Table

If men liked shopping, they'd call it research.
~Cynthia Nelms

I am not one who likes gambling unless you call life a gamble, and then all bets are off. I do not even play the lottery because I would end up paying out $1,987.14 in order to win ten dollars. I have a difficult time parting with my money because I am a Pennsylvania Dutchman; at least, that is my excuse.

That being said, there is only one area of my life where I indulge in a certain amount of gambling. That area is Mother's Day cards. I am at a complete loss when it comes to this.

Now, part of my quandary is in the loose interpretation of Mother's Day. When we celebrate Mother's Day, who in the world are we celebrating?

I can remember when the "Gracious Mistress of the Parsonage" and yours truly were first married. It was so long ago that I do not have enough fingers or toes to count the years. When we were first married, we bought two Mother's Day cards: one for her mother and one for mine. Oh, how I long for those simple days.

A little over a year after we were married, a little tyke came into our lowly domicile. Our first daughter was born in the month of August, and I really did not understand the significance until the following Mother's Day.

That year, we had to buy three Mother's Day cards: one for my wife's mother, one for my mother, and one for my daughter to give to her mother.

Now what I want to know is, how in the world was I roped into buying a Mother's Day card for my wife? After all, she is not *my* mother. And I do not know how many times I have reminded her of that very fact.

I was conned into buying that Mother's Day card for my wife after being told that I was buying it for my daughter to give to her mother. I bought the card, all right, and when I gave it to my daughter, she immediately put it in her mouth. She had no idea what in the world a Mother's Day card was.

Several years later, we added to our family — our son was born.

Now I have more Mother's Day cards to buy. One for my mother, one for my wife's mother, one for my daughter to give to her mother, and one for my son to give to his mother. These Mother's Day cards are getting to be rather expensive.

A few years later, a third child became a member of our family. Our second daughter was born. And you guessed it: My Mother's Day card buying increased.

Now I need to buy a Mother's Day card for my mother, one for my wife's mother, one for my first daughter to give to her mother, one for my son to give to his mother, and one for my second daughter to give to her mother.

I once suggested that I buy one Mother's Day card for my three children to give to their mother. I was quickly and soundly outvoted on that issue. And so, I begin saving up right after Christmas for my Mother's Day card extravaganza.

If this was not bad enough, each Mother's Day card has to be specifically chosen in respect to the person who is giving it. That person, not being *me*. How many times and how many different ways can you say "Happy Mother's Day"?

I thought I had reached the height of my Mother's Day card purchasing, but in a few years it took on a different perspective.

Not only was I to buy all of these Mother's Day cards, but I was to take the respective children along with me and allow them to personally pick out the card they wanted to give their mother. And, of course, their mother could not be along to supervise these purchases. Taking two toddlers and one semi-toddler into a store to select appropriate Mother's Day cards is as close as I have ever come to gambling away my fortune.

Between the three of them, they had each boiled down their choice to ninety-seven cards. Of course, the youngest just grabbed as many as she possibly could. The other two had to look at each card and discuss the contents, meaning of course that I had to read each card to them.

Not once, but over and over again.

Looking back on that time, I realize that my children had an ingenious strategy all worked out. After four hours of going through all of these cards, I would say to them, "If you pick a card right now, I'll take you all to get ice cream."

Now, those children are all grown up and married, which has added to my long list of Mother's Day card purchases.

But of all the thousands of Mother's Day cards I have purchased throughout the years, I must honestly confess they have all been worth it.

~James L. Snyder

The Necklace

Sometimes, only one person is missing, and
the whole world seems depopulated.
~Alphonse de Lamartine, Méditations Poétiques

When my mother-in-law, who had been a close part of my life for more than fifty years, died, I felt a sense of loss that had to do not only with missing her, but also with missing that part of myself that expressed itself when I was with her. That part — that unique piece of how she and I related and interacted — was forever gone, at least in the physical form.

I also missed her listening. At the age of ninety-nine, she still devoted much of her time to talking with (and listening to) friends and family, being both a sounding board and cheerleader. No matter what was going on, she had a way of simply being with people that made them feel better.

One of our last conversations together had been about jewelry. For years, she had attended "home parties" given by Mary, a neighbor, and had bought necklaces, bracelets, and earrings. I had received some as gifts, but knew she kept an entire dresser drawer full of these items, even though she seldom wore them. They were all neatly tucked into their separate boxes, stacked up nearly to the top of the drawer.

"They're a way I can contribute to Mary," she said when I questioned her. "And I think of them as a way to connect to the people who receive them as gifts."

“What about all those others you have in your drawer?” I said. Her answer gave me a new reason to appreciate her love of jewelry.

“Oh, I like to revisit them from time to time. They’re like old friends. I can usually remember when I bought them and who was there with me.”

As I moved through the days following her death, every day felt heavy and grief-filled as we did what had to be done to prepare for her memorial service. I wondered when I would ever feel good again without this overlay of sadness. I had lost my own parents long ago (they both died relatively young by today’s standards), and my mother-in-law was truly like another mother to me.

My husband and I drove out the day before her memorial service to check final details and had an early dinner before heading for Mom’s house to spend the night. Although I dreaded being in the empty house, it seemed comforting to be surrounded by all of her favorite things. Thanks to a neighbor who had come in to clean, the house had its familiar welcoming smells of orange-scented furniture polish and the lemony kitchen counter spray she used. I sat in her favorite chair, watched the news, and had no trouble falling asleep.

The day of her memorial service arrived. The gray clouds echoed my mood, and I felt both empty and exhausted. I got dressed and put on the necklace I had brought with me, but for some reason I didn’t like how it looked. It no longer seemed to fit what I was wearing. I decided to look in Mom’s jewelry drawer.

I didn’t have the energy to go through every box. Feeling sad and frustrated, I spoke out loud. “Mom, I need your help. Would you guide me to the right thing for me to wear today?”

My fingers seemed to have a will of their own. Instantly, they reached out and plucked a box — seemingly at random — from the drawer. I opened it. There lay a silver heart necklace, just the right length for the neckline of my dress. The next thing I noticed was that it was an open heart, not solid in the middle. I felt joyful just holding it in my hand. I knew then that she really had shown me much more than what necklace to wear.

I received the message directly from her — from her heart to mine:

I love you, although I am no longer physically with you. Keep an open heart, and you will know I'm around.

That necklace has become a touchstone for the way we can now relate through time and space, and a way for me to know that our hearts are linked forever.

~Maril Crabtree

I Lubbyou

To love is nothing. To be loved is something.
But to love and be loved, that's everything.
~T. Tolis

My parents left Puerto Rico, my mother's home, soon after they were married. My father was in the military, so they moved from base to base as they had their children. Shortly after World War II, they lived in Japan for three years. During the boat trip home across the Pacific, a typhoon hit the boat. That was when my mother, pregnant with me and terrified by the storm, began her descent into mental illness.

Stateside, once I was born, my mother refused to take care of me or my sisters. She was hospitalized, drugged and physically survived several electric shock treatments, but her spirit was broken, and she never fully recovered. She continued to be hospitalized on and off throughout my youth.

At the age of seventeen, I was off into the world. I found a job as a secretary at the Buffalo Psychiatric Center. As I stepped off the bus and walked toward the campus, I remembered that my mother had been a patient there when I was a child. I saw the road that tunneled under a walkway connecting two massive brick buildings, the same walkway I had viewed long ago with childlike wonder. I remembered the coffee shop above the tunnel, where my mother sat smoking cigarette after cigarette, eyes cast down, subdued by medication and shock treatments.

Dismay swept over me when I realized that the office was in

the same building where my mother had been housed, the one with the large concrete porch and bars from floor to ceiling. I recalled my father lifting me up to kiss my lifeless mother goodbye through those same bars.

For several years, I worked in the mental-health system, which enabled me to understand and even help my mother through her last psychiatric hospitalization. I was in my late twenties when my mother had her final breakdown. This time, the hospital didn't rely on heavy medications and shock therapy. Instead, my mother was given a new drug through injections. She could not refuse to take the meds. Slowly, she became more coherent, able to engage in short conversations, and show concern for herself and her children.

For the first time in my life, I could have lucid talks with my mother. At around this time, my youngest sister and her husband decided to tell their siblings and parents that they loved them. For our family, this was monumental. Kind words were rarely spoken in our home and we were not accustomed to displays of affection.

After being released from the hospital, my mother started phoning me at home. I'd never pick up the phone. She would always leave the same message: "Es mama from Nee-a-gra Falls." My husband and I laughed at this, as if her accent didn't give her away. Besides, what other mama would be from Niagara Falls? Then she would call again, leaving the same message, "Es mama from Nee-a-gra Falls." Still laughing, I'd return her call. We'd have a short exchange.

One time, she ended the call with "I lubbyou."

I froze. And then I said, "Huh?"

She repeated it.

"Okay, goodbye." I hung up, almost dropping the phone.

Again, a month later, she phoned and left the same message; I returned the call and had a short talk. It ended with her saying, "I lubbyou." This was too much to bear.

It took many months before I could say, "I love you too, Ma," but the way I said it was just in lieu of saying goodbye — a kind of casual "I love you."

I was confused about this new feeling. I decided that every time my mother said she loved me, I would use those words to heal myself. I let them wash over me and repair the jagged hole in my heart. I started telling her I loved her just so she would say those words back to me. Sometimes, I'd murmur "Huh?" to make her repeat the words. She never refused. She knew. She'd let those comforting words wrap around my heart and soul.

Through our discussions, I could see her life's circumstances and her personality more clearly. I came to understand and appreciate her fortitude, strength and faith. I was able to forgive her.

As she lay dying years later, I sat by her bedside. She confided she was afraid to die. I told her that she had loved God so much throughout her life, it was time to let him wrap his arms around her and to melt into his love. She closed her eyes. Her body relaxed.

It touches my heart and consoles me that my last words to my mother gave her comfort. Those words—"I love you—can heal a lifetime of wounds.

~Catherine Shavalier-Chernow

Chapter 8

My Amazing Mom

Thanks, Mom

My mother was the most beautiful woman I ever saw. All I am I owe to my mother. I attribute my success in life to the moral, intellectual, and physical education I received from her.
~George Washington

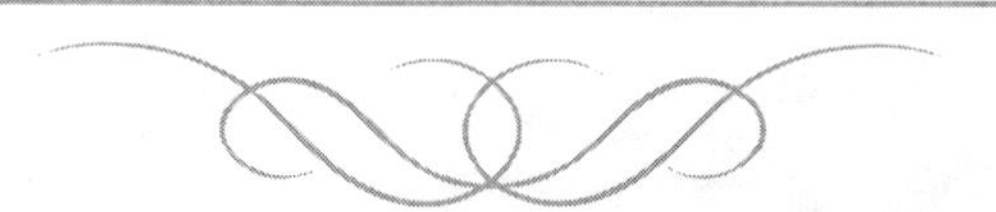

Lessons in Insecurity

Whatever is bringing you down, get rid of it.
Because you'll find that when you're free…
your true self comes out.
~Tina Turner

Mrs. D was one of those teachers who loved her job. Though I wasn't one of her students, she still invited me into her office during lunch to chat about life and what was going on in my fifteen-year-old mind.

She was a few inches shorter than I was, with long hair and glasses, and always had a smile on her face. Every student who crossed her path could agree that Mrs. D's gentle spirit and gift of encouragement could make even the most troubled of students believe in themselves.

I remember walking to her office one day for one of our regular lunchtime chats, rehearsing the day's topic in my head. That week had been particularly challenging because I was bogged down with honors coursework and midterms. On top of that, I had just found out the person I thought was my best friend blabbed my deepest secrets around school. It took all I had not to break down as I gently tapped on Mrs. D's office door.

Knock knock! "It's me, Jocelyn. Can I come in?"

Mrs. D motioned for me to step into her office just as she was finishing up a call.

"Hey, sweetie! How was your day today?"

"It's going okay, I guess. I did want to talk to you about something, though."

I pulled up a chair and plopped my book bag down on the floor beside me. As I began telling Mrs. D about my woes, tears welled up in the corners of my eyes. I told her that on top of everything going on at school, my best friend was actually *not* my friend at all, and I felt that I couldn't trust anyone.

"I understand that was your friend, and you thought she was treating you with the same kindness you were showing her," she told me, "but don't let that make you bitter. You shouldn't let what your friend has done stop you from giving love and being the sweet young lady that you are. The fact that she's mistreated you means she has unresolved issues within herself. This has nothing to do with you. Never let the insecurities of others determine who you are."

Just like that, my life was changed. *Never let the insecurities of others determine who you are.*

In that moment, Mrs. D stepped beyond her role as a teacher and gave me advice that I still carry with me today! As I went off to college and entered adulthood, I realized how true these words were. If I had allowed the cruelty of one person to change my entire disposition, I wouldn't have become the woman I am today. My life is full of joy. I'm surrounded by love and great people!

Every chance I get, I stop by to pay Mrs. D a visit and ask her, "Do you remember that time you talked to me about the insecurities of others?"

My life is so blessed, not only because of who Mrs. D was to me that day in her office, but because of who she's always been to me my entire life — my mom.

~Jocelyn Drawhorn

The Pink Wallet

My mother's love has always been a sustaining force for our family, and one of my greatest joys is seeing her integrity, her compassion, her intelligence reflected in my daughters.
~Michelle Obama

My mother was always very open with my siblings and me about being adopted. In addition to having three stepchildren and two biological children, my mother adopted eight of us. When I'd come home crying because kids in school would tease me about being adopted, my mother would look me in the eye and say, "You tell them 'my mom chose me out of hundreds of babies in the world, and your parents were stuck with you!'" I quickly learned to recite those words to anyone who teased me about being adopted.

Mom was tough. She became a single parent by the time I was a teenager and made it clear that it was not an excuse to abandon "the sense the good Lord gave us." So, at a very young age, we were taught to think before we reacted.

I'll never forget the time my sisters and I found a wallet in the park. The four of us were between the ages of eight and ten. We thought long and hard about what we wanted to do with our riches. We voted and decided it would be best to splurge on chips, candy, and pop with the few dollars that were inside. Oh yeah, we were going to go crazy in our neighborhood gas station!

We took the bright pink wallet home and stashed it in our room. It had about three dollars and no ID in it. Being rich was hard work, so we took shifts guarding the wallet. I'm sure my mother picked up on the slightly different attitudes we were all displaying because of our newfound treasure. When my mom fussed about making sure our chores were completed, the four of us would go into our room and talk smack about using the three bucks to buy a house of our own; none of us would have to do chores if we didn't want to. Yep, that's probably when she really caught onto something being "off."

When each of us was alone with her, she'd ask questions such as, "How was your day?" or "Do you have any homework?" We were convinced she was trying to see who would break first. So we met in our room and went back and forth trying to determine if she knew. Our meeting turned into each of us defending ourselves and the part we played in finding and keeping the wallet. There was only one thing left to do: bury the wallet in the sandbox and never discuss it again.

Whenever Mom felt like something was definitely off, she would call us into the family room. She would sit us down on the old church pew that served as extra seating when all the couch space was taken. Then she would walk from one end of the pew to the other, with a stern look on her face, lecturing us about the kind of children she didn't raise. She would repeatedly ask questions she had the answers to, such as "What's your name?" and "Where were you just a minute ago?" When these questions were asked, we knew any response would be taken as "getting smart," but remaining quiet would be seen as "disrespect." So… I'd cry. If no one cracked, she'd assign individual punishments. I can still hear her to this day saying, "Cash in every last Barbie, missy." Yep, everyone got what felt like a death sentence.

I'm not sure who broke down and told Mom about the wallet, but once she found out, she made us pile into our fifteen-passenger van, and she sped out of the driveway burning rubber.

We got out of the van with tear-filled eyes and walked into the Southfield Police Department station. Mom (who knew just about everyone in Southfield, Michigan) walked in like she had a badge of her own and told the officers to arrest us all. I was mortified. Begging and pleading between our sobs, we reassured our mother that we were sorry. Mom, who was famous for getting her point across, wasn't convinced. To ensure that we would "use the sense the good Lord gave us," she grabbed her fanny pack (because this was the '90s!) and left.

The police officers played along and gave us a firm talking-to. My siblings and I were so grateful when Mom came and picked us up after what felt like hours (but in reality was probably fifteen minutes). We were so happy to see her and to know that, no matter what we did, she was there for us. It didn't matter if we had gotten in trouble or did something she wasn't pleased with; she was there for us. That's all that mattered.

Many may think what my mom did was a bit extreme. Trust me, when my Barbies were taken away, so did I. But when I look back at Mom's methods, I understand that no matter how big or small the infraction, her mission was to teach us right from wrong. Because she cared about us, she drove her point home by exposing us to potential consequences. She preferred to show us while we were children instead of having "life" show us later on. But a mother's concern was coupled with compassion during the ride home from the police station that day. Her words of comfort broke the silence: "You are all good kids."

~Candace L. Parker

Susie's Babies

One good mother is worth a hundred schoolmasters.
~George Herbert

"Tonight, after your brother is asleep, you girls can come to my room. We're going to do something special." My sister and I were seven and nine when my mother whispered those words to us after supper one night. We were excited. My five-year-old brother wouldn't be included in whatever was going to happen. Mom's whisper indicated it was something very interesting indeed.

When my mother was sure my little brother was asleep, she poked her head into our room where we were waiting in anticipation and gestured it was time to come down to her bedroom. She invited us to jump onto her bed, and when we were sitting snugly tucked in on either side of her, she took out a book called *Susie's Babies*. There was a hamster on the front cover. She told us she would be reading us one chapter of the book every night, and we could stop her anytime to ask questions.

Susie's Babies is the story of an elementary-school class that has a pregnant pet hamster. The students in the story follow Susie the hamster through each day of her pregnancy and observe her nurturing her baby hamsters. My mother used the book as a springboard for talking to us frankly about sex. She told us exactly what would happen when we got our periods and showed us the supplies we would need.

After my mother finished reading *Susie's Babies,* she told us she was pregnant. In six months, we would have a new brother or sister. Throughout her pregnancy, Mom let us continue to ask questions and explained the changes that were taking place as our new sibling grew inside her. She talked to us about what would happen when the baby was born. The birth of my younger brother was such an important and meaningful event in our lives because Mom had shared the experience of her pregnancy with my sister and me.

I was on a vacation at my cousins' farm without my parents when I got my period for the first time. I was only ten years old, and if it hadn't been for the fact my mother had read me *Susie's Babies* and talked to me so openly and honestly about becoming a woman, I would have been terrified. Thanks to Mom, I knew what was happening and had the courage to ask my older cousin to help me.

Looking back, I realize how fortunate I was to have a mother who thought it was important to impart the "facts of life" in such a positive and honest way. I found out later that many of my friends had been left completely in the dark about the physical changes they would experience when they reached adolescence and had no idea how women got pregnant. This lack of information left them fearful and uninformed about sex, a reality that sometimes led to disastrous consequences. We lived in a small, very religiously conservative community, so there was no sex education in the schools.

When my mother was in her eighties, she told me that her own mother had never given her any information about sex. Consequently, her wedding night had been a shocking experience, and she had been anxious and scared when she became pregnant for the first time. Mom wanted things to be different for her own daughters. Thanks to her, they were.

~MaryLou Driedger

Heavenly Connections

God not only sends special angels into our lives, but sometimes Heaven sends them back again if we forget to take notes the first time!
~Eileen Elias Freeman

My heart sank as my sister said, "You need to come home right away. Mom is dying." My fifty-six-year-old mother lay severely ill in my hometown 230 miles away. How could that be?

Two months earlier, she'd helped with our wedding. She'd sewn the flower girl's dress for my niece, arranged food for the reception, attended bridal showers and offered advice for my future as a wife.

The drive home seemed to take forever. My husband, Dennis, consoled me, offering gentle words and tissues as he drove our banged-up Chevy Malibu over Highway 2. We arrived at the small-town hospital and entered her room. I couldn't grasp the situation. I knew a little bit about illness and caring for the infirm as I worked as an aide at a retirement home in Omaha. But none of that prepared me for seeing my mother, unconscious, with a large brown tube in her nose, IVs in her arms and neck, and the swishing sound of machines. I looked at the heart monitor, not knowing what the numbers and squiggly lines meant.

No one ran around yelling like on television shows. There were no shouts of "Clear!" Was she really dying? Wouldn't there be more drama?

The thought of losing Mom crushed me. Dad had died of a heart attack three years earlier at age sixty. So young.

My dreams of my parents meeting their grandchildren and growing old together vanished as I watched Mom take her last breath.

Throughout my childhood, Mom told me I should be a nurse. She and Dad were both registered nurses. They met in New York City while going to a Bellevue nursing school prior to World War II. Seeking a new start after the war, Dad moved the family to Nebraska where he became a hospital administrator.

"You should be a nurse," Mom badgered me throughout my childhood. "Why don't you become a nurse? You would be so good at it." I didn't agree.

I never wanted to be a nurse. I remembered all the holidays that Mom had to work, the night shifts, the gruesome dinner conversations about picking gravel out of a motorcyclist's brain or details of bloody surgical procedures. It didn't sound like the career for me.

Doris Day movies convinced me that a career in advertising would be fun. I enjoyed writing and drawing, so I decided to major in journalism. I soon discovered that my childhood dream of becoming an advertising executive was a fantasy. I floundered, wondering what career to choose. Then my dad died, and my grades plummeted. Three years later, I got married, leaving college behind.

Now I was beginning the long, arduous journey through grief. I went back to work at the nursing home. Dennis said, "You can't continue to work for minimum wage. You need a profession that will support you if anything happens to me."

What profession? And how could we pay for education? The questions overwhelmed me.

While caring for a lady in the nursing home, I got to know her granddaughter, who was a frequent visitor.

Even she told me: "You should be a nurse."

"You sound like my mother," I said.

A few days later, the woman began the conversation again. She asked me where I was from. "Broken Bow," I said.

"What do your parents do?"

"My parents are both dead," I said. "My dad was a hospital administrator, and my mom was a nurse."

The woman became more animated. "What were their names?"

I told her, and she started laughing. "I knew your parents," she said. "Your dad and my husband were good friends." Her husband was the administrator at one of the large hospitals in Omaha.

She continued to encourage me to become a nurse. Eventually, I confessed that we had no money for school, and my transcripts from the university weren't good. She persisted and arranged for me to talk to her husband about enrolling in the nursing school connected with his hospital.

A few days later, I found myself inside the large hospital, walking down the long marbled halls to the administrator's office. He greeted me from behind a large mahogany desk and invited me to sit in one of the plush chairs. He smiled as he told me about his friendship with my father. He recalled how Dad was president of the Nebraska Hospital Association in the 1950s and helped raise funds to build the hospital in which we sat. He said his wife described how I took care of her grandmother, and they were both convinced I should be a nurse.

"We'll find a scholarship for you." He made an appointment for me to see the director at the college of nursing.

Days later, I walked into the director's office. Taken aback, I stopped short. Sitting behind the desk was a petite, graying woman about my mother's age in a crisp white uniform. She wore the unique Bellevue School of Nursing upside-down "cupcake paper" nursing cap. I'd only seen that particular nursing cap on two other people — my mother and my aunt in Pennsylvania. The odds seemed incredible. The director of the Omaha nursing school was a graduate of the New York school my parents attended.

She agreed to allow me to enroll in the school, but sternly told me that I would have to prove myself and bring up my grades.

With only one car, Dennis drove me to school every day. Because of his work hours, I arrived an hour before classes started. I used the time to study in the student lounge. I noticed that our anatomy and physiology instructor would arrive early and write lengthy notes on the board. I decided to go into the classroom and get a head start on the notes.

One day, the instructor asked me where I was from. The conversation seemed very similar to those I had had with the nursing-home visitor and the director of the school.

It turned out that she knew my parents, too! She and her husband, a doctor, used to live in a small Nebraska town near my hometown. I thought it was very strange that I was meeting all these people who knew my parents. As a child, I didn't think about my parents having friends outside of our small community.

I excelled in school and graduated, beginning my career as an NICU nurse. Looking back, I believe my mother guided the conversations that led me to becoming a nurse.

Mom continues to help me, and I believe, in the end, she will be there at my deathbed, saying, "I told you so!"

~Susan Grady Bristol

My Mother's Daughter

We must value life and treasure each breath
we take. We must value each person
and how he or she touches
our lives every day.
~*Shadonna Richards,* A Gift of Hope

Last Saturday I attended a dear friend's wedding and it was gorgeous, colorful, and so much fun. Many of my friends and family members were there, and as always, I spent much of the evening being told how much I was like my mom. Throughout the night, and particularly on the dance floor, I heard basically the same thing from everyone: "Oh, my gosh, Bridget! You are your mother's daughter!"

I smiled politely and said thank you over and over again, but I wasn't really feeling it. I suppose that's because, despite my mother's exceptional accomplishments and incomparable character traits, I have spent too many of my twenty-eight years focusing on everything she *isn't*, instead of appreciating everything she *is*.

I have always loved my mom fiercely, but I haven't always shown it in the way she deserved. I used to think I shied away from being "just like her" because she really bugged me. Now I think it was because, in my heart, I couldn't quite appreciate her brand of pure goodness until I began to see how much I needed it in my life. I don't regret one thing about our mostly-amazing-but-sometimes-a-little-shaky relationship. It is the realest thing I have ever known.

Sometimes, I assumed she didn't understand me. I realize now, it was often *I* who misunderstood her.

Sometimes, I resented the perpetual positivity she prescribed for my teenage angst. I realize now she was teaching me resilience.

She is the most devoutly spiritual person I have ever met. She never tells me how to live, but she shows me all the time.

My mother practices the sort of kindness that softens people — the sort that I unsuccessfully try to emulate. It transforms stressful encounters into more personal, human-to-human interactions. She is arguably the best nurse in her hospital because she has the capacity to treat every patient with the same care she would provide to her own family.

Being "my mother's daughter," implies that I'm just like her? Never.

In fact, sometimes, during my adolescence, I thought of myself more as a "Daddy's Girl." And I unfairly used my mother as my emotional punching bag. I realize now that I did that because I knew she would love me anyway. I could rely on her steadfast support.

People like to say that once you're a mother, you begin to appreciate your own mother. I decided not to wait that long. So, let me say boldly and for the record: I am so proud to be my mother's daughter. We are, and always have been, the same in all the best ways.

Mom:
For all the times I rolled my eyes, I'm sorry.
For all the times I forgot to say it: Thank you. I love you. So very, very much.

~Bridget Chambers

My Eight Mothers

No one who achieves success does so without
the help of others. The wise and confident
acknowledge this help with gratitude.
~Alfred North Whitehead

I stood in the greeting-card section, searching for Mother's Day cards for my three daughters-in-law. Nothing expressed how much I loved them or how pleased I was at the way they were raising our grandchildren.

I thought of my own mothers. A lump in my throat told me to leave the card section. Unmovable, I stood. If my eight mothers were still living, which card would I send each one? Could cards even express all my love and gratitude?

Driving home, gratitude, sorrow, laughter, comfort, and pain all rushed through my memories. I began to compose love notes to my moms.

* * *

My mother who gave me life must have loved me, cradled me and laughed with me. I remember her taking care of my sister Sallie and me when we were sick. She read to us often. Mommy must have taught me things little girls need to know about being kind, quiet when necessary, and respectful toward adults. Most of all, she instilled a positive sense of security. Mommy died from polio when I was five years old so I don't remember much.

Thank you, Mommy, for taking care of me as a baby, toddler and kindergartner. We must have had fun times. You didn't know you were preparing me to be strong enough for my unusual life journey. I wish you could hold and play with my children and grandchildren. You would have loved them.

After Mommy died, Daddy took Sallie and me to live with his parents in Missouri. Grandmother, a gentle woman, enjoyed doing little-girl things with us. Her white hair with a blue rinse framed her beautiful, wrinkled face.

Because she knew we missed our mother, she taught us a prayer, "Father-Mother-God, loving me, guard me while I sleep. Guide my little feet up to thee." She told me God loved me.

Dear Grandmother, I now understand how hard it was for you to care for Sallie and me. We were sad little girls who nevertheless needed discipline. Your faith in God kept you strong. Thank you, Grandmother, for teaching me that God loves me, the most important fact I ever learned.

When I was in third grade, Dad remarried. We moved to Kansas with my stepmother. Dad and Janice, my third mother, were busy with difficulties in their own lives and struggled to care for two little girls. Therefore, I learned from Janice how to do things for myself.

Dear Janice, Taking care of us wasn't easy for you. But you tried. Through those tough times, you loved us. That's what held us together those six months. Thank you for my precious baby sister, your daughter.

We couldn't stay with Dad and Janice. Sallie went to live with our father's younger uncle and I went to live in New Jersey with his older brother. For three years, I lived in a real family unit with two cousins about my age. That was when my aunt, my fourth mother, taught me the joys of nature. I remember hiking through woods, stooping to inspect moss near the foot of trees. On dark nights, we trudged through snow, studying stars.

She stood up for me when I was insecure. I cried, telling her no one had asked me to be a partner in gym class. When she informed school officials, the choose-your-partner system changed.

Dear Aunt Betty, How I thank you for three years with your family. I loved those cross-country car trips when we played games and sang silly songs. You never told me I squeak off-key. Thank you for sticking up for this friendless girl. Your daughter and I are still like sisters.

I'm thankful for each mother who carried me through my shaky girlhood. Above all, I loved my mother's mother, Dee. Every summer, Sallie and I visited her in Illinois. One day, after Sallie had gone back to the uncle she lived with, Dee and I sat in her Oldsmobile. She asked, "Twink, would you like to live with me?" I jumped at the chance.

This skinny, timid adolescent moved in with her fifth mother. With Dee's encouragement, I became more outgoing, made friends, and even got good grades. I was elected president of the junior-high student council.

I lived with this wonderful woman for seven years before she sent me to college. Her optimistic outlook on life and her loving care and discipline transformed me into a new person.

Dear Dee, Thank you for your positive outlook. You changed my life. Mostly, thank you for being you. I treasure memories of us chatting about anything and everything. What would have happened to me without you?

Aunt Jan, my sixth mom, was Dee's best friend. She and her four children spent many afternoons at our house. Even though Dee and I lived down the street, we were part of her family. For seven Mother's

Days, I gave cards to both Dee and Aunt Jan.

When generation gaps caused problems, my sixth mom was there to talk us through misunderstandings.

Dear Aunt Jan, You truly were my other mother. I loved being part of your big family. I'm so glad you came to help when our third little boy was born. How could I have managed without your motherly care and concern?

Marriage gave me my wonderful mother-in-law, my seventh mom.

Thank you, Mom. I never thought of you as a mother-in-law. You've been my good friend as well as my mom. Thank you for coming to my rescue that time I had surgery when our three little guys were only one, two and four.

Every bride needs a mom to help her through uncharted waters. She turned out to be our precious landlady in Iowa, my eighth mother. She figured out I didn't know how to cook or clean. She taught me how to be a wife. She was the mother I needed to encourage me when I discovered I was pregnant a few months before my husband entered the Air Force.

Oh ZellaLea, I'm so thankful for your openness and love. Because you and your husband were there for us, Denny and I made it through those two years and still have a powerful marriage filled with love.

My eight mothers each took on a specific mother role I desperately needed. They fit together like a braided rope, each being my mom for a specific time and need, and together becoming the mother everyone would want to have.

~Twink DeWitt

My Mother the Travel Agent

Love is stronger than death even though it can't stop death from happening. But no matter how hard death tries, it can't separate people from love.
~Author Unknown

The text from my brother was brief: *I'm going to be at Disney World with Hannah and a few of her friends from April 1–5. You're going there too, right?*

I was delighted by his unexpected news. Two months earlier, I had booked a three-day vacation in Disney World for my son and me, with plans to be there from April 4–6. It would fall during our first visit to see my father in the United States since my mother had passed away the previous year, and I knew our trip would be fraught with mixed emotions. Orlando was less than a two-hour drive from the independent-living facility that my father had moved into shortly after my mother's death, and I liked the idea of breaking up our stay with a few days in the magical world of Disney. As a bonus, I was able to use points I'd accrued on my credit card to cover a significant portion of our booking costs, allowing us to choose a hotel we might not have selected otherwise.

I texted back quickly to let him know our dates and added that we'd be staying onsite at Disney's Pop Century Resort. His answer surprised me. "So are we," he responded, and asked if Yogev and I could arrive a day earlier so that we could spend more time together. I contacted the hotel and successfully changed our reservation, all the while marveling at this turn of events.

When I told my father that Josh and I would be meeting up at Disney World, he was ecstatic. He recounted his and my mother's fear that my brother and I would lose our connection once they were both gone, and he was thrilled that we were seizing this opportunity to vacation together with our children. His voice choked up as he spoke of my mother and how happy it would have made her to know that we were doing this.

Josh and I had always gotten along well when we visited, but we didn't speak often and saw one another even less. In the days before our mother died, though, we managed to connect on a level that had eluded us for years — a connection that deepened as our family dynamic turned upside-down while we faced our mother's illnesses and subsequent death.

My brother and I made restaurant reservations and park plans, re-arranging schedules as needed to maximize our time together. I was excited at the prospect of having fun with my brother, and looked forward to Yogev and Hannah having this rare opportunity to hang out. Despite their two-year age difference and the miles that separated them, they enjoyed each other's company, and I wanted them to develop their relationship even further. They hadn't seen one another since the days surrounding my mother's funeral, keeping each other company during the day and sleeping on matching sofas in my parents' living room at night. I loved the idea of us wandering around Disney World with my brother and one of my nieces, making memories together.

But even as my excitement grew, like my father, I was deeply saddened by the fact that my mother wasn't alive to witness what was happening. I, too, knew how happy it would have made her to see her children and grandchildren planning and taking a trip together. My grief over her loss was palpable and still felt fresh; knowing that she was missing it all made my heart ache and filled my eyes with tears.

And yet, I couldn't help but wonder if my mother somehow had a spiritual hand in bringing my brother and me together in this way. After all, what were the chances that Josh and I — completely independently of one another — would make plans to be in Disney World at the same time *and* choose to stay at the same hotel?

I didn't know what to think. On one hand, I wanted — perhaps even desperately needed — to believe that our mother had been the guiding force, that she was watching over us from wherever she was, doing her best to help us celebrate our sibling relationship. I was utterly devastated by her death, and I missed her terribly. The idea that she was somehow responsible for bringing us together was soothing. On the other hand, the cynic in me was skeptical, unwilling to accept the possibility that what had happened was nothing more than an incredibly wonderful coincidence.

My friends were more confident than I was. "It does sound like something your mom would help to orchestrate," noted Sheri, one of my oldest friends who had known my mother since we were kids. "You know she did," exclaimed Denise, whose wisdom and friendship during the previous year had been a lifeline when my grief was overwhelming and I needed a confidante. My friend Debbie called it "mom serendipity" — a term that brought a smile to my face.

I allowed myself to accept the possibility that my mother had intervened to create this unexpected family reunion. I liked what my friend Roni had to say: "It doesn't matter what the situation is. If you felt that your mother was there and helped you, then she was! Your mother is always with you."

And my mother was clearly with us as we traveled, hovering in our thoughts as we stopped for lunch at her favorite roadside restaurant chain on the way to Orlando. I felt her with me when I hugged my brother in the hotel lobby and as we watched the sunset from the balcony of our room. Perhaps we couldn't see or touch her, but my mother was definitely with us at Disney World, and the one thing I knew for certain was that she was happy.

~Liza Rosenberg

To Thine Own Self Be True

One of the most important relationships we'll have is the relationship we have with our mothers.
~Iyanla Vanzant

The country roads are horrendously icy this evening, so I take extra care driving home. As my small, tin-can car moves steadily down our long driveway, I realise it's not just the harsh British weather that's slowing me down.

I'm reluctant to arrive. So nervous to tell her what's happened.

The situation I now find myself in will change my life forever. I've just been offered a new job, hundreds of miles from home. In less than a month, I'll be gone. For some people, these decisions are no big deal, but those of us who are deeply connected to those who raised us can feel their hearts breaking before we've even packed our bags.

"She has to understand," I whisper to myself as I pull up outside the house. "It's her influence, after all."

My love for literature and theatre is directly inherited from my mum. Whilst other kids my age were opening new make-up on their sixteenth birthdays, I was hugging the heavy anthologies of William Shakespeare, Edgar Allan Poe, Sylvia Plath… to name a few.

Now, one of those great names would drag me across our country quite literally. I'd secured a position working for the largest theatre company in the world, dedicated to performing the works of The Bard.

I was going to live in his hometown—quaint little Stratford-upon-Avon in Warwickshire.

Throughout the whole recruitment process, I kept telling myself that it was my destiny. An emotional force constantly re-assured me that this was where I was meant to go. This upheaval would allow me to truly become myself.

I started talking before I'd finished walking through the door. "Mum, I need to tell you something."

"Me, too."

I looked puzzled. "Um, okay. You first."

She walked off into the next room and returned with a small parcel, wrapped in light blue paper, and handed it to me.

"I bought this for you yesterday," she muttered. "I don't know... don't know why, but I thought it was important that... I give you this." She looked uncomfortable, like something was troubling her. I tore open the package like that sixteen-year-old version of myself.

Inside was a beautiful silver chain, and from it dangled a ring. Inside the ring, I could see the inscription: *This above all—to thine own self be true.* My jaw dropped. My new boss had spoken.

"Why did you get this?"

"I just felt compelled to buy it, like I said. I don't know why. I can't explain it. Do you like it? Do you recognise the words from *Hamlet*, one of our favourite plays?" She looked into my eyes. "I just... wanted to let you know that you must always be true to yourself, no matter what."

I burst into tears. Then, at a million miles an hour, I told her everything.

That I was leaving.

That we wouldn't live together anymore.

That I was scared.

That, for some reason, I just knew this was my path.

That I was going to work for the man whose words were inscribed on this piece of metal.

That I would miss her terribly.

That I was, just as the engraving stated, going to be true to the voices in my head.

She was overjoyed. And shocked. Not at the move, but the synchronicity of our thoughts. This sentence, spoken by Polonius, is the last piece of advice that Laertes hears from his father before he goes overseas.

They were now my own parting gift from the woman closest to me in the world. A woman who, until a few seconds ago, had no idea I was even considering this move.

Language can hold a power that is, ironically, inexplicable. A small saying can pick us up when we're at our lowest. A quote can inspire us to make life-changing decisions. Books written by these legends remain in our bedrooms throughout our lives, tucked away in a sea of our favourite stories lined up on our shelves. We sleep alongside their voices; perhaps that's why they find their way into our dreams. I had always believed that words could change lives, but had never even considered that they could predict the future.

The following week, I would be late for my goodbye dinner — too busy getting those nine words tattooed on the back of my neck. I would contemplate the perplexing experience my mother and I shared that day, how it transcended the worlds of literature and motherhood. Our spiritual connection could only be remembered with a permanent reminder on my body.

This inky mark, now on my skin, will be with me until the day I die. For me, these will always be powerful words. Not because they were spoken by Shakespeare, or Polonius… but because they were a message from my mother.

~Rebecca Rimmer

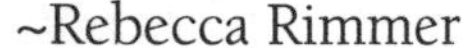

Milk Lady

Any sufficiently advanced technology is indistinguishable from magic.
~Arthur C. Clarke

"Here comes the Milk Lady," my roommate said as my mom walked up the porch steps, lugging a gallon of milk. Mom came twice a week to my college house to use my computer. As she believed my roommate and I weren't eating properly, the milk was her contribution to our wellbeing.

My mother owned an ancient manual typewriter. But when I started high school, she bought me an electric typewriter. She proudly announced, "This will last you all the way through college!"

Well, it lasted through eleventh grade, anyway. Then my mother bought me a Tandy computer. "Now this will last you all the way through college," she said.

Next, she wanted me to teach her how to use that computer.

Back when I was five, I had asked my mother to teach me how to read. I was determined to sit on the couch until I'd mastered reading. Now my mother was coming to me with twenty-five years of scientific research, complete with chemical equations, and she wanted to summarize it on my computer right then.

I owed her one, so we got started. This was a situation where technology did not make life easier. Mom was furious with the cursor. It was never where she thought it should be.

After a couple of hours of her struggle I suggested, "Why don't you come back on another day and I'll help you some more?"

And thus began my mother's twice a week visits. She'd bring us a gallon of milk and I'd tutor her for an hour on the computer. Gradually I retreated from looking over her shoulder and got back to my French homework, merely in the same room in case she had a question.

I should mention that tutoring my mom on the computer was one of the best investments of my time in college. By the end of my sophomore year she said, "You need a better computer. This Tandy is too slow. You need to upgrade." She kept me in the latest computers through graduate school.

Now Mom has her own cottage industry making greeting cards on her laptop from pictures she takes with her digital camera.

As for me, I'm still reading. And I drink my milk. Thanks, Mom.

~C. J. Godwin

My Mom and My Mother

All that I am or ever hope to be,
I owe to my angel Mother.
~Abraham Lincoln

I never knew my mother. I don't know what her laugh sounded like or if she was afraid of the dark or if she liked the beach. The Catholic adoption agency she surrendered me to didn't know very much about her either.

But I know that she loved me enough to make sure I had a good home.

I grew up in a house full of laughter and hugs, with church on Sundays, a back yard with pink rosebushes, chocolate bunnies on Easter, and stockings to hang on Christmas Eve. I attended dance lessons, voice lessons, swim team, and softball, and we said grace as a family before every meal.

In the room I shared with my sister, I slept in the top bunk, and I had my own desk with my own plastic typewriter that I used to tap out lists of dreams. My mom took us to the library every week, volunteered as room mother for my class every year, and let me lick the spoon when she baked cookies. I remember her preparing me for my classmates' taunts that she wasn't my "real mother" and that it was "too bad my biological mother didn't want me." And when they came, I was ready for them. I fiercely defended a woman I had never met because my mom let me know how much that woman loved me.

I was raised to understand the sacrifice my mother made for me. I learned of her frequent visits to the foster home I was in before deciding on an official placement for me. She knew she could not provide a life for me, and as hard as it was, she decided to give me a chance at a real one. My mom discussed all this with me and helped me understand how much love it took to make the choice my mother did.

Every year on my birthday, my mom would tell me with a hug, "Say a prayer for your mother today. I know she is thinking of you." And after she left, I would pray for the mother I didn't know. I hoped she could somehow know that I was happy and healthy, loved and secure.

I have two amazing moms. One put herself last in order to give me a life full of love, experiences and security. And one wrapped her arms around me and never let me forget how much both of them loved me.

~Beth Rice

Second Chance

Cherish your yesterdays, dream your tomorrows and live your todays.
~Author Unknown

I was making my mom's bed when she walked in. Quickly, I asked the instinctive question, "How did it go?" expecting her to tell me everything was fine. When she hesitated, I thought she was joking, like when you ask children if they received good grades on their report card and they frown—only to say "gotcha!" before revealing straight A's. But that was not my mom's sense of humor. She didn't like to scare me, especially when it concerned a doctor's visit.

"Good? Bad?" I prodded, feeling like I was slipping into a nightmare. "What? It isn't cancer, is it?"

She leaned against her old desk, in her pastel bedroom with the Paris theme, and told me something so ugly it was completely contrary to the surroundings. Possible cancer. A "painful" biopsy in one week, followed by two more weeks of waiting.

I stared at the woman before me, whose face I had looked into nearly every day for twenty-six years, and felt like I was seeing a stranger. Nearly sixty, my mom was more beautiful and full of life than anyone I had ever known. She had been published in a *Chicken Soup for the Soul* book, started a website dedicated to helping motivate and encourage people, and had plans to visit friends in Provence in France—a place she had always wanted to visit.

I had plans, too. I had grown up without a grandmother and was determined that, when I had children someday, they would not miss out on having one. My beautiful mother would be the one to make them laugh like she made me laugh every day. Her smile would make them smile; they would feel the comfort in her arms and experience the kindness of her spirit and her deep faith. They would be as blessed as I had been to know this woman who never raised a hand or her voice to me, and who was my best friend.

Of course, I cried, but then I got angry. I was angry that a disease could take away the woman who had homeschooled me and my two brothers, taking us to the science center with a lunch bag full of peanut-butter sandwiches every other weekend, and on field trips to the grocery store. She would stop someone to compliment them, regardless of what language they spoke, and invite people into her home despite their religious beliefs. She went to the Netherlands when people from our church tried to tell her it was impossible, our pastor at the time being her biggest opponent. When we returned after two successful weeks of her being booked solid to speak in Bible colleges and churches, despite knowing no one when we went over, a crowd was waiting to welcome us at the airport. She's been back seven times, adding more countries along the way. The details of her trip to Paris were published in *FRANCE*—her favorite magazine.

Not everyone saw her the way I did, and it was their loss. I watched men treat this rare diamond as if she were a plastic ring in a Cracker Jack box. Watched as she went back to work after my dad was arrested for attacking her. Watched her fight for us in court, and pace the hallway in prayer outside the operating room when my brother was having surgery, while simultaneously making phone calls to find us a place to live after my dad took our house. We should have spent her birthday in Paris or watching a movie together at home—she would have been happy with either. But we spent the day moving the rest of our belongings into a storage unit. Her beloved library was packed into dirty boxes, a padlock the only security.

In that darkest moment, thinking she might die, I realized some things I wished every child with a good mother knew before it was too late. Having a good mom was my greatest blessing. Instead of daydreaming while she spoke, I should listen gladly to her voice. Even when I was tired or wallowing in self-pity, I should make the effort to do something when she asked me — whether performing a chore or playing *Minecraft* with her.

That news of the biopsy was meant to change us, and it did. She turned out to be fine — no cancer. And now, when I do that thing that daughters do, and I start to get frustrated with her, I take a breath and thank God that she is here, so grateful for the second chance I've been given.

~April Pollack

A Painting of You

I paint the spirit and soul of what I see.
~Brian Froud

If I were to paint a picture of you
I would need to find the right colour for grace.
Not the dainty kind — the deep touching-your-soul kind.
I'd use deep warm red for the colour of love,
the unconditional kind that conveys appreciation, hope and joy.
I would need some deep blue to convey inner strength, courage and
will, and a soft spring green for being young at heart.
With a sprinkling of pink for laughter and fun.
Rich burgundy for your appreciation of beauty and goodness
around you.
A deeper green, like jade or forests tall, might convey your
intelligence, caring wisdom, and keen interest in people and
the world.
If I were to paint you, I would need every colour of the rainbow
To reflect the music in your heart, the sparkle in your eyes,
Both humble and vulnerable, understanding and forgiving.
Even with all the colours of the rainbow, I would not be
able to capturethe wonder and beauty of you.

~Trudy M. Davies

A Lasting Legacy

What you leave behind is not what is engraved
in stone monuments, but what is woven
into the lives of others.
~Pericles

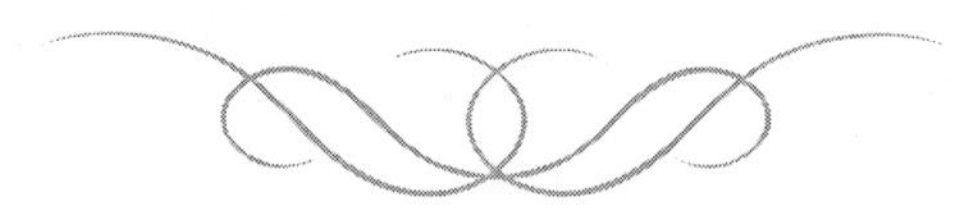

Mother's Handbag

The more a daughter knows the details of her mother's life, the stronger the daughter.
~Anita Diamant

I reach down into the wicker storage basket and pull out the large handbag. I brush off a little bit of dust and unclasp the lock. The first thing I find inside is a green packet of Wrigley's Doublemint gum. I slip out a foil-wrapped piece and sniff; a faint scent lingers. Memories of my mother waft over me along with the minty fragrance. Her purse still carries a part of her identity, bits and pieces of her unique personality.

A paperback book is in the middle of the pocketbook, with a rubber band wrapped securely around it. Mom rubber-banded everything, including the pigtails on my older sister and the braids on my own head when we were young. I think she would have rubber-banded both of us to keep us still if she could have found one large enough. The title of the book makes me smile, *Overcoming the Shake, Rattle and Roll in Your Life!* My mother was an overcomer, a strong yet tender woman of solid Polish descent.

I riffle through several medical prescriptions, pill bottles, doctor appointment cards and health insurance papers. These items are a painful reminder of all the health problems she stoically endured. Yet in the middle of the medical paraphernalia lies a slim volume titled *A Rainbow of Hope,* reflecting her steadfast optimism and sincere faith in the face of her daily struggles. Tucked in a corner of the bag is a rolled-up rain bonnet, a thin strip of colorful, polka-dotted plastic in case of a sudden downpour. It might rain, but she was ready with some funky colors to brighten a dreary day. An address sticker is clearly taped inside the purse in case it wandered away from the owner and needed to be returned. She was even ready for that.

There is a flat case enclosing a square mirror to be sure she was always presentable. My fingers touch a filmy blue scarf, and I draw it out. It unfurls a bright banner of color. I grin, picturing her with the scarf tied securely around her neck or over her head.

There are other papers in the purse, including several religious tracts. She was determined to convert the world and would leave a trail of little booklets wherever she went. Without a doubt, she influenced far more lives than we would ever realize. I pull out all the tissues, causing a blur of soft whiteness. She was always ready for a sudden sneeze or to clean up an accidental spill. Usually, they were used to dry someone's tears as she comforted them in their distress and offered compassion in the form of a clean white tissue and a warm hug.

I remember so many examples of strong character just from the perusal of Mother's handbag. She gave me valuable life lessons to guide my way. I can hear the determination in her voice. "Cynthia, be courageous, fight for the right and look on the bright side! Always be prepared, look your best, reach out to others." I'd smile and roll my eyes. How could I hope to live up to her standards? "Be loving, be kind, and remember to truly listen to others…." Yes, Mother, I'm working on it.

Was she perfect? Excuse me, I just heard her laugh floating through the clouds. She would have been the first one to say no. She had a temper she struggled with daily. She possessed a quirky sense of humor, and she wasn't overly concerned with the opinions of others. This fact was more obvious in the winter when she constantly wore mismatched mittens. I still wonder if she really couldn't find the proper match or if it was a deliberate ploy to challenge the norm.

On days when I miss her deeply and the loss is more poignant, I pull out the handbag and allow the bittersweet nostalgia to soothe my soul. Every item carries significance, a slice of my mother's life within the simple confines of her handbag. Clean it out? Throw out that stale, old gum? I think not. I carefully place it back in storage with a gentle pat, knowing that I'll return again for more memories and life lessons from Mother's handbag.

~Cynthia A. Lovely

An Enduring Love

Love as powerful as your mother's for you leaves its own mark. To have been loved so deeply, even though the person who loved us is gone, will give us some protection forever.
~*J.K. Rowling,* Harry Potter and the Sorcerer's Stone

I've faced many tragedies in my life, but none as overwhelming as the death of my mother. She passed away a couple of years ago, and my life hasn't been the same since. But from this loss has come a realization that I didn't think would come so quickly to me: I haven't really lost her at all.

Mom had been chronically ill for quite a while, but she was a courageous woman, possessed of an inner strength and a positive outlook that enabled her to have many more wonderful years with her children, grandchildren, and great-grandchildren than the doctors had predicted. Many wonderful memories and tender moments came from those years, and we were all grateful for them.

But Mom's passing left a huge hole in my life, one that seemed impossible to fill. My wife and I had cared for my mom for several years, sharing the good days and helping her through the bad ones. We came to learn how, when you truly love someone, being there for them when they need you the most is the reason we are all here on earth. When she was no longer there, it seemed as if a part of my heart had been torn away.

My mom, however, always lived with great cheer and happiness.

She would never have spent a moment holding onto sadness when there is such great reason in life for joy. In the dozens and dozens of pictures I have of her with our family, her friends and the people she'd known and loved in her life, she had a heartfelt and genuine smile in almost every one of them. She taught me to find the good in life, in people, and in all that we do.

Soon after Mom's passing, my brothers and sister, my wife and kids, and everyone in our family began to spend more time together. We had always been close, but now it seemed as if there was a great need to get to know each other better. It was as if we had come to recognize there was now a great emptiness in our lives, and we had decided to honor our mother's memory and our love for each other by taking on the roles that she had so often played in the past.

The first time we celebrated a holiday without her, I expected it to be a sad occasion. Without my mother there, how could any occasion be happy? But somewhere deep inside me, I seemed to hear my mother's laughter, and feel her joy at all of us coming together again to celebrate life and each other. I realized she would never want her memory to be full of sadness, but of love and happiness. As I looked at the faces of the family I loved, I suddenly saw her face in all of theirs. We celebrated that day with my mom's spirit in full attendance.

Shortly afterward, I went to visit my mom's grave. My sister had planted flower bulbs in the ground around her headstone, and over the cold, hard winter, they had worked their way up through the frozen soil. They stood unfurled in the sun, their colors bright and cheery, reflecting the happiness I knew Mom would have felt knowing that her family had remained close. The memory of her glorious and loving spirit had shown us the way.

Even though there are days when I look around and miss her laughter and seeing her smile at the sight of her children and their families being together, that same laughter can be heard in the voices of her grandchildren and great-grandchildren. I know that the love she so selflessly and gladly shared with us all her life will live on forever in her family.

My mom is still close, watching over us and loving us. Her spirit will always be a part of me, guiding me and showing me the way to better care for those I love. I know that every time I want to feel her arms around me again and make me feel that all is right with the world, all I have to do is wrap my arms around the people I love, and care for them with the joy and happiness she always shared with me.

~John P. Buentello

Mom's Cards from Beyond

What is a mom but the sunshine of our days and the north star of our nights.
~Robert Brault

In 2010, about three months before my wife died, she decided to write birthday, holiday, graduation, and wedding cards to our two children as nuggets of herself they would have to share for many years after her death. At first, she tackled the project with energy and enthusiasm. She researched what was going on in the world when she turned ten, eleven, twelve… eighteen, etc., so she could share with either Miguel or Maya what her life was like when she was their ages.

Because she was taking steroids and narcotics for pain, I asked her if I could be her secretary.

"No," she insisted. "I want the kids to know what I went through, how I wrote the cards for them."

Even when her handwriting, which was never all that legible, deteriorated as her metastatic breast cancer progressed, she never wavered from her task.

I am convinced that our children — Miguel, who was twelve, and Maya, who was four, when Verna Wefald, wife and mother, died — appreciate the amazing gift she left them.

For Maya's tenth birthday in 2016, Verna wrote:

One of the typical projects for 4th grade is to write a report on one of California's missions. I used to love history, and one of my favorite ways to learn about it is to travel and visit historic sites. Some of my favorite ones were to Israel in 1992, to Italy, Portugal, and France with Grandma (it was a religious pilgrimage for her), Costa Rica in 1990 after I got my teaching credential, and Washington, D.C., in 2004.

She added:

I hope you will always love traveling the world.

Verna would sit in her sliding recliner chair in our living room, use one of her special colored pens, do her research, write the card, and then stuff a savings bond, which she'd collected when she was a paralegal for the city of San Francisco, into it when she was finished.

She wrote cards for each kid's first Easter, Thanksgiving, Christmas, and Hanukkah after she died. She wrote birthday cards they will receive until they turn eighteen. There is one for Maya's sweet sixteen, and ones for Miguel's and Maya's high-school graduations. She knew she wouldn't be there for any of the celebrations, but she left part of herself for each child to savor.

For their first Thanksgiving after her death, Verna wrote one for Miguel and Maya together.

I always loved Thanksgiving because we all got packed into our car and drove wherever the whole family wanted to be. Thanksgiving is a time of thanks. I'm forever grateful I got a chance to be your mother and I brought you into this world.

On the first Easter after she died, Verna wrote to Maya:

I had fun coloring eggs with you. And I loved watching you run through the park to find the eggs. Don't eat all the candy at once. Save it so you can eat it for many more days, even months.

Each night before a birthday or holiday or important life event, I pull the card out of the plastic zippered bag and bring it down for either Maya or Miguel. I have to read most of them because I am the best at deciphering her handwriting.

For Miguel's fifteenth birthday in 2013, Verna wrote in purple ink:

You're going to be able to get your learner's permit soon, and I can't believe it. I expect you to maintain good grades and a good attitude if you want to be a driver in the Friedman-Wefald household.

She said she took driver's education training with three other teenagers, one of whom was a bad driver.

I had to close my eyes every time she got behind the wheel. Whenever she would take a right turn she would overturn and almost run over a curb. One time she almost plowed into a bus stop full of people. Thank God the instructor had the ability to apply his own brake.

She used the cards as opportunities to share love and advice for years to come even after she was gone. The void from her absence will always be so stark and painful, but I do believe her cards help ease our suffering by bringing her into our lives during important celebrations.

For Miguel's seventeenth birthday in 2015, the last birthday card she wrote for him, she said:

I applied to one college only—San Francisco State. One of the regrets in my life is that I didn't apply to other colleges. I never got to experience living in a dormitory.

She'd chosen a local college and lived at home.

Stuffed into the two plastic bags in our closet are dozens of cards she bought for birthdays and other celebrations that she never filled out. She purchased an eighteenth- birthday card for Miguel, but never had the chance to write anything in it. But the card alone was so sweet I gave it to him anyway. The Hallmark writer said:

> *Son, every once in a while in your running-everywhere childhood, I'd see you in a moment of quiet and catch a glimpse of the man you'd one day be… I knew I'd be proud of you. I just never could have guessed how much.*

Tears filled my eyes as I read the unfilled card the night before and again when I shared it with Miguel on the morning of his eighteenth birthday.

Being a parent was the greatest joy in Verna's life. She adored being a mother, spending time with her kids, watching them grow, and playing with them. When her oncologist told us she probably had three months to live, she dedicated herself to leaving a legacy for Miguel and Maya (and me) that they would have for their entire lives, even without her.

She may be gone, but the cards she wrote to each child mean she will never be forgotten or absent from their lives.

~Steven Friedman

Mirror Magic

Mirror Mirror on the wall, I am my mother after all.
~Author Unknown

I step out of the shower, dry off, and slip into my undies, then glance at the big mirror over the vanity. It's then I realize that something strange has been happening in our house lately.

Whenever I look in the mirror, someone else looks back. I peer closely and shake my head. The person in the mirror is my mother, *not* me. How can that be? She has been gone for many years, but there she is. If I wave my hand, she waves right back. If I smile, so does she. When I frown, Mom scrunches up her face, too.

"Face it," I tell myself. "It's you in that mirror. It's not the person you think you are. Ah no, you think of yourself as that redhead who flew across the college campus to classes and back to the dorm for meals and studying. You are the girl who left Chicago and went to college in a downstate teacher-education university. You are the girl who thrilled to be independent after living with a strict father who curtailed everything you thought to be fun and a mother who convinced him you should have more privileges. You are that young woman who fell in love half a dozen times in the four years of study time."

I apply moisturizer and lean closer to the mirror. The woman with the circles under her eyes, the white hair and wrinkled neck is *me*. Dear Lord, when did it happen? When did I begin to look like my mother? I was minding my own business, going about my busy life, when Mom slipped in and waved a magic wand. *Zap! You're me.* And without so much as an *Alakazam!*, the deed was done.

Next, I put on make-up. Not too much, just enough to enhance what God already bestowed upon me. That will help. I will be back in the mirror, not Mom.

First, a little foundation, then eyebrow pencil to help where my eyebrows have vanished, a bit of mascara, a light dusting of powder and blush, and finish with a lipstick. Look in the mirror again. My mother is *still* there. She looks better, I think, but it's *her*, not *me*.

Where is the bride who walked down the aisle in a wedding gown and bridal veil? Where is the young mother who raised two babies using the wisdom her mother had instilled by example? Where is the thirty-something woman who attended dinners and conventions with her husband to help his career? Where is the mother of teens who fretted and fumed over many a late night, auto accident, and prom? She's no longer in that mirror. All I see is the woman who raised me long ago, the one who gave me the foundation for all that I've done over the years.

It's not such a bad thing, I think. My mother was a pretty neat lady, right up to the day she died. She passed on more to me than a physical resemblance. I have her sense of humor, love of reading, baking ability, and positive outlook on life. Suddenly, I am quite happy to look like my mother.

I straighten up, stand tall, and stare back at Mom in the mirror. We smile at each other. We share a secret. We both know that my daughter is going to look in the mirror one day and see *me*. I won't tell her now. Let it be a surprise.

~Nancy Julien Kopp

Go Home and See Your Mother

There's nothing more vital to the bond you share with someone than simply being there for them.
~Suman Rai

During the first week of September 1992, I had a dream that Jesus spoke to me. In my dream, Jesus said very firmly, "Go home and see your mother." I was so startled, it woke me up.

When I got up the next morning, I packed a suitcase and called Mom to tell her I would be home for the Labor Day weekend. I planned it as a spur-of-the-moment weekend for just the two of us to spend time together, although I had a feeling of unease about that dream.

When I arrived late Friday, all was right with the world. Mom and I went out to dinner and visited with friends at the Elks Club. It was a wonderful evening. The next day, we went shopping and ended up at an estate sale. We laughed as we picked through all the bargain items for sale, especially when Mom picked up a statue of Our Lady of the Immaculate Heart. Mom was an avid devotee of Our Lady, and her rosary was always at hand. The poor statue had seen better days, though, and really should have been discarded. Mom insisted she was buying it for me to repair, as she never could pass up anything that had to do with Our Lady. I fell into peals of giggles over that one. It hardly had any paint left on it, and it had no nose. But it would become one of the most precious gifts my mother ever gave me.

The following day, as we were getting ready for Mass, Mom was suddenly overwhelmed with a terrible fit of vomiting. I called the ambulance against her wishes, and it was good I was there, because the following day, in the hospital, Mom suffered a stroke that destroyed her eyesight. The next day, an abdominal aneurysm almost killed her. Following surgery for that, she suffered blood clots in both legs and more surgery. By the time this cascading medical crisis had concluded, Mom went from a healthy, vibrant woman to being blind and a double-amputee.

When Mom went to rehab for prostheses, they said she would never walk again. They were wrong. Mom worked doggedly to overcome this challenge and she did learn to walk again. While she was in rehab, she met a young man who had lost his leg in a farming accident. Jeff was despondent and angry at the world. No one could make him hope and believe he still had a wonderful life to live. No one, that is, except my mom. She was relentless in making him go to therapy, challenging him at every turn. She refused to be put off by his angry responses.

On the day I went to pick her up from rehab, a young, handsome man came running down the hall to wish us goodbye and tell Mom how much he loved her. That young man was Jeff. With joy, he exclaimed how Mom was the best running partner he had ever had. She was a seventy-one-year-old who could not be beat, and refused to let him give up either.

Four years later, Mom got breast cancer and lost her last fight. But her can-do spirit lives on... in Jeff and the lives of many others Mom met along the way. If I had not obeyed the dream I had, Mother would never have survived that stroke, as she lived alone. I'm so grateful for that special dream that put me in the right place to save her and give her four more years and to touch so many lives.

~Christine Trollinger

The Journal

By writing personal and family histories, we are helped immeasurably in gaining a true, eternal perspective of life.
~John H. Groberg

Some of the world's most talented and beloved authors are never published. Margaret Peterson was one of them. She will never make *The New York Times* bestseller list or host a book signing, but her words are cherished, read and re-read, and then passed on to others all the same. She was my grandmother, and she left us one of the most personal gifts of all.

In 1940, Margaret started a journal in the pages of a brown spiral stenographer's notebook. Maybe she meant it to be something else — more of a log book to mark notable dates, or to keep track of the family's farm expenses — but it became so much more. When my grandmother started writing, she was already thirty-eight years old. She was the wife of a blacksmith, and they owned a small farm. Five of her six children had already been born. In the initial entries, she wrote about logging and farming. She wrote about her family, which would later include two additional generations. And she used her pen to document world affairs and a war that would affect everyone.

For fifty-four years she wrote daily. Some of the entries were merely a sentence recounting the temperature of the day, an unusual measurement of snow or rain, or a mention of how nice it was that one of the neighbors had come to call. Sometimes, she remarked on the high cost of gasoline, and noted the date and price if they were lucky enough to purchase a new piece of farm equipment.

If someone in her growing family did something notable—whether good or bad—they might warrant their own personal comment in a sidebar. She would use the pages of her life story to deliver a soft scolding if someone had misbehaved or embarrassed the family. And she would use those same places to thank her family for Christmas gifts and birthday parties, and would always note her surprise that so many people cared.

Throughout the years, she would chronicle heartbreak, too.

Three of her sons were required to register during wartime and were called to serve. In separate journal entries, she wrote of each of her sons' enlistments and call to active duty. She described how afraid she was for them, and in later pages she would note who had sent word for them with one of the neighbor boys home on leave, or who was able to send a letter or a gift and news of the war.

In March 1944, her third son was called to serve at eighteen years old. Grandma wrote often of his whereabouts, a glorious trip he made home that July, and the many cherished letters he had written while he was away.

Within that year, my grandmother would log an excruciatingly painful entry. A letter had come to tell the couple that their son was missing. And then, in multiple entries, she wrote her prayers. She prayed they would find him, and that he would return to their little farm safely. On a cold night, a terrified mother wrote of her hope that wherever he was, her son had found a way to stay warm. Word had reached them that the conditions they were fighting in were terrible.

Sadly, just pages later, my grandmother would write another painful entry. With a broken heart, she wrote in her journal that her youngest son, who had been gone from home for only a year, had been confirmed killed in action. Laid to rest temporarily overseas, he would be sent home following the war for a proper burial. Though they later received his Purple Heart, it was little consolation to a mother who had lost one of her sons.

There were many happy times documented as well. She enjoyed words and had a wicked sense of humor. She delighted in telling stories. "Margaretisms" are sprinkled throughout the pages.

In November 1963, Margaret wrote of the President's assassination. In 1974, when her husband passed away, there was an entry to both assure and warn her children. "I'm fine," she wrote. "I will stay in my own home. 'Til I get lonesome. Then, watch out kids!"

As she entered her eighties and nineties, and arthritis began to cripple her fingers and make it hard to spend as much time writing, Margaret's entries were often shortened to one or two lines. But still she managed to give readers a sense of the times and anything of note.

My children have fuzzy memories of their great-grandmother. My daughters remember visiting, as preschoolers, and that they would sit on her lap or perch on the arm of her rocking chair. They remember her coming to their birthday parties. I was wearing maternity clothes the day I attended her funeral. I always feel bad that my son doesn't have his own memories of her. But as future members of her family are born, each generation is getting to know her. They are able to hold in their hands the book that took her fifty-four years to write. When they are ready, they, too, will read the tangible, cherished gift to her family that is what we call The Journal.

~Sheila Helmberger

The Gift of the Bumblebees

Love is missing someone whenever you're apart,
but somehow feeling warm inside because
you're close in heart.
~Kay Knudsen

Since my mother's passing, I had been searching for a sign from her. I prayed every day for a sign that she was still watching over me. I also wanted to know that she was happy and free of the burden of Alzheimer's disease.

My mom loved children, especially her children and grandchildren. She was loving and silly with all of us. She was known for holding her finger high in the air and twirling it down to them, making a *zzzzzz* sound and tickling them wherever she could find a spot. It stuck with me so much over the years that I continued to do it to my own daughter, and now my grandchildren. I tell them each time when I do it that it's what my mother used to do to me, and now I get to do it to them.

Shortly after I began praying for a sign, I started to see bumblebees wherever I went. I'm talking about those big, fat, black ones with thick, yellow stripes. All of a sudden, they appeared everywhere — flying in my yard, hovering near me, and once even following my grandson and me in a playground. It was never a couple of bumblebees together — it was always a single one.

I noted the connection between the buzzing bees and the tickle game my mother would play, and I decided that was my sign. I even began saying "Hi, Mom" every time I saw one. But I still had my doubts. Was this Mommy giving me a sign? Or was I just reading too much into a few bumblebees?

I also began to feel that I needed to "honor" her in some way. But how? I wanted something that I could look at every day. I planted a tree, but it wasn't enough. A piece of jewelry or a picture wasn't going to cut it. So I decided I wanted a tattoo! It's funny to think about how against them I had always been, but a tattoo would actually work perfectly because I wanted something small that was just for her and me. A tattoo on my foot was a perfect idea, and it would have to be a bumblebee. I even went so far as to draw one on my ankle with swirling lines behind it to get used to the idea.

One day following the drawing of my fake tattoo, the mail arrived. I am always getting packages, so I thought nothing of it. Once again, I had ordered another unnecessary item for my kitchen, an apron with a red-apple pattern. But someone had made a mistake and sent me an apron with a bumblebee pattern! It even looked the same as the bumblebee picture I had drawn on my ankle. And by the way, the apron arrived on my mother's birthday!

A few weeks later, I awoke early one morning feeling down and looked out the window. A bumblebee was flying at the screen. I said "Hi, Mom," and it landed right on the screen. It stayed there for over an hour as I sat with it, and we had a nice conversation. Visiting with that little bee filled me with happiness. I think Mom knew I needed a little help getting through that particular day because it was Mother's Day!

I did get that tattoo after all. I designed a little bumblebee with twirling lines coming from a heart. This is Mommy. And she continues on.

My mother gave me the best gift of all that she couldn't give me in this life: She told me in her way that she was happy and free, and she was with me.

She gave me the gift of the bumblebees.

~Patty Benz

A Well-Timed Message

Perhaps they are not stars, but rather openings in heaven where the love of our lost ones pours through and shines down upon us to let us know they are happy.
~Eskimo Proverb

Despite all of the Mother's Day reminders and marketing messages that appear all over TV and social media, I try to remain calm. But the truth is, it hurts to realize that I'll not see my mom again in this lifetime. It's my first Mother's Day without her.

Sometimes, perusing the books on my shelves can have a calming effect on me. I thought it would be a good diversion from the sadness I was feeling. I noticed some of the books were sticking out further than others, and there were gaps here and there in the rows. Perhaps one of my sons borrowed a book, or maybe I lent some to a neighbor. But they were definitely not in their usual neat order. Strange, I thought.

As I started straightening them, I pulled out a worn, yellowing paperback called *Summer on Blossom Street* by Debbie Macomber. Holding the book, I clearly remembered why it had earned a spot on my shelves among the hardcovers. It had been a gift from Mom six years earlier. She often bought secondhand books at the Salvation Army store.

As I opened the book, her familiar handwriting spoke the words my heart needed to hear that night. Her note read:

May 2010
Happy Mother's Day… and all the Mother's Days to come…
Love, Mom

"And all the Mother's Days to come…"

In her wisdom, Mom must have known that there'd come a time when she would not be here. And to bring some measure of comfort, she hand-scrawled a simple message in my favorite thing—a book!

I don't know what drove me to my bookshelves and that particular paperback, as it had likely sat undisturbed for six years. But stumbling across my mom's gift and timely message reminded me to never lose hope, for my mother's love will always be with me.

~Anita Gogno

In Lieu of Flowers

There are few things that are more beautifully infectious than true kindness. It spreads like a magnificent wildfire.
~Keith Wynn

My cell phone vibrated on the oak dresser next to my bed. Why was someone calling so early in the morning? Squeezing my eyes shut, I inhaled a whiff of cinnamon and remembered my mom's favorite potpourri nestled in a glass jar next to my phone. I'd knelt next to my mom when she took her last breath only two days earlier. I couldn't listen to one more statement of sympathy followed by a list of the countless ways the random caller missed my mom. I pressed my face into my pillow and groaned. "I can't do this, Lord. Give me a little help here."

After a few moments of silence, the relentless caller struck again. I wanted to reach for the phone and turn off the ringer. Instead, I picked it up. I felt guilty when I heard the voice of another woman who missed my mama.

Doctors had diagnosed my mom with leukemia only ten months ago. We rejoiced when we found her a one-hundred-percent match for a bone-marrow transplant. When the transplant failed, my mom refused more treatment, saying, "I'm at peace. God's will be done. I don't want to suffer anymore. No more hospitals. No more pain."

She'd been healthy her whole life. She'd been a kind person her whole life. And now I had to sum up her sixty-six years in an obituary.

The morning call was a reminder that stabbed me in the heart with one more reason my mother would be missed. In lieu of flowers, our family decided to honor my mom by carrying on her yearly tradition of providing new winter coats, hats, and gloves for students in need. My job was to add the request at the end of her obituary.

I curled into a fetal position and pressed the phone to my ear. *Help me, Lord.* Arranging a funeral left no time for being a big wimp. Grief mingled with joy as I nodded my approval to the fundraiser organizer. Gratitude streaked my cheeks. "It's exactly what Mom would want."

With my smile widening, I hung up the phone. School district employees would team up with the staff from the elementary school where my mom had served as a teacher's aide for over thirty years. They would help spread the word and decorate two large collection barrels to be placed at the funeral home.

A few of the shattered pieces of my heart had been set properly back in place, making it feel a little less broken. My mother's legacy of kindness would be honored as we grieved our loss and celebrated her life. The children she faithfully loved and cared for would be warm this winter. Alone, she would have been able to afford to help two or three students a year. Surely, we could collect more than two or three new coats.

I arrived early on the day of the service. Two decorated containers stood ready to receive our gifts, one already stuffed to the brim with colorful, brand-spanking-new coats, gloves, and hats. The ladies who worked at the school already packed the kitchen, helping prepare the food for the repast. I admired a pink, puffy coat with a fur-lined hood. There were definitely over twenty coats already collected.

The next few hours whisked me into a whirl of condolences. We hosted a handful of family members, outnumbered by Mom's co-workers, neighbors, and community acquaintances. I greeted friends from her past, friends she'd known for decades, and friends she'd encouraged since she started battling cancer.

A few people shared how much her handwritten cards and hospitality meant to them. Others told me how she provided meals when they were sick or recovering from surgery. Some of Mom's old students, now adults, remembered the small candies she'd used to reward them for meeting goals and making good choices. Co-workers raved about how she decorated the teachers' lounge and spoiled them with treats and vegetables from her garden. Almost all recounted how my mom generously offered timely words of encouragement and prayers, how she listened and made people feel less alone, less invisible.

After the service, one of my mom's co-workers said the teachers wanted to collect coats the following year, too. I thanked her for everything they'd done to make the week easier for our family. When she walked away, I thanked God for that moment and the woman I now consider my friend.

My mom made a difference with her genuine kindness, offered through simple words and ordinary actions. The standing-room-only Celebration of Life service and the hundreds of new coats, gloves, and hats donated that day and the following school year evidenced her impact. One woman lived to give, still inspiring others to follow her lead… in lieu of flowers.

~Xochitl E. Dixon

Thank You, Mom

Mama was my greatest teacher, a teacher of compassion, love and fearlessness. If love is sweet as a flower, then my mother is that sweet flower of love.
~Stevie Wonder

I call myself a writer, a poet,
and some say I'm pretty good
but I'm troubled by a feeling
I never write the things I should.
I can write about adventures
or social problems all day long
but words sometimes fail me
when emotions run too strong.
The most important words are hoarded.
The most sacred tears are never shed.
Our deepest pains and greatest loves
are rarely written down or said.
Maybe that is why the strongest love
is such a challenge to convey
and why I'm struggling, Mother,
with this poem for you today.
How can I ever begin to thank you
for the faith in me you've always had
and the strength your love has given me

through the good times and the bad.
How can I thank you with only words
for the countless deeds you have done
or express how proud I've always been
to tell the world that I'm your son?
For thousands of small, heroic deeds
performed without a single complaint.
For always listening to my problems
with the love and patience of a saint.
For the presents under the Christmas tree
wrapped with love in red and gold;
For all the happy birthday parties;
For the bedtime stories that you told.
My childhood was so happy and peaceful
and the world such a wonderful place
when the last sight I'd see before sleeping
was your beautiful, smiling face.
So how can I show my appreciation?
I don't even know where to start,
For healing my cuts and bruises
and, at times, my broken heart.
I'd give you everything that I own
if you told me you wanted me to,
but I know you would only say
that my love is enough for you.
And that's you in a nutshell, Mom,
unselfish above and beyond the call.
That's also why a mother's love
is the purest, richest love of all.
The fact is it's an impossible task
to thank you for all you've given me
and for being my strongest supporter
through all of life's adversity.

So all I can give you is this little poem
written with a humble, helpless hand.
And all I can say is "Thank you, Mom,"
and hope that you understand.

~Mark Rickerby

My Amazing Mom

Meet Our Contributors
Meet Amy Newmark
Thank You
About Chicken Soup for the Soul

Meet Our Contributors

Lorraine Allison received her Master of Arts in English, with honors, from Salem State University in 1993 where she now teaches composition and literature. She has one son and a Shetland Sheepdog. Lorraine enjoys book collecting, listening to jazz music, and taking walks by the shore. She plans to write a historical novel.

Tammy Allison has a BA in gerontology and her MBA. She also writes feature stories for her local newspaper. Tammy has worked in long-term care for sixteen years and loves working with the older generation. She is married to her high school sweetheart and has two children who are the inspiration for her writing.

Michelle Armbrust lives in Virginia with her husband, Brian, daughter, Isabella, and son, Isaiah. She is passionate about leading women into becoming lovers of God's Word, which will enable them to live the abundant life they were meant to lead. She is working on creating her own line of Bible study journals for women.

Natasha Basinger lives in Northern Indiana with her husband of ten years. She has two young children, Ava and Andrew. Natasha enjoys vacationing in Traverse City, MI and taking her children to Disney World each year. She hopes to one day publish her own children's and/or young adult book. E-mail her at btbasinger@gmail.com.

Emily Bednarz received her Bachelor of Arts, with honors, from Wilfrid Laurier University in 2012. She completed her Master's degree in English at the University of Western Ontario, and is currently pursuing her Ph.D. at Wilfrid Laurier. She resides in Kitchener, Ontario, but loves visiting Cape Breton, Nova Scotia whenever she can.

Brooke Bent resides in Bozeman, MT with her husband Tim and daughter Zoey. She uses her passion for writing along with her degrees in Spanish Education and English Literature to write about her life experiences. Follow her blog at www.fruitscakesandnuts.tumblr.com.

Patty Benz is now the proud Grammy of four and still continues to be visited by the bumblebees.

David L. Bishop was raised in a small Missouri town by loving parents who both worked in education. This instilled in him a respect for education and books. After graduating with a degree in political science, he turned to his passion of writing. When not writing, David enjoys watching sports and having conversations with good friends.

Lil Blosfield is the CFO for The Counseling Center of Columbiana County in Ohio. She has been writing since she was a young girl and has accumulated an eclectic collection of stories and poems. Lil also enjoys seeing people smile and a good laugh! E-mail her at LBlosfield40@msn.com.

Susan Grady Bristol is a retired pediatric/NICU nurse. She and her husband, Dennis, have three grown sons and four grandchildren. Besides family, writing is her passion. She has written several short stories and articles in professional journals. She belongs to the Nebraska Writers Guild.

John P. Buentello has published essays, fiction, nonfiction and poetry. He's the co-author of *Reproduction Rights*, *Binary Tales* and *Night Rose of the Mountain*. He's at work on a mystery novel and a picture book for children. E-mail him at jakkhakk@yahoo.com.

Jill Burns lives in the mountains of West Virginia with her wonderful family. She's a retired piano teacher and performer. She enjoys writing, music, gardening, nature, and spending time with her grandchildren.

Emily H. Cappo is a mom to three sons, married to her college sweetheart, and a writer, blogger and Essay Specialist for a college prep company where she works with high school students on their college application essays. Emily is also an iced tea junkie and a tennis-playing fanatic whose game never improves.

Cynthia Siems Carlson is a wife, mother, grandmother, and special education teacher in Rochester, MN. She loves quilting, reading, and writing about family history.

Eva Carter is a freelance writer living in Dallas, TX with her Canadian-born husband. She was born in Czechoslovakia, raised in New York and is an avid photographer with a background in finance. E-mail her at evacarter@sbcglobal.net.

Savannah D. Cassel is a registered nurse living in Central Pennsylvania. She is honored to be publishing her second story in the *Chicken Soup for the Soul* series and is married to the man that inspired her first story featured in *Chicken Soup for the Soul: The Power of Gratitude*.

Bridget Chambers is a Life Coach and writer at BridgetChambers.com. Her advice has been featured in outlets such as *Teen Vogue*, *Elite Daily*, *SheKnows*, and *Huffington Post*. Through coaching, speaking engagements, and contributions to the media, Bridget is regarded as a go-to personal development expert for Generation Y.

Teri Anne Conrad grew up riding on the back of her mom's motorcycle and has been riding her own bike since 2003. She is an avid writer, editor, and photographer. She enjoys traveling, hiking, and stand-up paddle boarding. Her work has appeared in numerous print and online magazines.

Maril Crabtree grew up in Memphis and New Orleans but calls the Midwest home. Her most recent poetry book is *Fireflies in the Gathering Dark* (Kelsay Books, 2017). Her poetry, short stories, and essays have appeared in numerous journals and anthologies. More of her work can be seen at www.marilcrabtree.com.

Elaine D'Alessandro enjoys writing fiction for children, and nonfiction short stories for adults. Her work has appeared in children's magazines, and a child anthology. She lives in New Hampshire with her husband. She has four children and five grandchildren. Elaine enjoys gardening, snowshoeing, hiking, and walking by the ocean.

Trudy M. Davies enjoys writing for adults and children. She has written and illustrated three children's books and published a collection of her poetry for adults paired with her husband's beautiful photography. Writing poetry is a way of sharing smiles, ideas, and saving special moments. Learn more at www.TrudyMDavies.wordpress.com.

Twink DeWitt and her husband raised three sons while he served in the Air Force. They then volunteered with Mercy Ships and Youth With A Mission (YWAM). Twink speaks about her book, *The Trust Diamond*. She has five stories published in the *Chicken Soup for the Soul* series. E-mail her at Twinkdewitt@gmail.com.

Xochitl (so-cheel) E. Dixon serves as a writer for *Our Daily Bread*. She is currently working on a devotional for dog lovers who desire deeper relationships with God and others. She enjoys being a mom, traveling with her husband, Alan, and encouraging spiritual growth at www.xedixon.com and www.odb.org/subscriptions.

Jocelyn Drawhorn is a creative writing professional and photographer who calls North Carolina home. Aside from photography and corporate work, Jocelyn dabbles in poetry, music, and marketing. She is an upbeat, resilient individual who loves to create. Regardless of the avenue, she'll find a way to squeeze something out of it!

MaryLou Driedger is a newspaper columnist, art gallery tour guide, and university faculty supervisor who lives in Winnipeg, Manitoba. She and her husband love to travel. They have two grandsons. MaryLou is currently trying to find publishers for a middle-grade novel and a picture book she has written.

Laurie Carnright Edwards enjoys writing and working with children. She has degrees from Berkshire Christian College and Gordon-Conwell Theological Seminary. She is a proud mom and mother-in-law, and the happy wife of her husband Dale. She has had stories in the *Chicken Soup for the Soul* series and *Leadership Journal* online.

Penny Fedorczenko is a retired teacher living in Ontario, Canada. She enjoys traveling, cooking, gardening, reading, and, of course, writing in her spare time. She has had several other stories published in the *Chicken Soup for the Soul* series and is currently working on some children's stories and a romance novel.

A native of Atlanta who now lives in Sugar Hill, GA, **Timothy Freeman** loves his wife, his family, his Coonhound, Georgia Tech Sports, Atlanta Braves baseball and southern rock & roll (in that order). He spends his time piddling with his guitar, writing songs, and writing short stories.

Steven Friedman has a Master's of Arts in Anthropology, and currently teaches middle school social studies in Northern California. Widowed in 2010, he has two children, and recently remarried. Steven enjoys cycling, running, music, and books.

BJ Gallagher is an inspirational speaker and author of more than thirty books, including an international bestseller *A Peacock in the Land of Penguins* and *Everything I Need to Know I Learned from Other Women* and *The Power of Positive Doing*. Learn more at www.bjgallagher.com.

Kevin Gerard lives with two feline friends, Jesse and Jelly. When not writing or teaching, he enjoys the San Diego Zoo, South Cardiff State Beach, and the local Pizza Port. He also enjoys playing *Halo* on the Internet; look for him in the rocket games as one of the characters from Diego's Dragon or Conor and the Crossworlds.

Pamela Gilsenan is the mother of five adult children whose names all start with the letter "J."

Besides her Master's thesis in archaeology, **C. J. Godwin** has written for college journals, local papers, and community newsletters, and currently ghostwrites online media for a handful of local businesses. C. J. graduated from the University of Florida and lives in St. Augustine with her family.

Anita Gogno has been a writer, editor, hospital PR Director, and columnist for local newspapers. Her stories have been published in *Chicken Soup for the Couple's Soul* and *Chicken Soup for the Sports Fan's Soul*. She lives in Pennsylvania with her husband Charlie and their beloved dog, Roosie.

Karen Gorback is a former college dean with a doctorate in education from the University of California, Santa Barbara. Her award-winning novel, *Freshman Mom,* tells the story of a single parent's struggles and joys in returning to college. Learn more at www.karengorback.com.

Arlene Rains Graber is an award-winning journalist, novelist, and devotional writer in Wichita, KS. She is published in magazines, newspapers, and periodicals, and is the author of seven books. When not writing, she enjoys scrapbooking and yoga. Visit her at www.arlenerainsgraber.com.

Brenda Davis Harsham lives in New England with her husband and three kids. When she isn't writing, she photographs nature and scarfs chocolate. Her award-winning poetry and prose have been published in numerous anthologies and journals. Visit her popular website at FriendlyFairyTales.com or on Twitter at @BrendaDHarsham.

Maureen Hart is a retired teacher who enjoys reading, time spent with family, friends and pup, frozen mochas, and smelling the roses. She is a literacy volunteer.

Suzan Teall Headley is a former small business owner. She lives part-time in Kona, HI, part-time in Bozeman, MT, and part-time at their respective airports. When she's not traveling, she dedicates her time to writing novels, painting, and making ceramic art in her studio.

Sheila Helmberger has a Bachelor of Science in Journalism and has been a freelance writer for nearly twenty years. She lives in Minnesota and has three children and three grandchildren. She enjoys telling stories of everyday life and is currently working on a handful of children's books. E-mail her at skhelm@brainerd.net.

Christine L. Henderson's stories have been featured in numerous anthologies including *Chicken Soup for the Soul*, *Heaven Touching Earth*, *21 Days of Love*, and *Life Lessons from Dads*. She is an active member of the Children's Writers Workshop and Christian Writers Group of San Antonio.

Eileen Melia Hession is a former teacher and publisher's rep whose writing has appeared in many publications. Her book, *Vittles in Verse*, was published in 2017. She loves running, yoga, and her fabulous daughter. She believes there is a need for more levity in life and her writing reflects that belief.

Cindy Hudson is the author of *Book by Book: The Complete Guide to Creating Mother-Daughter Book Clubs*. She lives in Portland, OR, with her husband and two daughters and enjoys writing about things that inspire her: family life, her community, reading, and family literacy. Learn more at www.CindyHudson.com.

David Hull is a retired teacher who enjoys writing, reading, and spoiling his nieces and nephews. He lives in Holley, NY.

Jeanie Jacobson is on the Wordsowers Christian Writers leadership team. She has been published in ten *Chicken Soup for the Soul* titles. Jeanie loves visiting family and friends, reading, hiking, praise dancing, and gardening. Grab her fun book, *Fast Fixes for the Christian Pack-Rat*, online. Learn more at www.jeaniejacobson.com.

Cassie Jones graduated from Texas A&M University in 2014 and now teaches in Houston, TX. She enjoys writing, reading, and playing video games in her spare time.

Jean Jones enjoys hiking, horseback riding, and reading, and is eternally grateful for the incredible gift of second chances.

Jill Keller is a novelist who lives in a small town in Pennsylvania with her husband and two children. When not writing, she enjoys pursuing her passions of cooking, visiting the library, taking walks on the Appalachian Trail and reading to her children. Learn more at kellerjf.wixsite.com/authorjillkeller.

James Kinneen is a freelance writer from Braintree, MA. His writing has appeared on Cracked.com and thehardtimes.net.

Kathleen Kohler writes about the ups and downs of family life for numerous magazines and anthologies. She and her husband live in the Pacific Northwest, and have three children and seven grandchildren. Visit www.kathleenkohler.com to read more of her articles or enter her latest contest.

Nancy Julien Kopp is a Kansan, originally from Chicago but she has lived in the Flint Hills of Kansas for many years. She writes creative nonfiction, memoir, inspirational, award-winning children's fiction, poetry and articles on the writing craft. She's published in eighteen *Chicken Soup for the Soul* books, other anthologies, ezines and Internet radio.

Dr. Beth Krone-Downes is a licensed clinical psychologist, an Assistant Professor of Psychology and clinical educator, a scientific researcher, a pet rescuer, an organic gardener, a music enthusiast, a pretty good cook, and a mother of three wonderful human beings. This is her first published literary work outside of academia.

D.K. Laidler has two Bachelor degrees plus a Master's in Literacy from the University of Michigan. She is a special education teacher with the Department of Corrections and enjoys traveling, photography, and writing. She is currently working on her first novel.

From the time her mother taught her to read at age three, **Traci E. Langston** has read everything she could get her hands on. Now her reading has led her into being an author. She writes in a variety of genres from children's books to romance. She enjoys travel and spending time with her husband and their three cats.

Denise LaRosa is a children's book author, educator and CEO/founder of Mom Talk with Denise LaRosa, LLC. A devoted wife and mother of two precious girls, Denise earned her Bachelor of Arts degree in dance from Radford University in 2003 and graduated from Carlow University in 2008 with a Master of Education degree.

Brenda Leppington lives in Saskatchewan, Canada and works as an Information Manager within the healthcare system. She is a previous contributor to the *Chicken Soup for the Soul* series. Brenda enjoys traveling, writing, and spending time with her horses.

Barbara LoMonaco has worked for Chicken Soup for the Soul as an editor since 1998. She has co-authored two *Chicken Soup for the Soul* book titles and has had stories published in numerous other titles. Barbara is a graduate of the University of Southern California and has a teaching credential.

Donna Lorrig is a writer and an award-winning photographer, with articles and photos appearing in Colorado's Front Range news publications, including *The Gazette* and the *Colorado Springs Independent*. She is a homeschooling mother of seven, and previous contributor to the *Chicken Soup for the Soul* series. She thrives on the creative process.

Cynthia A. Lovely, of New York, is a freelance writer, musician and minister's wife. Published in magazines, newspapers, and anthologies, she is working on a novel and a non-fiction title. She is forever grateful for the God-gift of her husband and the gain of a lovely signature. Learn more at www.cynthialovely.com.

Katherine Mabb is a teacher, a freelance writer, previous contributor to the *Chicken Soup for the Soul* series, and a proud mother—not necessarily in that order!

Crissy Martin received her Bachelor of Arts degree from Texas Wesleyan University in 2007. She currently works as an art teacher in Fort Worth, TX. Cristin enjoys writing, painting and photography. She plans on writing children's books in the future.

Carolyn McCartney is a teacher in Jersey, UK. She was born in Belfast and has published a novel set during the troubles in the 1980s. Carolyn also writes pantomimes, loves Elves and Leonard Cohen, has a wonderful son and a long-suffering soul mate of some twenty years. Her mission is to make poetry popular!

Christine McCleod is a lawyer and treaty negotiator in Canada's far north. She lives in the Thousand Islands region of Ontario with her husband, and they enjoy road trips, playing guitar, canoeing on their mill pond, and a good craft beer in front of the woodstove.

Ronni Meier received her Bachelor of Science at Taylor University, majoring in Professional Writing and minoring in Christian Education and Youth Ministry. She loves to write, sing, cheer for the Indianapolis Colts, and encourage others. Ronni plans to write inspirational young adult books and become a public speaker.

Cindy J. Morris received her Bachelor of Arts from Boise State University in 2013. She enjoys biking and hiking with Rob, her husband of twenty-eight years. She has two daughters, Jessica and Brittney, who live near her in Boise, ID. Her weekends are often spent with her three grandchildren spending the night and going on adventures.

Nicole Muchowski has been writing fiction for four years, in the spare moments between raising children to school age — not yet there, but very close. Prior to that, she wrote scientific reports as an environmental consultant. Writing full-time will be the next big chapter for Nicole.

Elaine Herrin Onley, a retired public relations professional and former missionary, has written extensively for religious publications. Elaine is the author of three books and co-author of a fourth. Her writing has appeared in *Chicken Soup for the Soul: The Cancer Book* and *Chicken Soup for the Soul: True Love*.

Blogger, lover of Jesus, and Detroit native! **Candace L. Parker** is thirty years old and lives by the motto, "You miss 100% of the shots you don't take!" Connect with Candace on her blog, www.spillthesalt.com, where she spills about life, love, and so much more!

Kesha Phillips is a passionate creator and consumer of art and media. You'll find her all around the web sharing her parenting journey, which includes everything from hilarious family videos to her refreshing takes on raising kids today. She currently resides in Atlanta, GA with her husband and twins.

April Pollack has enjoyed writing for the past fourteen years. She recently received her AA in Liberal Arts from Bismarck State College and is currently pursuing her life-long dream of attending cosmetology school. She is blogging her way through it at apriltheswift.blogspot.com so future cosmetologists know what to expect.

Kay Presto's stories have been published in numerous *Chicken Soup for the Soul* books. She recently published a middle grade go-karting mystery novel, *Chasing the Checkered Flag*, which has recently won two national awards. Kay loves writing, and has written ten additional children's books. E-mail her at prestoprod6@yahoo.com.

Jilly Pretzel earned her MFA in creative writing from Chapman University and her BA in Philosophy from the University of Redlands. She is a California native, and enjoys loitering in bookstores, watching Netflix with her fiancé, and hanging out with her cat, Kierkegaard.

Beth Rice never became a journalist. Working odd jobs, she married and raised a family. When her father intervened with a request for her to return to writing, she did. Beth has one children's book, *I'm Adopted, I'm Special,* to her name. She works as a content writer for JMX Brands, contributing to the DutchCrafters blog.

Mark Rickerby has contributed eighteen stories to the *Chicken Soup for the Soul* series. He is co-creator and head writer of a western TV series in development, co-author of his father's memoir *The Other Belfast: An Irish Youth*, and he wrote/sang fifteen songs on *Great Big World*, a CD inspired by and dedicated to his daughters Marli and Emma.

Rebecca Rimmer is a writer and blogger who lives in Warwickshire, England. She likes to look closer at things, contemplating the world around her, through the power of words. This philosophical outlook is also why she is an avid tattoo collector, and is covered in memories and meanings that she will wear forever.

Liza Rosenberg is an American expat living in Israel with her husband and thirteen-year-old son. Tech writer by day and freelance writer by night, Liza writes for a variety of local and international publications. Her passions include music, escaping to the desert, and making ice cream. Learn more at www.lizarosenberg.com.

A nationally-published essayist and public speaking instructor, **Joel Schwartzberg** is the author of two award-winning personal essay collections: *The 40-Year-Old Version* and *Small Things Considered*. Learn more at www.joelschwartzberg.net.

Cathy Shavalier-Chernow received her BA in Anthropology and her M.Ed. in Learning Disabilities. Retiring after thirty years of teaching, she now has the time to pursue her creative spirit in other avenues: painting and writing.

Angelena Shepard lives in Los Angeles with her husband and cat. She is currently earning her Bachelor of Arts degree in Creative Writing/Screenwriting. During her down time, you will likely find her at the beach (weather permitting), or watching Hallmark movies. E-mail her at angeshepard@live.com.

Leigh Smith is a middle-age life voyager who currently resides in South Carolina with her enduring confidant and husband of twenty-three years, a wickedly intelligent and visionary teenage son who lights up their world, and two feline entertainers. She plans to keep dreaming and continue writing.

Reverend James L. Snyder is an award-winning author whose writings have appeared in more than eighty periodicals including *Guideposts*. *In Pursuit of God: The Life of A.W. Tozer*, Snyder's first book, won the Reader's Choice Award in 1992 from *Christianity Today*. Snyder has authored and edited thirty books altogether.

Sandeep Sreedharan lives and works in New Jersey. He used to do the same in India, Africa, and the Middle East, marketing a range of consumer products along the way. Sandeep and his wife love travel, food, and traveling for food. He revels in translating experiences into words.

Diane Stark is a wife, mother of five, and freelance writer. She is a frequent contributor to the *Chicken Soup for the Soul* series. Diane loves to write about the important things in life: her family and her faith. E-mail her at DianeStark19@yahoo.com.

Gary Stein has enjoyed a long career on Wall Street and in media. He built a thirty-time Emmy-winning kids TV firm and has consulted for Lionsgate, Miramax and Seventh Generation. A frequent contributor to the *Chicken Soup for the Soul* series, Gary's blessed with a loving wife and some amazing mentees.

Lynn Sunday is an artist, writer, and animal advocate who lives near San Francisco with her husband and two senior rescue dogs. Eleven of her stories appear in ten *Chicken Soup for the Soul* books, and numerous other publications. E-mail her at Sunday11@aol.com.

Annmarie B. Tait lives in Conshohocken, PA with her husband Joe Beck. Annmarie has been published in more than twenty *Chicken Soup for the Soul* books as well as various other magazines and anthologies. Annmarie and her husband enjoy singing and recording Irish and American folk music. E-mail her at irishbloom@aol.com.

Johnny Tan is a keynote speaker, talk show host, award-winning and bestselling author, and founder of *From My Mama's Kitchen*. His radio show has amassed over one million listeners. From My Mama's Kitchen Inspirational Signs are available online. Johnny welcomes comments at www.FromMyMamasKitchen.com.

Two years ago, **Sylvia Brich Thompson** and her husband moved to San Luis Obispo, CA. SLO (slow) is what the locals call this ideal central coast college town. Sylvia enjoys writing, nature, and cooking. Gardening is a challenge, sharing vegetables with pesky ground squirrels! And, with her remarkable family, Sylvia is always grateful.

Christine Trollinger is a freelance author who has had many of her stories published in the *Chicken Soup for the Soul* series. After retiring from the insurance business she took up writing for pleasure and was soon being published. She is a widow with three grown children.

Dawn Turzio is an award-winning writer whose work has been featured in many publications including *The New York Times*, *MSN Lifestyle*, *Yahoo! News*, and *Salon*, which can be found at www.dawnturzio.com.

Ed VanDeMark has three previous stories published in the *Chicken Soup for the Soul* series. He has a new book titled *We May Have Done It Sort Of, Almost Exactly Like This*, available online. He lives in Owego, NY with his wife Linda. They have three adult children and nine grandchildren. E-mail him at elvdm16@gmail.com.

Lizette Vega received a Bachelor of Arts degree in Christian Ministries from The Master's University in California. She is the author of *NINE! The Nine Virtues Known as the Fruit of the Spirit*, and two children's books, *Alligator Loose in the City!* and its sequel *Alligator Loose in the Train Depot!*

Dorann Weber is a freelance photographer for a southern New Jersey newspaper and a contributor for Getty Images. She has a newfound love for writing, especially for *Chicken Soup for the Soul* books. She lives in the Pine Barrens of South Jersey with her family and loves taking long walks. E-mail her at Dorann_weber@yahoo.com.

Marcia Wells taught middle and high school students for twenty years. After encouraging them to follow their dreams, she decided to retire early to pursue her own. She has since written two young adult fantasy novels and is working on two others. Marcia lives in Eastern Washington with her husband and family.

Audrey RL Wyatt is a multi-award-winning author, writing instructor, and speaker. Audrey's novel, *Poles Apart*, has been honored with five awards and her essays and short fiction have been published in various forums, both in print and online. Learn more at www.audreyrlwyatt.com.

Charlie Wyatt was born in Alabama and received a BA in English Literature from Auburn University. He served in the Navy including in Vietnam as skipper of a PCF (Swift Boat). He has been writing short stories and memoirs for the past ten years. He currently lives in Southern California.

Hannah Yoder is a misplaced Tennessean wandering the foreign lands of Southern Ohio. She is a full-time crazy horse lady, part-time trainer of retired racehorse Thoroughbreds, and part-time freelance writer.

Luanne Tovey Zuccari is the mother of three and the grandmother of eight who lives in western New York. She is an online freelance copywriter and a retired community relations specialist for public schools. Her memories of growing up in Kansas include many of her mother's lessons in kindness and empathy for others.

Meet Amy Newmark

Amy Newmark is the bestselling author, editor-in-chief, and publisher of the *Chicken Soup for the Soul* book series. Since 2008, she has published more than 150 new books, most of them national bestsellers in the U.S. and Canada, more than doubling the number of Chicken Soup for the Soul titles in print today. She is also the author of *Simply Happy*, a crash course in Chicken Soup for the Soul advice and wisdom that is filled with easy-to-implement, practical tips for enjoying a better life.

Amy is credited with revitalizing the Chicken Soup for the Soul brand, which has been a publishing industry phenomenon since the first book came out in 1993. By compiling inspirational and aspirational true stories curated from ordinary people who have had extraordinary experiences, Amy has kept the twenty-five-year-old Chicken Soup for the Soul brand fresh and relevant.

Amy graduated *magna cum laude* from Harvard University where she majored in Portuguese and minored in French. She then embarked on a three-decade career as a Wall Street analyst, a hedge fund manager, and a corporate executive in the technology field. She is a Chartered Financial Analyst.

Her return to literary pursuits was inevitable, as her honors thesis in college involved traveling throughout Brazil's impoverished northeast region, collecting stories from regular people. She is delighted to have come full circle in her writing career—from collecting stories "from the people" in Brazil as a twenty-year-old to, three decades later, collecting stories "from the people" for Chicken Soup for the Soul.

When Amy and her husband Bill, the CEO of Chicken Soup for the Soul, are not working, they are visiting their four grown children and their first grandchild.

Follow Amy on Twitter @amynewmark. Listen to her free podcast, The Chicken Soup for the Soul Podcast, at www.chickensoup.podbean.com, or find it at Apple Podcasts, Google Play, the Podcasts app on iPhone, or using your favorite podcast app on other devices.

Thank You

We are grateful to all our story contributors and fans, who shared thousands of stories about their mothers, grandmothers, stepmothers, mothers-in-law, and honorary mothers. Ronelle Frankel, Mary Fisher, Barbara LoMonaco, Kristiana Pastir, and D'ette Corona read all the stories that were submitted and narrowed down the list to a few hundred finalists that ended up filling this collection and our 2017 collection, *Chicken Soup for the Soul: Best Mom Ever*.

Kristiana Pastir and Susan Heim did the preliminary round of editing and Associate Publisher D'ette Corona continued to be Amy's right-hand woman in creating the final manuscript and working with all our wonderful writers. Barbara LoMonaco and Kristiana Pastir, along with outside proofreader Elaine Kimbler, jumped in at the end to proof, proof, proof. And yes, there will always be typos anyway, so feel free to let us know about them at webmaster@chickensoupforthesoul.com and we will correct them in future printings.

The whole publishing team deserves a hand, including Senior Director of Marketing Maureen Peltier, Senior Director of Production Victor Cataldo, and graphic designer Daniel Zaccari, who turned our manuscript into this beautiful book.

Sharing Happiness, Inspiration, and Hope

Real people sharing real stories, every day, all over the world. In 2007, *USA Today* named *Chicken Soup for the Soul* one of the five most memorable books in the last quarter-century. With over 100 million books sold to date in the U.S. and Canada alone, more than 250 titles in print, and translations into nearly fifty languages, "chicken soup for the soul®" is one of the world's best-known phrases.

Today, twenty-five years after we first began sharing happiness, inspiration and hope through our books, we continue to delight our readers with new titles, but have also evolved beyond the bookstore with super premium pet food, television shows, podcasts, positive journalism from aplus.com, and licensed products, all revolving around true stories, as we continue "changing the world one story at a time®." Thanks for reading!

Share with Us

We all have had Chicken Soup for the Soul moments in our lives. If you would like to share your story or poem with millions of people around the world, go to chickensoup.com and click on "Submit Your Story." You may be able to help another reader and become a published author at the same time. Some of our past contributors have launched writing and speaking careers from the publication of their stories in our books!

We only accept story submissions via our website. They are no longer accepted via mail or fax. Visit our website, www.chickensoup.com, and click on Submit Your Story for our writing guidelines and a list of topics we are working on.

To contact us regarding other matters, please send us an e-mail through webmaster@chickensoupforthesoul.com, or fax or write us at:

Chicken Soup for the Soul
P.O. Box 700
Cos Cob, CT 06807-0700
Fax: 203-861-7194

One more note from your friends at Chicken Soup for the Soul: Occasionally, we receive an unsolicited book manuscript from one of our readers, and we would like to respectfully inform you that we do not accept unsolicited manuscripts and we must discard the ones that appear.

Chicken Soup for the Soul®

Grandmothers

101 Stories of Love, Laughs, and Lessons from Grandmothers and Grandchildren

Jack Canfield, Mark Victor Hansen & Amy Newmark

Paperback: 978-1-935096-64-1

eBook: 978-1-61159-187-3

More tales of family

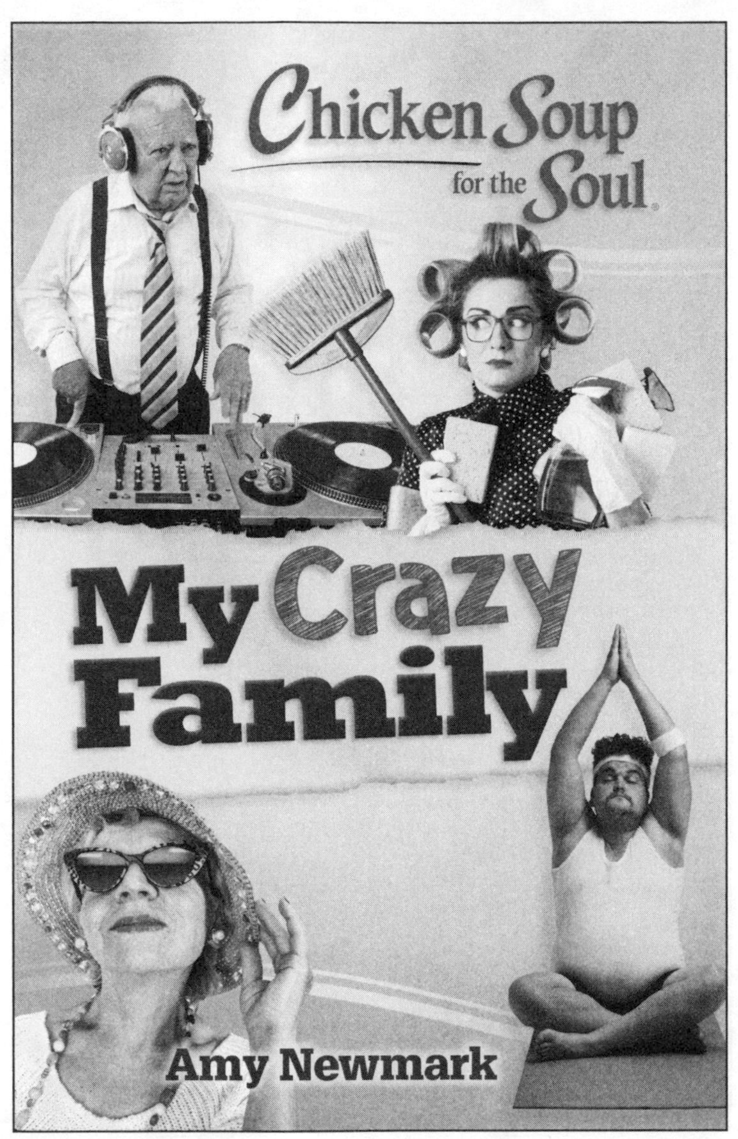

Paperback: 978-1-61159-977-0
eBook: 978-1-61159-277-1

love, laughter, and lessons

Paperback: 978-1-61159-927-5
eBook: 978-1-61159-229-0

More family fun,

The Multitasking Mom's Survival Guide

101 Inspiring and Amusing Stories for Mothers Who Do It All

Jack Canfield,
Mark Victor Hansen
& Amy Newmark

Paperback: 978-1-61159-933-6
eBook: 978-1-61159-234-4

wisdom and tips

Changing your life one story at a time®
www.chickensoup.com